SELECTED ESSAYS

R L S

SELECTED ESSAYS

ROBERT LOUIS STEVENSON

*Edited and with an Introduction
by George Scott-Moncrieff*

A GATEWAY EDITION

HENRY REGNERY COMPANY · CHICAGO

CONTENTS

INTRODUCTION

Robert Louis Stevenson was born in Edinburgh on November 13, 1850. His father, Thomas Stevenson, an able and distinguished engineer, was a member of a firm that designed and built many lighthouses off the coast of Scotland. His mother, the daughter of a Presbyterian minister and the granddaughter of a university professor, seems to have had both the delicate health and the vivacity inherited by her son.

Ill-health plagued Stevenson's life. He nearly died of gastric fever at the age of eight, and his education was much interrupted by illness. He went to many schools, had many tutors, and described himself, moreover, as an inveterate idler and truant, even after he went to Edinburgh University at the age of seventeen. Although a reluctant schoolboy, he was always an avid reader of books in both English and French. He was also a keen student of Scottish history and had thoughts of becoming a historian, but in practice, he simply used the material as the basis of several of his best novels, stories, and essays.

It was originally intended that Stevenson should go into his father's firm, and as a young man, he actually won a silver medal from the Edinburgh Society of Arts for a paper on the improvement of lighthouse apparatus. However, he turned from science to law and was called to the bar in 1875, but he never practiced.

All his life, Stevenson was drawn toward literature. As a boy, he edited and wrote family and school magazines. At the University, he launched a magazine with several other young men, including my grandfather, but he had occasion to be grateful when his father settled the resulting debts. One of the essays in this selection is a tribute Stevenson paid his father, to whom he was devoted, although theirs was often a difficult relationship. The young Stevenson was too gay and lively to take kindly to the narrow Calvinism that still largely prevailed in nineteenth-century Scotland. As Edwin Muir has observed in his *Autobiography*, every important Scottish writer since the beginning of the eighteenth century, "with the exception of Carlyle, who, like Knox, admired power," has revolted against John Knox, the central figure of the Scottish Reformation, finding his bitter narrowness antipathetic.

Bouts of illness took Stevenson to the Riviera and other places abroad. He began writing and first became known as an essayist for his work in the *Cornhill Magazine*, afterwards collected under the title *Virginibus Puerisque*. He began to make literary friends, including W. E. Henley, a writer of ability but a certain sourness of character. Collaborating with Henley, Stevenson tried his hand at a number of plays, hoping, as so many other writers have hoped, to be able to make some money with drama. In this he was unsuccessful, and until he was in his middle thirties, he was never able to earn much more than £300 a year by his pen. In 1886, however, he had two successes. One was the publication, as a "shilling shocker," of *Dr. Jekyll and Mr. Hyde*, which had an immediate vogue. The other was *Kidnapped*, a romance based upon an incident in Scottish history.

During his visits to France, Stevenson got to know an American lady, Mrs. Osbourne, who was separated from her husband and living in Europe with her children. Although she was ten years older than he, Stevenson fell deeply in love with her, and in 1879, he followed her to America. He sailed on an emigrant ship, for economy as well as experience, and had some difficult times with poverty and illness. Mrs. Osbourne obtained her divorce, and they were married the following year. Stevenson's parents had been distressed at the idea of his marrying a divorcee, but when the two returned to Scotland, his wife was well received and much liked by the family.

Recurrent hemorrhages kept Stevenson in a state of continual physical weakness. He lived in various places, including Davos in Switzerland, in the hope that his health might improve, but with no lasting success. When his father died in 1887, he felt free to leave Scotland for America, believing that he might find health there.

An American publisher, S. S. McClure, commissioned Stevenson to write a volume of letters from the South Seas. For this he was to receive £2,000, a handsome sum in those days. Although the resulting book was not one of his best, the commission gave his life a decisive turn. He travelled a great deal, first by yacht and then on island steamers, and finally bought a small property, which he named Vailima, in Samoa. Here he had a house built for him and eventually settled down in 1891.

Although Stevenson was to die within four years, the days in Samoa were filled with intense activity. He not only wrote hard but also took an active interest in the lives of the islanders, who became devoted to him. He vigorously exposed abuses in the colonial administration, and because of his letters to the London *Times,* some of the leading officials were removed from office. And he worked on a number of books. *Catriona,* a sequel to *Kidnapped,* was completed, but both *St. Ives* and *Weir of Hermiston* were unfinished at the time of his death. It is particularly sad that he was unable to finish *Weir of Hermiston,* for there is no doubt that as a novelist, he was finding new depth and power. Yet for all his bad health, the last years in Samoa were fruitful and happy. He was surrounded by people he loved; his wife and her son and daughter by her first marriage, his mother, and, from time to time, visiting friends provided a happy communal life, and the natives were his willing servants.

Robert Louis Stevenson died on December 3, 1894, from a burst blood vessel in the brain. Sixty natives hacked their way through dense jungle the next day to take his body to the top of Mount Vaea, where he had wished to be buried. He had written his own epitaph:

Under the wide and starry sky,
Dig the grave and let me lie.
Glad did I live and gladly die,
  And I laid me down with a will.
This be the verse you grave for me:
Here he lies where he longed to be;
Home is the sailor, home from sea,
  And the hunter home from the hill.

It is probably as a novelist that Stevenson is best remembered, but his poems and essays are still widely read. He was always a conscientious writer. Sometimes, indeed, his style is a little over-studied; it is never careless or slapdash. It was often said of him that he wrote more like a Frenchman than an Englishman, taking great de-liberation over the words he used. In the realm of fiction, he may be said to have reintroduced the element of action at a time when, as so often happens, the novel had become static and psycho-logical. *Treasure Island*, although primarily a boys' book, shows a splendidly vital handling of action and is a masterpiece amongst its kind. Nor does this enthusiasm for action detract from a more pensive quality in Stevenson's work, for he was highly intelligent and perceptive of the inner workings of men's minds. Throughout his life, as far as his health would permit, he was a man of action himself.

Much has been made of Stevenson's "double life" in his youth. Besides the hours of respect-ability in his parents' home, he spent much of his time in less correct society and was considered a "Bohemian," which to some people was downright shocking. It does not seem to me that there is anything very remarkable in this. Victorian society, on the surface at least, leaned toward a hyper-respectability. It was natural enough that a gifted young man should seek wider experience than was offered in the drawing rooms of the day. It is plain, moreover, that young Stevenson's quest, through whatever strange alleys it may have led him, was the true idealism that is not satisfied with experience for its own sake but seeks it primarily as a means toward a fuller comprehension of life. The loftiness of Stevenson's ideal for man is apparent in "An Open Letter to the Reverend Dr. Hyde of Honolulu," which is reprinted here. In this we also see his exasperation at a hypocrisy that he must first have resented amongst the people of his native Edinburgh.

In an imperfect world, revolt is natural to the ardent young; it is where it leads them that discloses the degree of their integrity. For Stevenson, his revolt was to lead him to his life's work as a conscientious artist, with an undimmed indignation at injustice and hypocrisy of all kinds. He could see too keenly to subscribe to a political solution, and his essay "The Day after To-morrow," with its indictment of authoritarian socialism, shows remarkable vision for the times in which it was written. Yet is it not simply the expression of a man of integrity who knows that political and economic theories will not save a world in which good will is lacking?

Of the other essays I have selected, "An Apology for Idlers" is a defense of a non-materialistic approach to life made by one who combined the capacity for intense hard work with the capacity for what might be said to be an equally creative idleness. "The Morality of the Profession of Letters" remains a sensible summing up of a writer's responsibilities, and "A Note on Realism" touches on the same topic. "A Gossip on Romance" is more purely concerned with one aspect of creative literature. The essays on Whitman and Thoreau are studies of American writers whose works are included in the essay "Books Which Have Influenced Me." The two studies of John Knox reflect both Stevenson's historical sense and knowledge and his humorous understanding of human nature. "Nuits Blanches," "Memoirs of an Islet," "Some College Memoirs," and "Penny Plain and Twopence Coloured" are sensitive evocations of childhood and youth, as is much of the two essays on "Talk and Talkers."

Between them, these essays give, I think, a fair picture of Stevenson's manner, which, as he would have had it himself, was constantly changing and developing, and his thought, the thought of a true artist, a man profoundly religious and heroic in adversity who possessed undying joy and hope in the potentialities of mankind, both in greater aspirations and in smaller delights.

GEORGE SCOTT-MONCRIEFF

Edinburgh
1959

SELECTED ESSAYS

AN APOLOGY FOR IDLERS

BOSWELL: *We grow weary when idle.*

JOHNSON: *That is, sir, because others being busy, we want company; but if we were idle, there would be no growing weary; we should all entertain one another.*

JUST now, when every one is bound, under pain of a decree in absence convicting them *lèse*-respectability, to enter on some lucrative profession, and labour therein with something not far short of enthusiasm, a cry from the opposite party who are content when they have enough, and like to look on and enjoy in the meanwhile, savours a little of bravado and gasconade. And yet this should not be. Idleness so called, which does not consist in doing nothing, but in doing a great deal not recognised in the dramatic formularies of the ruling class, has as good a right to state its position as industry itself. It is admitted that the presence of people who refuse to enter in the great handicap race for sixpenny pieces, is at once an insult and a disenchantment for those who do. A fine fellow (as we see so many) takes his determination, votes for sixpences, and in the emphatic Americanism, "goes for" them. And while such an one is ploughing distressfully up the road, it is not hard to understand his resentment, when he perceives cool persons in the meadows by the wayside, lying with a handkerchief over their ears and a glass at their elbow. Alexander is touched in a very delicate place by the disregard of Diogenes. Where was the glory of having taken Rome for those tumultuous barbarians, who poured into the Senate house, and found the Fathers sitting silent and unmoved by their success? It is a sore thing to have laboured along and scaled the arduous hilltops, and when all is done find humanity indifferent to your achievement. Hence physicists condemn the unphysical; financiers have only a superficial toleration for those who know little of stocks; literary persons despise the unlettered; and people of all pursuits combine to disparage those who have none.

But though this is one difficulty of the subject, it is not the greatest. You could not be put in prison for speaking against industry, but you can be sent to Coventry for speaking like a fool. The greatest difficulty with most subjects is to do them well; therefore, please to remember this is an apology. It is certain that much may be judiciously argued in favour of diligence; only there is something to be said against it, and that is what, on the present occasion, I have to say. To state one argument is not necessarily to be deaf to all others, and that a man has written a book of travels in Montenegro, is no reason why he should never have been to Richmond.

It is surely beyond a doubt that people should be a good deal idle in youth. For though here and there a Lord Macaulay may escape from school honours with all his wits about him, most boys pay so dear for their medals that they never afterwards have a shot in their locker, and begin the world bankrupt. And the same holds true during all the time a lad is educating himself, or suffering others to educate him. It must have been a very foolish old gentleman who addressed Johnson at Oxford in these words: "Young man, ply your book diligently now, and acquire a stock of knowledge; for when years come upon you, you will find that poring upon books will be but an irksome task." The old gentleman seems to have been unaware that many other things besides reading grow irksome, and not a few become impossible, by the time a man has to use spectacles and cannot walk without a stick. Books are good enough in their own way, but they are a mighty bloodless substitute for life. It seems a pity to sit like the Lady of Shalott, peering into a mirror, with your back turned on all the bustle and glamour of reality. And if a man reads very hard, as the old anecdote reminds us, he will have little time for thought.

If you look back on your own education, I am sure it will not be the full, vivid, instructive hours of truantry that you regret; you would rather cancel some lack-lustre periods between sleep and waking in the class. For my own part, I have attended a good many lectures in my time. I still remember that the spinning of a top is a case of Kinetic Stability. I still remember that Emphyteusis is not a disease, nor Stillicide a crime. But though I would not willingly part with such

3

scraps of science, I do not set the same store by them as by certain other odds and ends that I came by in the open street while I was playing truant. This is not the moment to dilate on that mighty place of education, which was the favourite school of Dickens and of Balzac, and turns out yearly many inglorious masters in the Science of the Aspects of Life. Suffice it to say this: if a lad does not learn in the streets, it is because he has no faculty of learning. Nor is the truant always in the streets, for if he prefers, he may go out by the gardened suburbs into the country. He may pitch on some tuft of lilacs over a burn, and smoke innumerable pipes to the tune of the water on the stones. A bird will sing in the thicket. And there he may fall into a vein of kindly thought, and see things in a new perspective. Why, if this be not education, what is? We may conceive Mr. Worldly Wiseman accosting such an one, and the conversation that should thereupon ensue:—

"How now, young fellow, what dost thou here?"

"Truly, sir, I take mine ease."

"Is not this the hour of the class? and should'st thou not be plying thy Book with diligence, to the end thou mayest obtain knowledge?"

"Nay, but thus also I follow after Learning, by your leave."

"Learning, quotha! After what fashion, I pray thee? Is it mathematics?"

"No, to be sure."

"Is it metaphysics?"

"Nor that."

"Is it some language?"

"Nay, it is no language."

"Is it a trade?"

"Nor a trade neither."

"Why, then, what is't?"

"Indeed, sir, as time may soon come for me to go upon Pilgrimage, I am desirous to note what is commonly done by persons in my case, and where are the ugliest Sloughs and Thickets on the Road; as also, what manner of staff is of the best service. Moreover, I lie here, by this water, to learn by root-of-heart a lesson which my master teaches me to call Peace, or Contentment."

Hereupon Mr. Worldly Wiseman was much commoved with passion, and shaking his cane with a very threatful countenance, broke forth upon this wise: "Learning, quotha!" said he; "I would have all such rogues scourged by the Hangman!"

And so he would go his way, ruffling out his cravat with a crackle of starch, like a turkey when it spread its feathers.

Now this, of Mr. Wiseman's, is the common opinion. A fact is not called a fact, but a piece of gossip, if it does not fall into one of your scholastic categories. An inquiry must be in some acknowledged direction, with a name to go by; or else you are not inquiring at all, only lounging; and the workhouse is too good for you. It is supposed that all knowledge is at the bottom of a well, or the far end of a telescope. Sainte-Beuve, as he grew older, came to regard all experience as a single great book, in which to study for a few years ere we go hence; and it seemed all one to him whether you should read in Chapter xx., which is the differential calculus, or in Chapter xxxix., which is hearing the band play in the gardens. As a matter of fact, an intelligent person, looking out of his eyes and hearkening in his ears, with a smile on his face all the time, will get more true education than many another in a life of heroic vigils. There is certainly some chill and arid knowledge to be found upon the summits of formal and laborious science; but it is all round about you, and for the trouble of looking, that you will acquire the warm and palpitating facts of life. While others are filling their memory with a lumber of words, one-half of which they will forget before the week be out, your truant may learn some really useful art: to play the fiddle, to know a good cigar, or to speak with ease and opportunity to all varieties of men. Many who have "plied their book diligently," and know all about some one branch or another of accepted lore, come out of the study with an ancient and owl-like demeanour, and prove dry, stockish, and dyspeptic in all the better and brighter parts of life. Many make a large fortune, who remain underbred and pathetically stupid to the last. And meanwhile there goes the idler, who began life along with them—by your leave, a different picture. He has had time to take care of his health and his spirits; he has been a great deal in the open air, which is the most salutary of all things for both body and mind; and if he has never read the great Book in very recondite places, he has dipped into it and skimmed it over to excellent purpose. Might not the student afford some Hebrew roots, and the business man some of his half-crowns, for a share of the idler's knowledge of life at large, and Art of Living? Nay, and the idler has another and more important quality than these. I mean his wisdom. He who has much looked on at the childish satisfaction of other people in their hobbies, will regard his own with only a very ironical indulgence. He will not be heard among the dogmatists. He will have a great and cool allowance for all sorts of people and opinions. If he finds no out-of-the-way truths, he will identify himself with no very burning falsehood. His way takes him along a by-road, not much frequented, but very even and pleasant, which is called Commonplace Lane, and leads to the Belvedere of Common-sense. Thence he shall command an agreeable, if no very noble prospect; and while others behold the East and West, the Devil and the Sunrise, he will be contentedly aware of a sort of morning hour upon all sublunary things, with an army of shadows running speedily and in many different directions into the great daylight of Eternity. The shadows and the generations, the shrill doctors and the plangent wars, go by into ultimate silence and emptiness; but underneath all this, a man may see, out of the Belvedere windows, much green and peaceful landscape; many fire-lit parlours; good people laughing, drinking, and making love as they did before the Flood or the French Revolution; and the old shepherd telling his tale under the hawthorn.

Extreme *busyness*, whether at school or college, kirk or market, is a symptom of deficient vitality; and a faculty for idleness implies a catholic appetite and a strong sense of personal identity. There is a sort of dead-alive, hackneyed people about, who are scarcely conscious of living except in the exercise of some conventional occupation. Bring these fellows into the country or set them aboard ship, and you will see how they pine for their desk or their study. They have no curiosity; they cannot give themselves over to random provocations; they do not take pleasure in the exercise of their faculties for its own sake; and unless Necessity lays about them with a stick, they will even stand still. It is no good speaking to such folk: they *cannot* be idle, their nature is not generous enough; and they pass those hours in a sort of coma, which are not dedicated to furious moiling in the gold-mill. When they do not require to go to office, when they are not hungry and have no mind to drink, the whole breathing world is a blank to them. If they have to wait an hour or so for a train, they fall into a stupid trance with their eyes open. To see them, you would suppose there was nothing to look at and no one to speak with; you would imagine they were paralysed or alienated; and yet very possibly they are hard workers in their own way, and have good eyesight for a flaw in a deed or a turn of the market. They have been to school

and college, but all the time they had their eye
on the medal; they have gone about in the world
and mixed with clever people, but all the time
they were thinking of their own affairs. As if a
man's soul were not too small to begin with, they
have dwarfed and narrowed theirs by a life of all
work and no play; until here they are at forty,
with a listless attention, a mind vacant of all
material of amusement, and not one thought to
rub against another, while they wait for the train.
Before he was breeched, he might have clambered
on the boxes; when he was twenty, he would have
stared at the girls; but now the pipe is smoked
out, the snuff-box empty, and my gentleman sits
bolt upright upon a bench, with lamentable eyes.
This does not appeal to me as being Success in
Life.

But it is not only the person himself who
suffers from his busy habits, but his wife and
children, his friends and relations, and down to
the very people he sits with in a railway-carriage
or an omnibus. Perpetual devotion to what a man
calls his business, is only to be sustained by perpetual neglect of many other things. And it is
not by any means certain that a man's business
is the most important thing he has to do. To
an impartial estimate it will seem clear that many
of the wisest, most virtuous, and most beneficent parts that are to be played upon the
Theatre of Life are filled by gratuitous perform-
ers, and pass, among the world at large, as phases
of idleness. For in that Theatre, not only the
walking gentlemen, singing chambermaids, and

diligent fiddlers in the orchestra, but those who look on and clap their hands from the benches, do really play a part and fulfil important offices towards the general result. You are no doubt very dependent on the care of your lawyer and stock-broker, of the guards and signalmen who convey you rapidly from place to place, and the police-men who walk the streets for your protection; but is there not a thought of gratitude in your heart for certain other benefactors who set you smiling when they fall in your way, or season your dinner with good company? Colonel Newcome helped to lose his friend's money; Fred Bayham had an ugly trick of borrowing shirts; and yet they were better people to fall among than Mr. Barnes. And though Falstaff was neither sober nor very honest, I think I could name one or two long-faced Barabbases whom the world could better have done without. Hazlitt mentions that he was more sensible of obligation to Northcote, who had never done him anything he could call a service, than to his whole circle of ostentatious friends; for he thought a good companion em-phatically the greatest benefactor. I know there are people in the world who cannot feel grateful unless the favour has been done them at the cost of pain and difficulty. But this is a churlish dis-position. A man may send you six sheets of letter-paper covered with the most entertaining gossip, or you may pass half an hour pleasantly, perhaps profitably, over an article of his; do you think the service would be greater if he had made the manuscript in his heart's blood, like a compact with the devil? Do you really fancy you should be more beholden to your correspondent, if he had been damning you all the while for your importunity? Pleasures are more beneficial than duties because, like the quality of mercy, they are not strained, and they are twice blest. There must always be two to a kiss, and there may be a score in a jest; but wherever there is an element of sacrifice, the favour is conferred with pain, and, among generous people, received with confusion. There is no duty we so much underrate as the duty of being happy. By being happy we sow anonymous benefits upon the world, which remain unknown even to ourselves, or when they are disclosed, surprise nobody so much as the benefactor. The other day, a ragged, barefoot boy ran down the street after a marble, with so jolly an air that he set everyone he passed into a good humour; one of these persons, who had been delivered from more than usually black thoughts, stopped the little fellow and gave him some money with this remark: "You see what sometimes comes of looking pleased." If he had looked pleased before, he had now to look both pleased and mystified. For my part, I justify this encouragement of smiling rather than tearful children; I do not wish to pay for tears anywhere but upon the stage; but I am prepared to deal largely in the opposite commodity. A happy man or woman is a better thing to find than a five-pound note. He or she is a radiating focus of goodwill; and their entrance into a room is as though another candle had been lighted. We

11

need not care whether they could prove the forty-seventh proposition; they do a better thing than that, they practically demonstrate the great Theorem of the Liveableness of Life. Consequently, if a person cannot be happy without remaining idle, idle he should remain. It is a revolutionary precept; but thanks to hunger and the workhouse, one not easily to be abused; and within practical limits, it is one of the most incontestable truths in the whole Body of Morality. Look at one of your industrious fellows for a moment, I beseech you. He sows hurry and reaps indigestion; he puts a vast deal of activity out to interest, and receives a large measure of nervous derangement in return. Either he absents himself entirely from all fellowship, and lives a recluse in a garret, with carpet slippers and a leaden inkpot; or he comes among people swiftly and bitterly, in a contraction of his whole nervous system, to discharge some temper before he returns to work. I do not care how much or how well he works, this fellow is an evil feature in other people's lives. They would be happier if he were dead. They could easier do without his services in the Circumlocution Office, than they can tolerate his fractious spirits. He poisons life at the well-head. It is better to be beggared out of hand by a scapegrace nephew, than daily hag-ridden by a peevish uncle.

And what, in God's name, is all this pother about? For what cause do they embitter their own and other people's lives? That a man should publish three or thirty articles a year, that he should finish or not finish his great allegorical picture, are questions of little interest to the world. The ranks of life are full; and although a thousand fall, there are always some to go into the breach. When they told Joan of Arc she should be at home minding women's work, she answered there were plenty to spin and wash. And so, even with your own rare gifts! When nature is "so careless of the single life," why should we coddle ourselves into the fancy that our own is of exceptional importance? Suppose Shakespeare had been knocked on the head some dark night in Sir Thomas Lucy's preserves, the world would have wagged on better or worse, the pitcher gone to the well, the scythe to the corn, and the student to his book; and no one been any the wiser of the loss. There are not many works extant, if you look the alternative all over, which are worth the price of a pound of tobacco to a man of limited means. This is a sobering reflection for the proudest of our earthly vanities. Even a tobacconist may, upon consideration, find no great cause for personal vainglory in the phrase; for although tobacco is an admirable sedative, the qualities necessary for retailing it are neither rare nor precious in themselves. Alas and alas! you may take it how you will, but the services of no single individual are indispensable. Atlas was just a gentleman with a protracted nightmare! And yet you see merchants who go and labour themselves into a great fortune, and thence into the bankruptcy court; scribblers who keep scribbling at little articles until

13

their temper is a cross to all who come about them, as though Pharaoh should set the Israelites to make a pin instead of a pyramid; and fine young men who work themselves into a decline, and are driven off in a hearse with white plumes upon it. Would you not suppose these persons had been whispered, by the Master of the Ceremonies, the promise of some momentous destiny? and that this lukewarm bullet on which they play their farces was the bull's-eye and centre-point of all the universe? And yet it is not so. The ends for which they gave away their priceless youth, for all they know, may be chimerical or hurtful; the glory and riches they expect may never come, or may find them indifferent; and they and the world they inhabit are so inconsiderable that the mind freezes at the thought.

NUITS BLANCHES

IF ANYONE should know the pleasure and pain of a sleepless night, it should be I. I remember, so long ago, the sickly child that woke from his few hours' slumber with the sweat of a nightmare on his brow, to lie awake and listen and long for the first signs of life among the silent streets. These nights of pain and weariness are graven on my mind; and so when the same thing happened to me again, everything that I heard or saw was rather a recollection than a discovery.

Weighed upon by the opaque and almost sensible darkness, I listened eagerly for anything to break the sepulchral quiet. But nothing came, save, perhaps, an emphatic crack from the old cabinet that was made by Deacon Brodie, or the dry rustle of the coals on the extinguished fire. It was a calm; or I know that I should have heard in the roar and clatter of the storm, as I have not heard it for so many years, the wild career of a horseman, always scouring up from the distance and passing swiftly below the window; yet always returning again from the place whence first he came, as though, baffled by some higher power, he had retraced his steps to gain impetus for another and another attempt.

As I lay there, there arose out of the utter stillness the rumbling of a carriage a very great way off, that drew near, and passed within a few streets of the house, and died away as gradually as it had arisen. This, too, was as a reminiscence.

I rose and lifted a corner of the blind. Over the black belt of the garden I saw the long line of Queen Street, with here and there a lighted window. How often before had my nurse lifted me out of bed and pointed them out to me, while we wondered together if, there also, there were children that could not sleep, and if these lighted oblongs were signs of those that waited like us for the morning.

I went out into the lobby, and looked down into the great deep well of the staircase. For what cause I know not, just as it used to be in the old days that the feverish child might be the better served, a peep of gas illuminated a narrow circle far below me. But where I was, all was darkness and silence, save the dry monotonous ticking of the clock that came ceaselessly up to my ear.

The final crown of it all, however, the last touch of reproduction on the pictures of my memory, was the arrival of that time for which, all night through, I waited and longed of old. It was my custom, as the hours dragged on, to repeat the question, 'When will the carts come in?' and repeat it again and again until at last those sounds arose in the street that I have heard once more this morning. The road before our house is a great thoroughfare for early carts. I know not, and I never have known, what they carry, whence they come, or whither they go. But I know that, long ere dawn, and for hours together, they stream continuously past, with the same rolling and jerking of wheels and the same clink of horses' feet. It was not for nothing that they made the burthen of my wishes all night through. They are really the first throbbings of life, the harbingers of day; and it pleases you as much to hear them as it must please a ship-wrecked seaman once again to grasp a hand of flesh and blood after years of miserable solitude. They have the freshness of the daylight life about them. You can hear the carters cracking their whips and crying hoarsely to their horses or to one another; and sometimes even a peal of healthy, harsh horse-laughter comes up to you through the darkness. There is now an end of mystery and fear. Like the knocking at the door in *Macbeth*,[1] or the cry of the watchman in the *Tour de Nesle*, they show that the horrible cæsura is over and the nightmares have fled away, because the day is breaking and the ordinary life of men is beginning to bestir itself among the streets.

In the middle of it all I fell asleep, to be wakened by the officious knocking at my door, and I find myself twelve years older than I had dreamed myself all night.

1. See a short essay of De Quincey's.

THE DAY AFTER TO-MORROW

HISTORY is much decried; it is a tissue of errors, we are told, no doubt correctly; and rival historians expose each other's blunders with gratification. Yet the worst historian has a clearer view of the period he studies than the best of us can hope to form of that in which we live. The obscurest epoch is today; and that for a thousand reasons of inchoate tendency, conflicting report, and sheer mass and multiplicity of experience; but chiefly, perhaps, by reason of an insidious shifting of landmarks. Parties and ideas continually move, but not by measurable marches on a stable course; the political soil itself steals forth by imperceptible degrees, like a travelling glacier, carrying on its bosom not only political parties but their flag-posts and cantonments; so that what appears to be an eternal city founded on hills is but a flying island of Laputa. It is for this reason in particular that we are all becoming Socialists without knowing it; by which I would not in the least refer to the acute case of Mr. Hyndman and his horn-blowing supporters, sounding their trumps of a Sunday within the walls of our individualist Jericho—but to the stealthy change that has come over the spirit of Englishmen and English legislation. A little while ago, and we were still for liberty; 'crowd a few more thousands on the bench of Government,' we seemed to cry; 'keep her head direct on liberty, and we cannot help but come to port.' This is over; *laisser faire* declines in favour; our legislation grows authoritative, grows philanthropical, bristles with new duties and new penalties, and casts a spawn of inspectors, who now begin, note-book in hand, to darken the face of England. It may be right or wrong, we are not trying that; but one thing it is beyond doubt: it is Socialism in action, and the strange thing is that we scarcely know it.

Liberty has served us a long while, and it may be time to seek new altars. Like all other principles, she has been proved to be self-exclusive in the long run. She has taken wages besides (like all other virtues) and dutifully served Mammon; so that many things we were accustomed to admire as the benefits of freedom and common to all were truly benefits of wealth, and took their value from our neighbours' poverty. A few shocks of logic, a few disclosures (in the journalistic phrase) of what the freedom of manufacturers, landlords, or shipowners may imply for operatives, tenants, or seamen, and we not unnaturally begin to turn to that other pole of hope, beneficent tyranny. Freedom, to be desirable, involves kindness, wisdom, and all the virtues of the free; but the free man as we have seen him in action has been, as of yore, only the master of many helots; and the slaves are still ill-fed, ill-clad, ill-taught, ill-housed, insolently treated, and driven to their mines and workshops by the lash of famine. So much, in other men's affairs, we have begun to see clearly; we have begun to despair of virtue in these other men, and from our seat in Parliament begin to discharge upon them, thick as arrows, the host of our inspectors. The landlord has long shaken his head over the manufacturer; those who do business on land have lost all trust in the virtues of the ship-owner; the professions look askance upon the retail traders and have even started their co-operative stores to ruin them; and from out the smoke-wreaths of Birmingham a finger has begun to write upon the wall the condemnation of the landlord. Thus, piece by piece, do we condemn each other, and yet not perceive the conclusion, that our whole estate is somewhat damnable. Thus, piece by piece, each acting against his neighbour, each sawing away the branch on which some other interest is seated, do we apply in detail our Socialistic remedies, and yet not perceive that we are all labouring together to bring in Socialism at large. A tendency so stupid and so selfish is like to prove invincible; and if Socialism be at all a practicable rule of life, there is every chance that our grandchildren will see the day and taste the pleasures of existence in something far liker an ant-heap than any previous human polity. And this not in the least because of the voice of Mr. Hyndman or the horns of his followers; but by the mere glacier movement of the political soil, bearing forward on its bosom, apparently undisturbed, the proud camps of Whig and Tory. If Mr. Hyndman were a man of keen humour, which is far from my conception of his character, he might rest from his troubling and look on: the walls of Jericho begin already to crumble and dissolve. That great servile war, the Armageddon of money and numbers, to which we looked forward when young, becomes more and more unlikely; and we may rather look to see a peaceable and blindfold evolution, the work of dull men immersed in political tactics and dead to political results.

The principal scene of this comedy lies, of course, in the House of Commons; it is there, besides, that the details of this new evolution (if it proceed) will fall to be decided; so that the state of Parliament is not only diagnostic of the present but fatefully prophetic of the future. Well, we all know what Parliament is, and we are all ashamed of it. We may pardon it some faults, indeed, on the ground of Irish obstruction—a bitter trial, which it supports with notable good humour. But the excuse is merely local; it cannot apply to similar bodies in America and France; and what are we to say of these? President Cleveland's letter may serve as a picture of the one; a glance at almost any paper will convince us of the weakness of the other. Decay appears to have seized on the organ of popular government in every land; and this just at the moment when we begin to bring to it, as to an oracle of justice, the whole skein of our private affairs to be unravelled, and ask it, like a new Messiah, to take upon itself our frailties and play for us the part that should be played by our own virtues. For that, in few words, is the case. We

cannot trust ourselves to behave with decency;
we cannot trust our consciences; and the remedy
proposed is to elect a round number of our neighbours, pretty much at random, and say to these:
'Be ye our conscience; make laws so wise, and
continue from year to year to administer them
so wisely, that they shall save us from ourselves
and make us righteous and happy, world without
end. Amen.' And who can look twice at the
British Parliament and then seriously bring it
such a task? I am not advancing this as an argument against Socialism: once again, nothing is
further from my mind. There are great truths in
Socialism, or no one, not even Mr. Hyndman,
would be found to hold it; and if it came, and
did one-tenth part of what it offers, I for one
should make it welcome. But if it is to come, we
may as well have some notion of what it will be
like; and the first thing to grasp is that our new
polity will be designed and administered (to put
it courteously) with something short of inspiration. It will be made, or will grow, in a human
parliament; and the one thing that will not very
hugely change is human nature. The Anarchists
think otherwise, from which it is only plain that
they have not carried to the study of history the
lamp of human sympathy.

Given, then, our new polity, with its new wag-
gon-load of laws, what headmarks must we look for
in the life? We chafe a good deal at that excellent
thing, the income-tax, because it brings into our
affairs the prying fingers, and exposes us to the tart
words, of the official. The official, in all degrees, is

already something of a terror to many of us. I would not willingly have to do with even a police-constable in any other spirit than that of kindness. I still remember in my dreams the eye-glass of a certain *attaché* at a certain embassy—an eye-glass that was a standing indignity to all on whom it looked; and my next most disagreeable remembrance is of a bracing, Republican postman in the city of San Francisco. I lived in that city among working folk, and what my neighbours accepted at the postman's hands—nay, what I took from him myself—it is still distasteful to recall. The bourgeois, residing in the upper parts of society, has but few opportunities of tasting this peculiar bowl; but about the income-tax, as I have said, or perhaps about a patient, or in the halls of an embassy at the hands of my friend of the eye-glass, he occasionally sets his lips to it; and he may thus imagine (if he has that faculty of imagination, without which most faculties are void) how it tastes to his poorer neighbours, who must drain it to the dregs. In every contact with authority, with their employer, with the police, with the School Board officer, in the hospital, or in the workhouse, they have equally the occasion to appreciate the light-hearted civility of the man in office; and as an experimentalist in several out-of-the-way provinces of life, I may say it has but to be felt to be appreciated. Well, this golden age of which we are speaking will be the golden age of officials. In all our concerns it will be their beloved duty to meddle, with what tact, with what obliging words, analogy will aid us to imagine. It is likely these gentlemen will be periodically elected; they will therefore have their turn of being underneath, which does not always sweeten men's conditions. The laws they will have to administer will be no clearer than those we know to-day, and the body which is to regulate their administration no wiser than the British Parliament. So that upon all hands we may look for a form of servitude most galling to the blood—servitude to many and changing masters, and for all the slights that accompany the rule of jack-in-office. And if the Socialistic programme be carried out with the least fulness, we shall have lost a thing, in most respects not much to be regretted, but as a moderator of oppression, a thing nearly invaluable—the newspaper. For the independent journal is a creature of capital and competition; it stands and falls with millionaires and railway bonds and all the abuses and glories of to-day; and as soon as the State has fairly taken its bent to authority and philanthropy, and laid the least touch on private property, the days of the independent journal are numbered. State railways may be good things and so may State bakeries; but a State newspaper will never be a very trenchant critic of the State officials.

But again, these officials would have no sinecure. Crime would perhaps be less, for some of the motives of crime we may suppose would pass away. But if Socialism were carried out with any fulness, there would be more contraventions. We see already new sins springing up like mustard— School Board sins, factory sins, Merchant Shipping Act sins—none of which I would be thought to except against in particular, but all of which, taken together, show us that Socialism can be a hard master even in the beginning. If it go on to such heights as we hear proposed and lauded, if it come actually to its ideal of the ant-heap, ruled with iron justice, the number of new contraventions will be out of all proportion multiplied. Take the case of work alone. Man is an idle animal. He is at least as intelligent as the ant; but generations of advisers have in vain recommended him the ant's example. Of those who are found truly indefatigable in business, some are misers; some are the practisers of delightful industries, like gardening; some are students, artists, inventors, or discoverers, men lured forward by successive hopes; and the rest are those who live by games of skill or hazard—financiers, billiard-players, gamblers, and the like. But in unloved toils, even under the prick of necessity, no man is continually sedulous. Once eliminate the fear of starvation, once eliminate or bound the hope of riches, and we shall see plenty of skulking and malingering. Society will then be something not wholly unlike a cotton plantation in the old days; with cheerful, careless, demoralised slaves, with elected overseers, and, instead of the planter, a chaotic popular assembly. If the blood be purposeful and the soil strong, such a plantation may succeed, and be, indeed, a busy ant-heap, with full granaries and long hours of leisure. But even then I think the whip will be in the overseer's hands, and not in vain. For, when it comes to be a question of each man doing his own share or the rest doing more, prettiness of sentiment will be forgotten. To dock the skulker's food is not enough; many will rather eat haws and starve on petty pilferings than put their shoulder to the wheel for one hour daily. For such as these, then, the whip will be in the overseer's hand; and his own sense of justice and the superintendence of a chaotic popular assembly will be the only checks on its employment. Now, you may be an industrious man and a good citizen, and yet not love, nor yet be loved by, Dr. Fell the inspector. It is admitted by private soldiers that the disfavour of a sergeant is an evil not to be combated; offend the sergeant, they say, and in a brief while you will either be disgraced or have deserted. And the sergeant can no longer appeal to the lash. But if these things go on, we shall see, or our sons shall see, what it is to have offended an inspector.

This for the unfortunate. But with the fortunate also, even those whom the inspector loves, it may not be altogether well. It is concluded that in such a state of society, supposing it to be financially sound, the level of comfort will be high. It does not follow: there are strange depths of idleness in man, a too-easily-got sufficiency, as in the case of the sago-eaters, often quenching the desire for all besides; and it is possible that the men of the richest ant-heaps may sink even into squalor. But suppose they do not; suppose our tricksy instrument of human nature, when we play upon it this new tune, should respond kindly; suppose no one to be damped and none exasperated by the new conditions, the whole enterprise to be financially sound—a vaulting supposition—and all the inhabitants to dwell together in a golden mean of comfort: we have yet to ask ourselves if this be what man desire, or if it be what man will even deign to accept for a continuance. It is certain that man loves to eat, it is not certain that he loves that only or that best. He is supposed to love comfort; it is not a love, at least, that he is faithful to. He is supposed to love happiness; it is my contention that he rather loves excitement. Danger, enterprise, hope, the novel, the aleatory, are dearer to man than regular meals. He does not think so when he is hungry, but he thinks so again as soon as he is fed; and on the hypothesis of a successful ant-heap, he would never go hungry. It would be always after dinner in that society, as, in the land of the Lotos-eaters, it was always afternoon; and food, which, when we have it not, seems all-important, drops in our esteem, as soon as we have it, to a mere prerequisite of living.

That for which man lives is not the same thing for all individuals nor in all ages; yet it has a common base; what he seeks and what he must have is that which will seize and hold his attention. Regular meals and weatherproof lodgings will not do this long. Play in its wide sense, as the artificial induction of sensation, including all games and all arts, will, indeed, go far to keep him conscious of himself; but in the end he wearies for realities. Study or experiment, to some rare natures, is the unbroken pastime of a life.

27

These are enviable natures; people shut in the house by sickness often bitterly envy them; but the commoner man cannot continue to exist upon such altitudes: his feet itch for physical adventure; his blood boils for physical dangers, pleasures, and triumphs; his fancy, the looker after new things, cannot continue to look for them in books and crucibles, but must seek them on the breathing stage of life. Pinches, buffets, the glow of hope, the shock of disappointment, furious contention with obstacles: these are the true elixir for all vital spirits, these are what they seek alike in their romantic enterprises and their unromantic dissipations. When they are taken in some pinch closer than the common, they cry, 'Catch me here again!' and sure enough you catch them there again—perhaps before the week is out. It is as old as *Robinson Crusoe*; as old as man. Our race has not been strained for all these ages through that sieve of dangers that we call Natural Selection, to sit down with patience in the tedium of safety; the voices of its fathers call it forth. Already in our society as it exists, the bourgeois is too much cottoned about for any zest in living; he sits in his parlour out of reach of any danger, often out of reach of any vicissitude but one of health; and there he yawns. If the people in the next villa took pot-shots at him, he might be killed indeed, but so long as he escaped he would find his blood oxygenated and his views of the world brighter. If Mr. Mallock, on his way to the publishers, should have his skirts pinned to a wall by a javelin, it would not

occur to him—at least for several hours—to ask
if life were worth living; and if such peril were
a daily matter, he would ask it never more; he
would have other things to think about, he would
be living indeed—not lying in a box with cotton, safe, but immeasurably dull. The aleatory,
whether it touch life, or fortune, or renown—
whether we explore Africa or only toss for half-
pence—that is what I conceive men to love best,
and that is what we are seeking to exclude from
men's existences. Of all forms of the aleatory, that
which most commonly attends our working men
—the danger of misery from want of work—is
the least inspiriting: it does not whip the blood;
it does not evoke the glory of contest; it is tragic,
but it is passive; and yet, in so far as it is aleatory,
and a peril sensibly touching them, it does truly
season the men's lives. Of those who fail, I do
not speak—despair should be sacred; but to those
who even modestly succeed, the changes of their
life bring interest: a job found, a shilling saved,
a dainty earned, all these are wells of pleasure
springing afresh for the successful poor; and it is
not from these but from the villa-dweller that
we hear complaints of the unworthiness of life.
Much, then, as the average of the proletariat
would gain in this new state of life, they would
also lose a certain something, which would not
be missed in the beginning, but would be missed
progressively and progressively lamented. Soon
there would be a looking back: there would be
tales of the old world humming in young men's
ears, tales of the tramp and the pedlar, and the

hopeful emigrant. And in the stall-fed life of the successful ant-heap—with its regular meals, regular duties, regular pleasures, an even course of life, and fear excluded—the vicissitudes, delights, and havens of to-day will seem of epic breadth. This may seem a shallow observation; but the springs by which men are moved lie much on the surface. Bread, I believe, has always been considered first, but the circus comes close upon its heels. Bread we suppose to be given amply; the cry for circuses will be the louder, and if the life of our descendants be such as we have conceived, there are two beloved pleasures on which they will be likely to fall back: the pleasures of intrigue and of sedition.

In all this I have supposed the ant-heap to be financially sound. I am no economist, only a writer of fiction; but even as such, I know one thing that bears on the economic question—I know the imperfection of man's faculty for business. The Anarchists, who count some rugged elements of common sense among what seem to me their tragic errors, have said upon this matter all that I could wish to say, and condemned beforehand great economical polities. So far it is obvious that they are right; they may be right also in predicting a period of communal independence, and they may even be right in thinking that desirable. But the rise of communes is none the less the end of economic equality, just when we were told it was beginning. Communes will not be all equal in extent, nor in quality of soil, nor in growth of population; nor will the surplus produce of all be equally marketable. It will be the old story of competing interests, only with a new unit; and, as it appears to me, a new, inevitable danger. For the merchant and the manufacturer, in this new world, will be a sovereign commune; it is a sovereign power that will see its crops undersold, and its manufactures worsted in the market. And all the more dangerous that the sovereign power should be small. Great powers are slow to stir; national affronts, even with the aid of newspapers, filter slowly into popular consciousness; national losses are so unequally shared, that one part of the population will be counting its gains while another sits by a cold hearth. But in the sovereign commune all will be centralised and sensitive. When jealousy springs up, when (let us say) the commune of Poole has overreached the commune of Dorchester, irritation will run like quicksilver throughout the body politic; each man in Dorchester will have to suffer directly in his diet and his dress; even the secretary, who drafts the official correspondence, will sit down to his task embittered, as a man who has dined ill and may expect to dine worse; and thus a business difference between communes will take on much the same colour as a dispute between diggers in the lawless West, and will lead as directly to the arbitrament of blows. So that the establishment of the communal system will not only reintroduce all the injustices and heart-burnings of economic inequality, but will, in all human likelihood, inaugurate a world of hedgerow warfare. Dorchester will march on Poole, Sherborne on Dorchester, Wimborne on both; the waggons will be fired on as they follow the highway, the trains wrecked on the lines, the ploughman will go armed into the field of tillage; and if we have not a return of ballad literature, the local press at least will celebrate in a high vein the victory of Cerne Abbas or the reverse of Toller Porcorum. At least this will not be dull; when I was younger, I could have welcomed such a world with relief; but it is the New-Old with a vengeance, and irresistibly suggests the growth of military powers and the foundation of new empires.

THOMAS STEVENSON

CIVIL ENGINEER

THE DEATH of Thomas Stevenson will mean
not very much to the general reader. His service
to mankind took on forms of which the public
knows little and understands less. He came seldom to London, and then only as a task, remaining always a stranger and a convinced provincial;
putting up for years at the same hotel where his
father had gone before him; faithful for long to
the same restaurant, the same church, and the
same theatre, chosen simply for propinquity;
steadfastly refusing to dine out. He had a circle
of his own, indeed, at home; few men were more
beloved in Edinburgh, where he breathed an air
that pleased him; and wherever he went, in railway carriages or hotel smoking-rooms, his strange,
humorous vein of talk, and his transparent honesty, raised him up friends and admirers. But to
the general public and the world of London,
except about the parliamentary committee-rooms,
he remained unknown. All the time, his lights
were in every part of the world, guiding the
mariner; his firm were consulting engineers to the
Indian, the New Zealand, and the Japanese Lighthouse Boards, so that Edinburgh was a world
centre for that branch of applied science; in Ger-

many, he had been called "the Nestor of light-house illumination"; even in France, where his claims were long denied, he was at last, on the occasion of the late Exposition, recognised and medalled. And to show by one instance the inverted nature of his reputation, comparatively small at home, yet filling the world, a friend of mine was this winter on a visit to the Spanish main, and was asked by a Peruvian if he "knew Mr. Stevenson the author, because his works were much esteemed in Peru?" My friend supposed the reference was to the writer of tales; but the Peruvian had never heard of *Dr. Jekyll*; what he had in his eye, what was esteemed in Peru, were the volumes of the engineer.

Thomas Stevenson was born at Edinburgh in the year 1818, the grandson of Thomas Smith, first engineer to the Board of Northern Lights, son of Robert Stevenson, brother of Alan and David; so that his nephew, David Alan Stevenson, joined with him at the time of his death in the engineership, is the sixth of the family who has held, successively or conjointly, that office. The Bell Rock, his father's great triumph, was finished before he was born; but he served under his brother Alan in the building of Skerryvore, the noblest of all extant deep-sea lights; and, in conjunction with his brother David, he added two—the Chickens and Dhu Heartach—to that small number of man's extreme outposts in the ocean. Of shore lights, the two brothers last named erected no fewer than twenty-seven; of beacons,[1] about twenty-five. Many harbours were successfully carried out: one, the harbour of Wick, the chief disaster of my father's life, was a failure; the sea proved too strong for man's arts; and after expedients hitherto unthought of, and on a scale hyper-cyclopean, the work must be deserted, and now stands a ruin in that bleak, God-forsaken bay, ten miles from John-o'-Groat's. In the improvement of rivers the brothers were likewise in a large way of practice over both England and Scotland, nor had any British engineer anything approaching their experience.

It was about this nucleus of his professional labours that all my father's scientific inquiries and inventions centred; these proceeded from, and acted back upon, his daily business. Thus it was as a harbour engineer that he became interested in the propagation and reduction of waves; a difficult subject in regard to which he has left behind him much suggestive matter and some valuable approximate results. Storms were his sworn adversaries, and it was through the study of storms that he approached that of meteorology at large. Many who knew him not otherwise, knew—perhaps have in their gardens—his louvre-boarded screen for instruments. But the great achievement of his life was, of course, in optics as applied to lighthouse illumination. Fresnel

1. In Dr. Murray's admirable new dictionary, I have remarked a flaw *sub voce* Beacon. In its express, technical sense, a beacon may be defined as "a founded, artificial sea-mark, not lighted."

had done much; Fresnel had settled the fixed light apparatus on a principle that still seems unimprovable; and when Thomas Stevenson stepped in and brought to a comparable perfection the revolving light, a not unnatural jealousy and much painful controversy rose in France. It had its hour; and, as I have told already, even in France it has blown by. Had it not, it would have mattered the less, since all through his life my father continued to justify his claim by fresh advances. New apparatus for lights in new situations was continually being designed with the same unwearied search after perfection, the same nice ingenuity of means; and though the holophotal revolving light perhaps still remains his most elegant contrivance, it is difficult to give it the palm over the much later condensing system, with its thousand possible modifications. The number and the value of these improvements entitle their author to the name of one of mankind's benefactors. In all parts of the world a safer landfall awaits the mariner. Two things must be said: and, first, that Thomas Stevenson was no mathematician. Natural shrewdness, a sentiment of optical laws, and a great intensity of consideration led him to just conclusions; but to calculate the necessary formulæ for the instruments he had conceived was often beyond him, and he must fall back on the help of others, notably on that of his cousin and lifelong intimate friend, *emeritus* Professor Swan, of St. Andrews, and his later friend, Professor P. G. Tait. It is a curious enough circumstance, and a great

encouragement to others, that a man so ill
equipped should have succeeded in one of the
most abstract and arduous walks of applied
science. The second remark is one that applies to
the whole family, and only particularly to
Thomas Stevenson from the great number and
importance of his inventions: holding as the
Stevensons did a Government appointment, they
regarded their original work as something due already to the nation, and none of them has ever
taken out a patent. It is another cause of the
comparative obscurity of the name: for a patent
not only brings in money, it infallibly spreads
reputation; and my father's instruments enter
anonymously into a hundred light-rooms, and
are passed anonymously over in a hundred re-
ports, where the least considerable patent would
stand out and tell its author's story.

But the life-work of Thomas Stevenson remains; what we have lost, what we now rather
try to recall, is the friend and companion. He
was a man of a somewhat antique strain: with a
blended sternness and softness that was wholly
Scottish and at first somewhat bewildering; with
a profound essential melancholy of disposition
and (what often accompanies it) the most humorous geniality in company; shrewd and childish; passionately attached, passionately prejudiced; a man of many extremes, many faults of
temper, and no very stable foothold for himself
among life's troubles. Yet he was a wise adviser;
many men, and these not inconsiderable, took
counsel with him habitually. "I sat at his feet,"

writes one of these, "when I asked his advice, and when the broad brow was set in thought and the firm mouth said his say, I always knew that no man could add to the worth of the conclusion." He had excellent taste, though whimsical and partial; collected old furniture and delighted specially in sunflowers long before the days of Mr. Wilde; took a lasting pleasure in prints and pictures; was a devout admirer of Thomson of Duddingston at a time when few shared the taste; and though he read little, was constant to his favourite books. He had never any Greek; Latin he happily re-taught himself after he had left school, where he was a mere consistent idler: happily, I say, for Lactantius, Vossius, and Cardinal Bona were his chief authors. The first he must have read for twenty years uninterruptedly, keeping it near him in his study, and carrying it in his bag on journeys. Another old theologian, Brown of Wamphray, was often in his hands. When he was indisposed, he had two books, *Guy Mannering* and *The Parent's Assistant*, of which he never wearied. He was a strong Conservative, or, as he preferred to call himself, a Tory; except in so far as his views were modified by a hot-headed chivalrous sentiment for women. He was actually in favour of a marriage law under which any woman might have a divorce for the asking, and no man on any ground whatever; and the same sentiment found another expression in a Magdalen Mission in Edinburgh, founded and largely supported by himself. This was but one of the many channels of his public generosity; his private was equally unstrained. The Church of Scotland, of which he held the doctrines (though in a sense of his own) and to which he bore a clansman's loyalty, profited often by his time and money; and though, from a morbid sense of his own unworthiness, he would never consent to be an office-bearer, his advice was often sought, and he served the Church on many committees. What he perhaps valued highest in his work were his contributions to the defence of Christianity; one of which, in particular, was praised by Hutchinson Stirling and reprinted at the request of Professor Crawford.

His sense of his own unworthiness I have called morbid; morbid, too, were his sense of the fleetingness of life and his concern for death. He had never accepted the conditions of man's life or his own character; and his inmost thoughts were ever tinged with the Celtic melancholy. Cases of conscience were sometimes grievous to him, and that delicate employment of a scientific witness cost him many qualms. But he found respite from these troublesome humours in his work, in his lifelong study of natural science, in the society of those he loved, and in his daily walks, which now would carry him far into the country with some congenial friend, and now keep him dangling about the town from one old book-shop to another, and scraping romantic acquaintance with every dog that passed. His talk, compounded of so much sterling sense and so much freakish humour, and clothed in language so apt, droll, and emphatic, was a perpetual delight to all who knew him before the clouds began to settle on his mind. His use of language was both just and picturesque; and when at the beginning of his illness he began to feel the ebbing of this power, it was strange and painful to hear him reject one word after another as inadequate, and at length desist from the search and leave his phrase unfinished rather than finish it without propriety. It was perhaps another Celtic trait that his affections and emotions, passionate as these were, and liable to passionate ups and downs, found the most eloquent expression both in words and gestures. Love, anger, and indignation shone through him and broke forth in imagery, like what we read of Southern races. For all these emotional extremes, and in spite of the melancholy ground of his character, he had upon the whole a happy life; nor was he less fortunate in his death, which at the last came to him unaware.

TALK AND TALKERS

Sir, we had a good talk.—JOHNSON.
As we must account for every idle word, so we must for every idle silence.—FRANKLIN.

I

THERE can be no fairer ambition than to excel in talk; to be affable, gay, ready, clear and welcome; to have a fact, a thought, or an illustration, pat to every subject; and not only to cheer the flight of time among our intimates, but bear our part in that great international congress, always sitting, where public wrongs are first declared, public errors first corrected, and the course of public opinion shaped, day by day, a little nearer to the right. No measure comes before Parliament but it has been long ago prepared by the grand jury of the talkers; no book is written that has not been largely composed by their assistance. Literature in many of its branches is no other than the shadow of good talk; but the imitation falls far short of the original in life, freedom and effect. There are always two to a talk, giving and taking, comparing experience and according conclusions. Talk is fluid, tentative, continually "in further search and progress"; while written words remain fixed, become idols even to the writer, found wooden dogmatisms, and preserve flies of

41

obvious error in the amber of the truth. Last and chief, while literature, gagged with linsey-woolsey, can only deal with a fraction of the life of man, talk goes fancy free and may call a spade a spade. Talk has none of the freezing immunities of the pulpit. It cannot, even if it would, become merely æsthetic or merely classical like literature. A jest intervenes, the solemn humbug is dissolved in laughter, and speech runs forth out of the contemporary groove into the open fields of nature, cheery and cheering, like schoolboys out of school. And it is in talk alone that we can learn our period and ourselves. In short, the first duty of a man is to speak; that is his chief business in this world; and talk, which is the harmonious speech of two or more, is by far the most accessible of pleasures. It costs nothing in money; it is all profit; it completes our education, founds and fosters our friendships, and can be enjoyed at any age and in almost any state of health.

The spice of life is battle; the friendliest relations are still a kind of contest; and if we would not forego all that is valuable in our lot, we must continually face some other person, eye to eye, and wrestle a fall whether in love or enmity. It is still by force of body, or power of character or intellect, that we attain to worthy pleasures. Men and women contend for each other in the lists of love, like rival mesmerists; the active and adroit decide their challenges in the sports of the body; and the sedentary sit down to chess or conversation. All sluggish and pacific pleasures are, to the same degree, solitary and selfish; and every

durable bond between human beings is founded
in or heightened by some element of competition.
Now, the relation that has the least root in matter is undoubtedly that airy one of friendship;
and hence, I suppose, it is that good talk most
commonly arises among friends. Talk is, indeed,
both the scene and instrument of friendship. It
is in talk alone that the friends can measure
strength, and enjoy that amicable counter-asser-
tion of personality which is the gauge of relations
and the sport of life.

A good talk is not to be had for the asking.
Humours must first be accorded in a kind of
overture or prologue; hour, company and circumstance be suited; and then, at a fit juncture, the
subject, the quarry of two heated minds, spring
up like a deer out of the wood. Not that the
talker has any of the hunter's pride, though he
has all and more than all his ardour. The genuine
artist follows the stream of conversation as an
angler follows the windings of a brook, not dallying where he fails to "kill." He trusts implicitly
to hazard; and he is rewarded by continual variety, continual pleasure, and those changing pros-
pects of the truth that are the best of education.
There is nothing in a subject, so called, that we
should regard it as an idol, or follow it beyond
the promptings of desire. Indeed, there are few
subjects; and so far as they are truly talkable,
more than the half of them may be reduced to
three: that I am I, that you are you, and that
there are other people dimly understood to be not
quite the same as either. Wherever talk may

range, it still runs half the time on these eternal lines. The theme being set, each plays on himself as on an instrument; asserts and justifies himself; ransacks his brain for instances and opinions, and brings them forth new-minted, to his own surprise and the admiration of his adversary. All natural talk is a festival of ostentation; and by the laws of the game each accepts and fans the vanity of the other. It is from that reason that we venture to lay ourselves so open, that we dare to be so warmly eloquent, and that we swell in each other's eyes to such a vast proportion. For talkers, once launched, begin to overflow the limits of their ordinary selves, tower up to the height of their secret pretensions, and give themselves out for the heroes, brave, pious, musical and wise, that in their most shining moments they aspire to be. So they weave for themselves with words and for a while inhabit a palace of delights, temple at once and theatre, where they fill the round of the world's dignities, and feast with the gods, exulting in Kudos. And when the talk is over, each goes his way, still flushed with vanity and admiration, still trailing clouds of glory; each declines from the height of his ideal orgie, not in a moment, but by slow declension. I remember, in the *entr'acte* of an afternoon performance, coming forth into the sunshine, in a beautiful green, gardened corner of a romantic city; and as I sat and smoked, the music moving in my blood, I seemed to sit there and evaporate *The Flying Dutchman* (for it was that I had been hearing) with a wonderful sense of life, warmth, well-being and pride; and the noises of the city, voices, bells and marching feet, fell together in my ears like a symphonious orchestra. In the same way, the excitement of a good talk lives for a long while after in the blood, the heart still hot within you, the brain still simmering, and the physical earth swimming around you with the colours of the sunset.

Natural talk, like ploughing, should turn up a large surface of life, rather than dig mines into geological strata. Masses of experience, anecdote, incident, crosslights, quotation, historical instances, the whole flotsam and jetsam of two minds forced in and in upon the matter in hand from every point of the compass, and from every degree of mental elevation and abasement— these are the material with which talk is fortified, the food on which the talkers thrive. Such argument as is proper to the exercise should still be brief and seizing. Talk should proceed by instances; by the apposite, not the expository. It should keep close along the lines of humanity, near the bosoms and businesses of men, at the level where history, fiction and experience intersect and illuminate each other. I am I, and You are You, with all my heart; but conceive how these lean propositions change and brighten when, instead of words, the actual you and I sit cheek by jowl, the spirit housed in the live body, and the very clothes uttering voices to corroborate the story in the face. Not less surprising is the change when we leave off to speak of generalities —the bad, the good, the miser, and all the char-

45

acters of Theophrastus—and call up other men, by anecdote or instance, in their very trick and feature; or trading on a common knowledge, toss each other famous names, still glowing with the hues of life. Communication is no longer by words, but by the instancing of whole biographies, epics, systems of philosophy, and epochs of history, in bulk. That which is understood excels that which is spoken in quantity and quality alike; ideas thus figured and personified, change hands, as we may say, like coin; and the speakers imply without effort the most obscure and intricate thoughts. Strangers who have a large common ground of reading will, for this reason, come the sooner to the grapple of genuine converse. If they know Othello and Napoleon, Consuelo and Clarissa Harlowe, Vautrin and Steenie Steenson, they can leave generalities and begin at once to speak by figures.

Conduct and art are the two subjects that arise most frequently and that embrace the widest range of facts. A few pleasures bear discussion for their own sake, but only those which are most social or most radically human; and even these can only be discussed among their devotees. A technicality is always welcome to the expert, whether in athletics, art or law; I have heard the best kind of talk on technicalities from such rare and happy persons as both know and love their business. No human being ever spoke of scenery for above two minutes at a time, which makes me suspect we hear too much of it in literature. The weather is regarded as the very nadir

and scoff of conversational topics. And yet the
weather, the dramatic element in scenery, is far
more tractable in language, and far more human
both in import and suggestion than the stable
features of the landscape. Sailors and shepherds,
and the people generally of coast and mountain,
talk well of it; and it is often excitingly presented
in literature. But the tendency of all living talk
draws it back and back into the common focus of
humanity. Talk is a creature of the street and
market-place, feeding on gossip; and its last resort
is still in a discussion on morals. That is the
heroic form of gossip; heroic in virtue of its high
pretensions; but still gossip, because it turns on
personalities. You can keep no men long, nor
Scotchmen at all, off moral or theological discussion. These are to all the world what law is
to lawyers; they are everybody's technicalities; the
medium through which all consider life, and the
dialect in which they express their judgments. I
know three young men who walked together daily
for some two months in a solemn and beautiful
forest and in cloudless summer weather; daily
they talked with unabated zest, and yet scarce
wandered that whole time beyond two subjects—
theology and love. And perhaps neither a court
of love nor an assembly of divines would have
granted their premises or welcomed their conclusions.

Conclusions, indeed, are not often reached by
talk any more than by private thinking. That is
not the profit. The profit is in the exercise, and
above all in the experience; for when we reason

at large on any subject, we review our state and history in life. From time to time, however, and specially, I think, in talking art, talk becomes effective, conquering like war, widening the boundaries of knowledge like an exploration. A point arises; the question takes a problematical, a baffling, yet a likely air; the talkers begin to feel lively presentiments of some conclusion near at hand; towards this they strive with emulous ardour, each by his own path, and struggling for first utterance; and then one leaps upon the summit of that matter with a shout, and almost at the same moment the other is beside him; and behold they are agreed. Like enough, the progress is illusory, a mere cat's cradle having been wound and unwound out of words. But the sense of joint discovery is none the less giddy and inspiriting. And in the life of the talker such triumphs, though imaginary, are neither few nor far apart; they are attained with speed and pleasure, in the hour of mirth; and by the nature of the process, they are always worthily shared.

There is a certain attitude, combative at once and deferential, eager to fight yet most averse to quarrel, which marks out at once the talkable man. It is not eloquence, not fairness, not obstinacy, but a certain proportion of all of these that I love to encounter in my amicable adversaries. They must not be pontiffs holding doctrine, but huntsmen questing after elements of truth. Neither must they be boys to be instructed, but fellow-teachers with whom I may wrangle and agree on equal terms. We must reach some solution, some shadow of consent; for without that, eager talk becomes a torture. But we do not wish to reach it cheaply, or quickly, or without the tussle and effort wherein pleasure lies.

The very best talker, with me, is one whom I shall call Spring-Heel'd Jack. I say so, because I never knew any one who mingled so largely the possible ingredients of converse. In the Spanish proverb, the fourth man necessary to compound a salad, is a madman to mix it: Jack is that madman. I know not which is more remarkable; the insane lucidity of his conclusions, the humorous eloquence of his language, or his power of method, bringing the whole of life into the focus of the subject treated, mixing the conversational salad like a drunken god. He doubles like the serpent, changes and flashes like the shaken kaleidoscope, transmigrates bodily into the views of others, and so, in the twinkling of an eye and with a heady rapture, turns questions inside out and flings them empty before you on the ground, like a triumphant conjuror. It is my common practice when a piece of conduct puzzles me, to attack it in the presence of Jack with such grossness, such partiality and such wearing iteration, as at length shall spur him up in its defence. In a moment he transmigrates, dons the required character, and with moonstruck philosophy justifies the act in question. I can fancy nothing to compare with the *vim* of these impersonations, the strange scale of language, flying from Shakespeare to Kant, and from Kant to Major Dyngwell—

"As fast as a musician scatters sounds
  Out of an instrument—"

the sudden, sweeping generalisations, the absurd
irrelevant particularities, the wit, wisdom, folly,
humour, eloquence and bathos, each startling in
its kind, and yet all luminous in the admired disorder of their combination. A talker of a different
calibre, though belonging to the same school, is
Burly. Burly is a man of a great presence; he commands a larger atmosphere, gives the impression
of a grosser mass of character than most men. It
has been said of him that his presence could be
felt in a room you entered blindfold; and the
same, I think, has been said of other powerful
constitutions condemned to much physical in-
action. There is something boisterous and piratic
in Burly's manner of talk which suits well enough
with this impression. He will roar you down, he
will bury his face in his hands, he will undergo
passions of revolt and agony; and meanwhile his
attitude of mind is really both conciliatory and
receptive; and after Pistol has been out-Pistol'd,
and the welkin rung for hours, you begin to perceive a certain subsidence in these spring torrents,
points of agreement issue, and you end arm-in-
arm, and in a glow of mutual admiration. The
outcry only serves to make your final union the
more unexpected and precious. Throughout there
has been perfect sincerity, perfect intelligence, a
desire to hear although not always to listen, and
an unaffected eagerness to meet concessions. You
have, with Burly, none of the dangers that attend

debate with Spring-Heel'd Jack; who may at any moment turn his powers of transmigration on yourself, create for you a view you never held, and then furiously fall on you for holding it. These, at least, are my two favourites, and both are loud, copious, intolerant talkers. This argues that I myself am in the same category; for if we love talking at all, we love a bright, fierce adversary, who will hold his ground, foot by foot, in much our own manner, sell his attention dearly, and give us our full measure of the dust and exertion of battle. Both these men can be beat from a position, but it takes six hours to do it; a high and hard adventure, worth attempting. With both you can pass days in an enchanted country of the mind, with people, scenery and manners of its own; live a life apart, more arduous, active and glowing than any real existence; and come forth again when the talk is over, as out of a theatre or a dream, to find the east wind still blowing and the chimney-pots of the old battered city still around you. Jack has the far finer mind, Burly the far more honest; Jack gives us the animated poetry, Burly the romantic prose, of similar themes; the one glances high like a meteor and makes a light in darkness; the other, with many changing hues of fire, burns at the sea-level, like a conflagration; but both have the same humour and artistic interests, the same unquenched ardour in pursuit, the same gusts of talk and thunderclaps of contradiction.

Cockshot[1] is a different article, but vastly enter-

1. The late Fleeming Jenkin.

taining, and has been meat and drink to me for many a long evening. His manner is dry, brisk and pertinacious, and the choice of words not much. The point about him is his extraordinary readiness and spirit. You can propound nothing but he has either a theory about it ready-made, or will have one instantly on the stocks, and proceed to lay its timbers and launch it in your presence. "Let me see," he will say. "Give me a moment. I *should* have some theory for that." A blither spectacle than the vigour with which he sets about the task, it were hard to fancy. He is possessed by a demoniac energy, welding the elements for his life, and bending ideas, as an athlete bends a horseshoe, with a visible and lively effort. He has, in theorising, a compass, an art; what I would call the synthetic gusto; something of a Herbert Spencer, who should see the fun of the thing. You are not bound, and no more is he, to place your faith in these brand-new opinions. But some of them are right enough, durable even for life; and the poorest serve for a cock-shy—as when idle people, after picnics, float a bottle on a pond and have an hour's diversion ere it sinks. Whichever they are, serious opinions or humours of the moment, he still defends his ventures with indefatigable wit and spirit, hitting savagely himself, but taking punishment like a man. He knows and never forgets that people talk, first of all, for the sake of talking; conducts himself in the ring, to use the old slang, like a thorough "glutton," and honestly enjoys a telling facer from his adversary. Cockshot is bottled

effervescency, the sworn foe of sleep. Three-in-
the-morning Cockshot, says a victim. His talk is
like the driest of all imaginable dry champagnes.
Sleight of hand and inimitable quickness are the
qualities by which he lives. Athelred, on the
other hand, presents you with the spectacle of a
sincere and somewhat slow nature thinking aloud.
He is the most unready man I ever knew to shine
in conversation. You may see him sometimes
wrestle with a refractory jest for a minute or two
together, and perhaps fail to throw it in the end.
And there is something singularly engaging, often
instructive, in the simplicity with which he thus
exposes the process as well as the result, the works
as well as the dial of the clock. Withal he has
his hours of inspiration. Apt words come to him
as if by accident, and, coming from deeper down,
they smack the more personally, they have the
more of fine old crusted humanity, rich in sedi-
ment and humour. There are sayings of his in
which he has stamped himself into the very grain
of the language; you would think he must have
worn the words next his skin and slept with them.
Yet it is not as a sayer of particular good things
that Athelred is most to be regarded, rather as the
stalwart woodman of thought. I have pulled on
a light cord often enough, while he has been
wielding the broad-axe; and between us, on this
unequal division, many a specious fallacy has
fallen. I have known him to battle the same
question night after night for years, keeping it in
the reign of talk, constantly applying it and re-
applying it to life with humorous or grave inten-

tion, and all the while, never hurrying, nor flagging, nor taking an unfair advantage of the facts. Jack at a given moment, when arising, as it were, from the tripod, can be more radiantly just to those from whom he differs; but then the tenor of his thoughts is even calumnious; while Athelred, slower to forge excuses, is yet slower to condemn, and sits over the welter of the world, vacillating but still judicial, and still faithfully contending with his doubts.

Both the last talkers deal much in points of conduct and religion studied in the "dry light" of prose. Indirectly and as if against his will the same elements from time to time appear in the troubled and poetic talk of Opalstein. His various and exotic knowledge, complete although unready sympathies, and fine, full, discriminative flow of language, fit him out to be the best of talkers; so perhaps he is with some, not *quite* with me—*proxime accessit*, I should say. He sings the praises of the earth and the arts, flowers and jewels, wine and music, in a moonlight, serenading manner, as to the light guitar; even wisdom comes from his tongue like singing; no one is, indeed, more tuneful in the upper notes. But even while he sings the song of the Sirens, he still hearkens to the barking of the Sphinx. Jarring Byronic notes interrupt the flow of his Horatian humours. His mirth has something of the tragedy of the world for its perpetual background; and he feasts like Don Giovanni to a double orchestra, one lightly sounding for the dance, one pealing Beethoven in the distance. He is not truly reconciled either with life or with himself; and this instant war in his members sometimes divides the man's attention. He does not always, perhaps not often, frankly surrender himself in conversation. He brings into the talk other thoughts than those which he expresses; you are conscious that he keeps an eye on something else, that he does not shake off the world, nor quite forget himself. Hence arise occasional disappointments; even an occasional unfairness for his companions, who find themselves one day giving too much, and the next, when they are wary out of season, giving perhaps too little. Purcel is in another class from any I have mentioned. He is no debater, but appears in conversation, as occasion rises, in two distinct characters, one of which I admire and fear, and the other love. In the first, he is radiantly civil and rather silent, sits on a high, courtly hilltop, and from that vantage-ground drops you his remarks like favours. He seems not to share in our sublunary contentions; he wears no sign of interest; when on a sudden there falls in a crystal of wit, so polished that the dull do not perceive it, but so right that the sensitive are silenced. True talk should have more body and blood, should be louder, vainer and more declaratory of the man; the true talker should not hold so steady an advantage over whom he speaks with; and that is one reason out of a score why I prefer my Purcel in his second character, when he unbends into a strain of graceful gossip, singing like the fireside kettle. In these moods he has an elegant homeliness that rings of the true Queen Anne. I know another person who attains, in his moments, to the insolence of a Restoration comedy, speaking, I declare, as Congreve wrote; but that is a sport of nature, and scarce falls under the rubric, for there is none, alas! to give him answer.

One last remark occurs: It is the mark of genuine conversation that the sayings can scarce be quoted with their full effect beyond the circle of common friends. To have their proper weight they should appear in a biography, and with the portrait of the speaker. Good talk is dramatic; it is like an impromptu piece of acting where each should represent himself to the greatest advantage; and that is the best kind of talk where each speaker is most fully and candidly himself, and where, if you were to shift the speeches round from one to another, there would be the greatest loss in significance and perspicuity. It is for this reason that talk depends so wholly on our company. We should like to introduce Falstaff and Mercutio, or Falstaff and Sir Toby; but Falstaff in talk with Cordelia seems even painful. Most of us, by the Protean quality of man, can talk to some degree with all; but the true talk, that strikes out all the slumbering best of us, comes only with the peculiar brethren of our spirits, is founded as deep as love in the constitution of our being, and is a thing to relish with all our energy, while yet we have it, and to be grateful for for ever.

TALK AND TALKERS[1]

II

IN THE last paper there was perhaps too much about mere debate; and there was nothing said at all about that kind of talk which is merely luminous and restful, a higher power of silence, the quiet of the evening shared by ruminating friends. There is something, aside from personal preference, to be alleged in support of this omission. Those who are no chimney-cornerers, who rejoice in the social thunderstorm, have a ground in reason for their choice. They get little rest indeed; but restfulness is a quality for cattle; the virtues are all active, life is alert, and it is in repose that men prepare themselves for evil. On the other hand, they are bruised into a knowledge of themselves and others; they have in a high degree the fencer's pleasure in dexterity displayed and proved; what they get they get upon life's terms, paying for it as they go; and once the talk is launched, they are assured of honest dealing from an adversary eager like themselves. The aboriginal man within us, the cave-dweller, still lusty as when he fought tooth and nail for roots and berries, scents this kind of equal battle from afar; it is like his old primæval days upon the crags, a return to the sincerity of savage life from

1. This sequel was called forth by an excellent article in *The Spectator*.

the comfortable fictions of the civilised. And if it be delightful to the Old Man, it is none the less profitable to his younger brother, the conscientious gentleman. I feel never quite sure of your urbane and smiling coteries; I fear they indulge a man's vanities in silence, suffer him to encroach, encourage him on to be an ass, and send him forth again, not merely contemned for the moment, but radically more contemptible than when he entered. But if I have a flushed, blustering fellow for my opposite, bent on carrying a point, my vanity is sure to have its ears rubbed, once at least, in the course of the debate. He will not spare me when we differ; he will not fear to demonstrate my folly to my face.

For many natures there is not much charm in the still, chambered society, the circle of bland countenances, the digestive silence, the admired remark, the flutter of affectionate approval. They demand more atmosphere and exercise; "a gale upon their spirits," as our pious ancestors would phrase it; to have their wits well breathed in an uproarious Valhalla. And I suspect that the choice, given their character and faults, is one to be defended. The purely wise are silenced by facts; they talk in a clear atmosphere, problems lying around them like a view in nature; if they can be shown to be somewhat in the wrong, they digest the reproof like a thrashing, and make better intellectual blood. They stand corrected by a whisper; a word or a glance reminds them of the great eternal law. But it is not so with all. Others in conversation seek rather contact with their fel-

low-men than increase of knowledge or clarity of
thought. The drama, not the philosophy, of life
is the sphere of their intellectual activity. Even
when they pursue truth, they desire as much as
possible of what we may call human scenery
along the road they follow. They dwell in the
heart of life; the blood sounding in their ears,
their eyes laying hold of what delights them with
a brutal avidity that makes them blind to all
besides, their interest riveted on people, living,
loving, talking, tangible people. To a man of this
description, the sphere of argument seems very
pale and ghostly. By a strong expression, a per-
turbed countenance, floods of tears, an insult
which his conscience obliges him to swallow, he
is brought round to knowledge which no syl-
logism would have conveyed to him. His own
experience is so vivid, he is so superlatively conscious of himself, that if, day after day, he is
allowed to hector and hear nothing but approving
echoes, he will lose his hold on the soberness of
things and take himself in earnest for a god. Talk
might be to such an one the very way of moral
ruin; the school where he might learn to be at
once intolerable and ridiculous.

This character is perhaps commoner than philosophers suppose. And for persons of that stamp
to learn much by conversation, they must speak
with their superiors, not in intellect, for that is
a superiority that must be proved, but in station.
If they cannot find a friend to bully them for
their good, they must find either an old man, a
woman, or some one so far below them in the

artificial order of society, that courtesy may be particularly exercised.

The best teachers are the aged. To the old our mouths are always partly closed; we must swallow our obvious retorts and listen. They sit above our heads, on life's raised daïs, and appeal at once to our respect and pity. A flavour of the old school, a touch of something different in their manner—which is freer and rounder, if they come of what is called a good family, and often more timid and precise if they are of the middle class—serves, in these days, to accentuate the difference of age and add a distinction to gray hairs. But their superiority is founded more deeply than by outward marks or gestures. They are before us in the march of man; they have more or less solved the irking problem; they have battled through the equinox of life; in good and evil they have held their course; and now, without open shame, they near the crown and harbour. It may be we have been struck with one of fortune's darts; we can scarce be civil, so cruelly is our spirit tossed. Yet long before we were so much as thought upon, the like calamity befell the old man or woman that now, with pleasant humour, rallies us upon our inattention, sitting composed in the holy evening of man's life, in the clear shining after rain. We grow ashamed of our distresses, new and hot and coarse, like villainous roadside brandy; we see life in aerial perspective, under the heavens of faith; and out of the worst, in the mere presence of contented elders, look forward and take patience. Fear shrinks before them "like a

thing reproved," not the flitting and ineffectual
fear of death, but the instant, dwelling terror of
the responsibilities and revenges of life. Their
speech, indeed, is timid; they report lions in the
path; they counsel a meticulous footing; but their
serene, marred faces are more eloquent and tell
another story. Where they have gone, we will go
also, not very greatly fearing; what they have en-
dured unbroken, we also, God helping us, will
make a shift to bear.

Not only is the presence of the aged in itself remedial, but their minds are stored with
antidotes, wisdom's simples, plain considerations
overlooked by youth. They have matter to communicate, be they never so stupid. Their talk is
not merely literature, it is great literature; classic
in virtue of the speaker's detachment, studded,
like a book of travel, with things we should not
otherwise have learnt. In virtue, I have said, of
the speaker's detachment,—and this is why, of
two old men, the one who is not your father
speaks to you with the more sensible authority;
for in the paternal relation the oldest have lively
interests and remain still young. Thus I have
known two young men great friends; each swore
by the other's father; the father of each swore by
the other lad; and yet each pair of parent and
child were perpetually by the ears. This is typical:
it reads like the gem of some kindly comedy.

The old appear in conversation in two characters: the critically silent and the garrulous anecdotic. The last is perhaps what we look for; it is
perhaps the more instructive. An old gentleman,

well on in years, sits handsomely and naturally in the bow-window of his age, scanning experience with reverted eye; and chirping and smiling, communicates the accidents and reads the lesson of his long career. Opinions are strengthened, indeed, but they are also weeded out in the course of years. What remains steadily present to the eye of the retired veteran in his hermitage, what still ministers to his content, what still quickens his old honest heart—these are "the real long-lived things" that Whitman tells us to prefer. Where youth agrees with age, not where they differ, wisdom lies; and it is when the young disciple finds his heart to beat in tune with his gray-bearded teacher's that a lesson may be learned. I have known one old gentleman, whom I may name, for he is now gathered to his stock—Robert Hunter, Sheriff of Dumbarton, and author of an excellent law-book still re-edited and republished. Whether he was originally big or little is more than I can guess. When I knew him he was all fallen away and fallen in; crooked and shrunken; buckled into a stiff waistcoat for support; troubled by ailments, which kept him hobbling in and out of the room; one foot gouty; a wig for decency, not for deception, on his head; close shaved, except under his chin—and for that he never failed to apologise, for it went sore against the traditions of his life. You can imagine how he would fare in a novel by Miss Mather; yet this rag of a Chelsea veteran lived to his last year in the plenitude of all that is best in man, brimming with human kindness, and staunch as

a Roman soldier under his manifold infirmities.
You could not say that he had lost his memory,
for he would repeat Shakespeare and Webster
and Jeremy Taylor and Burke by the page together; but the parchment was filled up, there
was no room for fresh inscriptions, and he was
capable of repeating the same anecdote on many
successive visits. His voice survived in its full
power, and he took a pride in using it. On his last
voyage as Commissioner of Lighthouses, he
hailed a ship at sea and made himself clearly
audible without a speaking trumpet, ruffling the
while with a proper vanity in his achievement. He
had a habit of eking out his words with interroga-
tive hems, which was puzzling and a little weari-
some, suited ill with his appearance, and seemed
a survival from some former stage of bodily port-
liness. Of yore, when he was a great pedestrian
and no enemy to good claret, he may have
pointed with these minute guns his allocutions to
the bench. His humour was perfectly equable, set
beyond the reach of fate; gout, rheumatism, stone
and gravel might have combined their forces
against that frail tabernacle, but when I came
round on Sunday evening, he would lay aside
Jeremy Taylor's *Life of Christ* and greet me with
the same open brow, the same kind formality of
manner. His opinions and sympathies dated the
man almost to a decade. He had begun life, under
his mother's influence, as an admirer of Junius,
but on maturer knowledge had transferred his
admiration to Burke. He cautioned me, with entire gravity, to be punctilious in writing English;

never to forget that I was a Scotchman, that
English was a foreign tongue, and that if I at-
tempted the colloquial, I should certainly be
shamed: the remark was apposite, I suppose, in
the days of David Hume. Scott was too new for
him; he had known the author—known him, too,
for a Tory; and to the genuine classic a contemporary is always something of a trouble. He had
the old, serious love of the play; had even, as he
was proud to tell, played a certain part in the
history of Shakespearian revivals, for he had successfully pressed on Murray, of the old Edinburgh
Theatre, the idea of producing Shakespeare's fairy
pieces with great scenic display. A moderate in
religion, he was much struck in the last years of
his life by a conversation with two young lads,
revivalists. "H'm," he would say—"new to me. I
have had—h'm—no such experience." It struck
him, not with pain, rather with a solemn philosophic interest, that he, a Christian as he hoped,
and a Christian of so old a standing, should hear
these young fellows talking of his own subject, his
own weapons that he had fought the battle of life
with,—"and—h'm—not understand." In this wise
and graceful attitude he did justice to himself
and others, reposed unshaken in his old beliefs,
and recognised their limits without anger or
alarm. His last recorded remark, on the last night
of his life, was after he had been arguing against
Calvinism with his minister and was interrupted
by an intolerable pang. "After all," he said, "of all
the 'isms, I know none so bad as rheumatism."
My own last sight of him was some time before,

when we dined together at an inn; he had been
on circuit, for he stuck to his duties like a chief
part of his existence; and I remember it as the
only occasion on which he ever soiled his lips
with slang—a thing he loathed. We were both
Roberts; and we took our places at table, he addressed me with a twinkle: "We are just what you
would call two bob." He offered me port, I remember, as the proper milk of youth; spoke of
"twenty-shilling notes"; and throughout the meal
was full of old-world pleasantry and quaintness,
like an ancient boy on a holiday. But what I recall chiefly was his confession that he had never
read *Othello* to an end. Shakespeare was his
continual study. He loved nothing better than to
display his knowledge and memory by adducing
parallel passages from Shakespeare, passages where
the same word was employed, or the same idea
differently treated. But *Othello* had beaten him.
"That noble gentleman and that noble lady—
h'm—too painful for me." The same night the
hoardings were covered with posters, "Burlesque
of *Othello*," and the contrast blazed up in my
mind like a bonfire. An unforgettable look it
gave me into that kind man's soul. His acquaintance was indeed a liberal and pious education. All the humanities were taught in that
bare dining-room beside his gouty footstool. He
was a piece of good advice; he was himself the
instance that pointed and adorned his various
talk. Nor could a young man have found elsewhere a place so set apart from envy, fear, dis-
content, or any of the passions that debase; a life

so honest and composed; a soul like an ancient violin, so subdued to harmony, responding to a touch in music—as in that dining-room, with Mr. Hunter chatting at the eleventh hour, under the shadow of eternity, fearless and gentle.

The second class of old people are not anecdotic; they are rather hearers than talkers, listening to the young with an amused and critical attention. To have this sort of intercourse to perfection, I think we must go to old ladies. Women are better hearers than men, to begin with; they learn, I fear in anguish, to bear with the tedious and infantile vanity of the other sex; and we will take more from a woman than even from the oldest man in the way of biting comment. Biting comment is the chief part, whether for profit or amusement in this business. The old lady that I have in my eye is a very caustic speaker, her tongue, after years of practice, in absolute command, whether for silence or attack. If she chance to dislike you, you will be tempted to curse the malignity of age. But if you chance to please even slightly, you will be listened to with a particular laughing grace of sympathy, and from time to time chastised, as if in play, with a parasol as heavy as a pole-axe. It requires a singular art, as well as the vantage-ground of age, to deal these stunning corrections among the coxcombs of the young. The pill is disguised in sugar of wit; it is administered as a compliment—if you had not pleased, you would not have been censured; it is a personal affair—a hyphen, a *trait d'union*, between you and your

censor; age's philandering, for her pleasure and
your good. Incontestably the young man feels
very much of a fool; but he must be a perfect
Malvolio, sick with self-love, if he cannot take
an open buffet and still smile. The correction of
silence is what kills; when you know you have
transgressed, and your friend says nothing and
avoids your eye. If a man were made of gutta-
percha, his heart would quail at such a moment.
But when the word is out, the worst is over; and
a fellow with any good-humour at all may pass
through a perfect hail of witty criticism, every
bare place on his soul hit to the quick with a
shrewd missile, and reappear, as if after a dive,
tingling with a fine moral reaction, and ready,
with a shrinking readiness, one-third loath, for a
repetition of the discipline.

There are few women, not well sunned and
ripened, and perhaps toughened, who can thus
stand apart from a man and say the true thing
with a kind of genial cruelty. Still there are some
—and I doubt if there be any man who can return the compliment. The class of man represented by Vernon Whitford in *The Egoist* says,
indeed, the true thing, but he says it stockishly.
Vernon is a noble fellow, and makes, by the
way, a noble and instructive contrast to Daniel
Deronda; his conduct is the conduct of a man of
honour; but we agree with him, against our consciences, when he remorsefully considers "its astonishing dryness." He is the best of men, but
the best of women manage to combine all that
and something more. Their very faults assist

them; they are helped even by the falseness of their position in life. They can retire into the fortified camp of the proprieties. They can touch a subject and suppress it. The most adroit employ a somewhat elaborate reserve as a means to be frank, much as they wear gloves when they shake hands. But a man has the full responsibility of his freedom, cannot evade a question, can scarce be silent without rudeness, must answer for his words upon the moment, and is not seldom left face to face with a damning choice, between the more or less dishonourable wriggling of Deronda and the downright woodenness of Vernon Whitford.

But the superiority of women is perpetually menaced; they do not sit throned on infirmities like the old; they are suitors as well as sovereigns; their vanity is engaged, their affections are too apt to follow; and hence much of the talk between the sexes degenerates into something unworthy of the name. The desire to please, to shine with a certain softness of lustre and to draw a fascinating picture of oneself, banishes from conversation all that is sterling and most of what is humorous. As soon as a strong current of mutual admiration begins to flow, the human interest triumphs entirely over the intellectual, and the commerce of words, consciously or not, becomes secondary to the commercing of eyes. But even where this ridiculous danger is avoided, and a man and woman converse equally and honestly, something in their nature or their education falsifies the strain. An instinct prompts them to agree; and where that is impossible, to agree to differ. Should they neglect the warning, at the first suspicion of an argument, they find themselves in different hemispheres. About any point of business or conduct, any actual affair demanding settlement, a woman will speak and listen, hear and answer arguments, not only with natural wisdom, but with candour and logical honesty. But if the subject of debate be something in the air, an abstraction, an excuse for talk, a logical Aunt Sally, then may the male debater instantly abandon hope; he may employ reason, adduce facts, be supple, be smiling, be angry, all shall avail him nothing; what the woman said first, that (unless she has forgotten it) she will repeat at the end. Hence, at the very junctures when a talk between men grows brighter and quicker and begins to promise to bear fruit, talk between the sexes is menaced with dissolution. The point of difference, the point of interest, is evaded by the brilliant woman, under a shower of irrelevant conversational rockets; it is bridged by the discreet woman with a rustle of silk, as she passes smoothly forward to the nearest point of safety. And this sort of prestidigitation, juggling the dangerous topic out of sight until it can be reintroduced with safety in an altered shape, is a piece of tactics among the true drawing-room queens.

The drawing-room is, indeed, an artificial place; it is so by our choice and for our sins. The subjection of women; the ideal imposed upon them from the cradle, and worn, like a hair-shirt, with so much constancy; their motherly, superior tenderness to man's vanity and self-importance; their managing arts—the arts of a civilised slave among good-natured barbarians—are all painful ingredients and all help to falsify relations. It is not till we get clear of that amusing artificial scene that genuine relations are founded, or ideas honestly compared. In the garden, on the road or the hillside, or *tête-à-tête* and apart from interruptions, occasions arise when we may learn much from any single woman; and nowhere more often than in married life. Marriage is one long conversation, chequered by disputes. The disputes are valueless; they but ingrain the difference; the heroic heart of woman prompting her at once to nail her colours to the mast. But in the intervals, almost unconsciously and with no desire to shine, the whole material of life is turned over and over, ideas are struck out and shared, the two persons more and more adapt their notions one to suit the other, and in process of time, without sound of trumpet, they conduct each other into new worlds of thought.

THE MORALITY OF THE PROFESSION OF LETTERS

THE PROFESSION of letters has been lately debated in the public prints; and it has been debated, to put the matter mildly, from a point of view that was calculated to surprise high-minded men, and bring a general contempt on books and reading. Some time ago, in particular, a lively, pleasant, popular writer[1] devoted an essay, lively and pleasant like himself, to a very encouraging view of the profession. We may be glad that his experience is so cheering, and we may hope that all others, who deserve it, shall be as handsomely rewarded; but I do not think we need be at all glad to have this question, so important to the public and ourselves, debated solely on the ground of money. The salary in any business under heaven is not the only, nor indeed the first, question. That you should continue to exist is a matter for your own consideration; but that your business should be first honest, and second useful, are points in which honour and morality are concerned. If the writer to whom I refer succeeds in persuading a number of young persons to adopt this way of life with an eye set singly on the livelihood, we must expect them in their works to follow profit only, and we must expect in conse-

1. Mr. James Payn.

71

quence, if he will pardon me the epithets, a slovenly, base, untrue, and empty literature. Of that writer himself I am not speaking: he is diligent, clean and pleasing; we all owe him periods of entertainment, and he has achieved an amiable popularity which he has adequately deserved. But the truth is, he does not, or did not when he first embraced it, regard his profession from this purely mercenary side. He went into it, I shall venture to say, if not with any noble design, at least in the ardour of a first love; and he enjoyed its practice long before he paused to calculate the wage. The other day an author was complimented on a piece of work, good in itself and exceptionally good for him, and replied, in terms unworthy of a commercial traveller, that as the book was not briskly selling he did not give a copper farthing for its merit. It must not be supposed that the person to whom this answer was addressed received it as a profession of faith; he knew, on the other hand, that it was only a whiff of irritation; just as we know, when a respectable writer talks of literature as a way of life, like shoemaking, but not so useful, that he is only debating one aspect of a question, and is still clearly conscious of a dozen others more important in themselves and more central to the matter in hand. But while those who treat literature in this penny-wise and virtue-foolish spirit are themselves truly in possession of a better light, it does not follow that the treatment is decent or improving, whether for themselves or others. To treat all subjects in the highest, the most honourable, and the pluckiest spirit, consistent with the fact, is the first duty of a writer. If he be well paid, as I am glad to hear he is, this duty becomes the more urgent, the neglect of it the more disgraceful. And perhaps there is no subject on which a man should speak so gravely as that industry, whatever it may be, which is the occupation or delight of his life; which is his tool to earn or serve with; and which, if it be unworthy, stamps himself as a mere incubus of dumb and greedy bowels on the shoulders of labouring humanity. On that subject alone even to force the note might lean to virtue's side. It is to be hoped that a numerous and enterprising generation of writers will follow and surpass the present one; but it would be better if the stream were stayed, and the roll of our old honest English books were closed, than that esurient book-makers should continue and debase a brave tradition, and lower, in their own eyes, a famous race. Better that our serene temples were deserted than filled with trafficking and juggling priests.

There are two just reasons for the choice of any way of life: the first is inbred taste in the chooser; the second some high utility in the industry selected. Literature, like any other art, is singularly interesting to the artist; and, in a degree peculiar to itself among the arts, it is useful to mankind. These are sufficient justifications for any young man or woman who adopts it as the business of his life. I shall not say much about the wages. A writer can live by his writing. If not so luxuriously as by other trades, then less luxuriously. The nature of the work he does all day will more affect his happiness than the quality of his dinner at night. Whatever be your calling and however much it brings you in the year, you could still, you know, get more by cheating. We all suffer ourselves to be too much concerned about a little poverty; but such considerations should not move us in the choice of that which is to be the business and justification of so great a portion of our lives; and like the missionary, the patriot, or the philosopher, we should all choose that poor and brave career in which we can do the most and best for mankind. Now Nature, faithfully followed, proves herself a careful mother. A lad, for some liking to the jingle of words, betakes himself to letters for his life; by-and-by, when he learns more gravity, he finds that he has chosen better than he knew; that if he earns little, he is earning it amply; that if he receives a small wage, he is in a position to do considerable services; that it is in his power, in some small measure to protect the oppressed and to defend the truth. So kindly is the world arranged, such great profit may arise from a small degree of human reliance on oneself, and such, in particular, is the happy star of this trade of writing, that it should combine pleasure and profit to both parties, and be at once agreeable, like fiddling, and useful, like good preaching.

This is to speak of literature at its highest; and with the four great elders who are still spared to our respect and admiration, with Carlyle, Ruskin, Browning, and Tennyson before us, it would be

cowardly to consider it at first in any lesser aspect.
But while we cannot follow these athletes, while
we may none of us, perhaps, be very vigorous,
very original, or very wise, I still contend that, in
the humblest sort of literary work, we have it in
our power either to do great harm or great good.
We may seek merely to please; we may seek, having no higher gift, merely to gratify the idle nine
days' curiosity of our contemporaries; or we may
essay, however feebly, to instruct. In each of these
we shall have to deal with that remarkable art
of words which, because it is the dialect of life,
comes home so easily and powerfully to the minds
of men; and since that is so, we contribute, in
each of these branches, to build up the sum of
sentiments and appreciations which goes by the
name of Public Opinion or Public Feeling. The
total of a nation's reading, in these days of daily
papers, greatly modifies the total of the nation's
speech; and the speech and reading, taken together, form the efficient educational medium of
youth. A good man or woman may keep a youth
some little while in clearer air; but the contemporary atmosphere is all-powerful in the end on
the average of mediocre characters. The copious
Corinthian baseness of the American reporter or
the Parisian *chroniquer*, both so lightly readable,
must exercise an incalculable influence for ill;
they touch upon all subjects, and on all with
the same ungenerous hand; they begin the consideration of all, in young and unprepared minds,
in an unworthy spirit; on all, they supply some
pungency for dull people to quote. The mere

body of this ugly matter overwhelms the rare utterances of good men; the sneering, the selfish, and the cowardly are scattered in broad sheets on every table, while the antidote, in small volumes, lies unread upon the shelf. I have spoken of the American and the French, not because they are so much baser, but so much more readable, than the English; their evil is done more effectively, in America for the masses, in French for the few that care to read; but with us as with them, the duties of literature are daily neglected, truth daily perverted and suppressed, and grave subjects daily degraded in the treatment. The journalist is not reckoned an important officer; yet judge of the good he might do, the harm he does; judge of it by one instance only: that when we find two journals on the reverse sides of politics each, on the same day, openly garbling a piece of news for the interest of its own party, we smile at the discovery (no discovery now!) as over a good joke and pardonable stratagem. Lying so open is scarce lying, it is true, but one of the things that we profess to teach our young is a respect for truth; and I cannot think this piece of education will be crowned with any great success, so long as some of us practise and the rest openly approve of public falsehood.

There are two duties incumbent upon any man who enters on the business of writing: truth to the fact and a good spirit in the treatment. In every department of literature, though so low as hardly to deserve the name, truth to the fact is of importance to the education and comfort of mankind, and so hard to preserve, that the faithful trying to do so will lend some dignity to the man who tries it. Our judgments are based upon two things: first, upon the original preferences of our soul; but, second, upon the mass of testimony to the nature of God, man, and the universe which reaches us, in divers manners, from without. For the most part these divers manners are reducible to one, all that we learn of past times and much that we learn of our own reaching us through the medium of books or papers, and even he who cannot read learning from the same source at second-hand and by the report of him who can. Thus the sum of the contemporary knowledge or ignorance of good and evil is, in large measure, the handiwork of those who write. Those who write have to see that each man's knowledge is, as near as they can make it, answerable to the facts of life; that he shall not suppose himself an angel or a monster; nor take this world for a hell; nor be suffered to imagine that all rights are concentred in his own caste or country, or all veracities in his own parochial creed. Each man should learn what is within him, that he may strive to mend; he must be taught what is without him, that he may be kind to others. It can never be wrong to tell him the truth; for, in his disputable state, weaving as he goes his theory of life, steering himself, cheering or reproving others, all facts are of the first importance to his conduct; and even if a fact shall discourage or corrupt him, it is still best that he should know it; for it is in this world as it is, and not in a world made easy by educational suppressions, that he must win his way to shame or glory. In one word, it must always be foul to tell what is false; and it can never be safe to suppress what is true. The very fact that you omit may be the fact which somebody was wanting, for one man's meat is another man's poison, and I have known a person who was cheered by the perusal of *Candide*. Every fact is a part of that great puzzle we must set together; and none that comes directly in a writer's path but has some nice relations, unperceivable by him, to the totality and bearing of the subject under hand. Yet there are certain classes of fact eternally more necessary than others, and it is with these that literature must first bestir itself. They are not hard to distinguish, nature once more easily leading us; for the necessary, because the efficacious, facts are those which are most interesting to the natural mind of man. Those which are coloured, picturesque, human, and rooted in morality, and those, on the other hand, which are clear, indisputable, and a part of science, are alone vital in importance, seizing by their interest, or useful to communicate. So far as the writer merely narrates, he should principally tell of these. He should tell of the kind and wholesome and beautiful elements of our life; he should tell unsparingly of the evil and sorrow of the present, to move us with instances; he should tell of wise and good people in the past, to excite us by example; and of these he should tell soberly and truthfully, not glossing faults, that we may neither grow discouraged with ourselves nor exacting to our neighbours. So the body of contemporary literature, ephemeral and feeble in itself, touches in the minds of men the springs of thought and kindness, and supports them (for those who will go at all are easily supported) on their way to what is true and right. And if, in any degree, it does so now, how much more might it do so if the writers chose! There is not a life in all the records of the past but, properly studied, might lend a hint and a help to some contemporary. There is not a juncture in to-day's affairs but some useful word may yet be said of it. Even the reporter has an office, and, with clear eyes and honest language, may unveil injustices and point the way to progress. And for a last word: in all narration there is only one way to be clever, and that is to be exact. To be vivid is a secondary quality which must presuppose the first; for vividly to convey a wrong impression is only to make failure conspicuous.

But a fact may be viewed on many sides; it may be chronicled with rage, tears, laughter, indifference, or admiration, and by each of these the story will be transformed to something else. The newspapers that told of the return of our representatives from Berlin, even if they had not differed as to the facts, would have sufficiently differed by their spirits; so that the one description would have been a second ovation, and the other a prolonged insult. The subject makes but a trifling part of any piece of literature, and the view of the writer is itself a fact more important because less disputable than the others. Now this spirit in which a subject is regarded, important in all kinds of literary work, becomes all-important in works of fiction, meditation, or rhapsody; for there it not only colours but itself chooses the facts; not only modifies but shapes the work. And hence, over the far larger proportion of the field of literature, the health or disease of the writer's mind or momentary humour forms not only the leading feature of his work, but is, at bottom, the only thing he can communicate to others. In all works of art, widely speaking, it is first of all the author's attitude that is narrated, though in the attitude there be implied a whole experience and a theory of life. An author who has begged the question and reposes in some narrow faith cannot, if he would, express the whole or even many of the sides of this various existence; for, his own life being maim, some of them are not admitted in his theory, and were only dimly and unwillingly recognised in his experience. Hence the smallness, the triteness, and the inhumanity in works of merely sectarian religion; and hence we find equal although unsimilar limitation in works inspired by the spirit of the flesh or the despicable taste for high society. So that the first duty of any man who is to write is intellectual. Designedly or not, he has so far set himself up for a leader of the minds of men; and he must see that his own mind is kept supple, charitable, and bright. Everything but prejudice should find a voice through him; he should see the good in all things; where he has even a fear that he does not wholly understand, there he should be wholly silent; and he should recognise from the first that he has only one tool in his workshop, and that tool is sympathy.[2]

The second duty, far harder to define, is moral. There are a thousand different humours in the mind, and about each of them, when it is uppermost, some literature tends to be deposited. Is this to be allowed? Not certainly in every case, and yet perhaps in more than rigourists would fancy. It were to be desired that all literary work, and chiefly works of art, issued from sound, human, healthy, and potent impulses, whether grave or laughing, humorous, romantic or religious. Yet it cannot be denied that some valuable books are partially insane; some, mostly religious, partially inhuman; and very many tainted with morbidity and impotence. We do not loathe a masterpiece although we gird against its blemishes. We are not, above all, to look for faults, but merits. There is no book perfect, even in design; but there are many that will delight, improve, or encourage the reader. On the one hand, the Hebrew psalms are the only religious poetry on earth; yet they contain sallies that savour rankly of the man of blood. On the other hand, Alfred de Musset had a poisoned and a contorted na-

2. A footnote, at least, is due to the admirable example set before all young writers in the width of literary sympathy displayed by Mr. Swinburne. He runs forth to welcome merit, whether in Dickens or Trollope, whether in Villon, Milton, or Pope. This is, in criticism, the attitude we should all seek to preserve, not only in that, but in every branch of literary work.

ture; I am only quoting that generous and frivolous giant, old Dumas, when I accuse him of a bad heart; yet when the impulse under which he wrote was purely creative, he could give us works like *Carmosine* or *Fantasio*, in which the last note of the romantic comedy seems to have been found again to touch and please us. When Flaubert wrote *Madame Bovary*, I believe he thought chiefly of a somewhat morbid realism; and behold! the book turned in his hands into a masterpiece of appalling morality. But the truth is, when books are conceived under a great stress, with a soul of ninefold power, nine times heated and electrified by effort, the conditions of our being are seized with such an ample grasp, that, even should the main design be trivial or base, some truth and beauty cannot fail to be expressed. Out of the strong comes forth sweetness; but an ill thing poorly done is an ill thing top and bottom. And so this can be no encouragement to knock-kneed, feeble-wristed scribes, who must take their business conscientiously or be ashamed to practise it.

Man is imperfect; yet, in his literature, he must express himself and his own views and preferences; for to do anything else is to do a far more perilous thing than to risk being immoral; it is to be sure of being untrue. To ape a sentiment, even a good one, is to travesty a sentiment; that will not be helpful. To conceal a sentiment, if you are sure you hold it, is to take a liberty with truth. There is probably no point of view possible to a sane man but contains some truth and, in the true connection, might be profitable to the race. I am not afraid of the truth, if any one could tell it me, but I am afraid of parts of it impertinently uttered. There is a time to dance and a time to mourn; to be harsh as well as to be sentimental; to be ascetic as well as to glorify the appetites; and if a man were to combine all these extremes into his work, each in its place and proportion, that work would be the world's masterpiece of morality, as well as of art. Partiality is immorality; for any book is wrong that gives a misleading picture of the world and life. The trouble is that the weakling must be partial; the work of one proving dank and depressing; of another, cheap and vulgar; of a third, epileptically sensual; of a fourth, sourly ascetic. In literature as in conduct, you can never hope to do exactly right. All you can do is to make as sure as possible; and for that there is but one rule. Nothing should be done in a hurry that can be done slowly. It is no use to write a book and put it by for nine or even ninety years; for in the writing you will have partly convinced yourself; the delay must precede any beginning; and if you meditate a work of art, you should first long roll the subject under the tongue to make sure you like the flavour, before you brew a volume that shall taste of it from end to end; or if you propose to enter on the field of controversy, you should first have thought upon the question under all conditions, in health as well as in sickness, in sorrow as well as in joy. It is this nearness of examination necessary for any true and kind writing, that makes practice of the art a prolonged and noble education for the writer.

There is plenty to do, plenty to say, or to say over again, in the meantime. Any literary work which conveys faithful facts or pleasing impressions is a service to the public. It is even a service to be thankfully proud of having rendered. The slightest novels are a blessing to those in distress, not chloroform itself a greater. Our fine old sea-captain's life was justified when Carlyle soothed his mind with *The King's Own* or *Newton Forster*. To please is to serve; and so far from its being difficult to instruct while you amuse, it is difficult to do the one thoroughly without the other. Some part of the writer or his life will crop out in even a vapid book; and to read a novel that was conceived with any force is to multiply experience and to exercise the sympathies. Every article, every piece of verse, every essay, every *entre-filet*, is destined to pass, however swiftly, through the minds of some portion of the public, and to colour, however transiently, their thoughts. When any subject falls to be discussed, some scribbler on a paper has the invaluable opportunity of beginning its discussion in a dignified and human spirit; and if there were enough who did so in our public press, neither the public nor the Parliament would find it in their minds to drop to meaner thoughts. The writer has the chance to stumble, by the way, on something pleasing, something interesting, something encouraging, were it only to a single reader. He will be unfortunate, indeed, if he suit no one. He has the chance, besides, to stumble on something that a dull person shall be able to comprehend; and for a dull person to have read anything and, for that once, comprehended it, makes a marking epoch in his education.

Here, then, is work worth doing and worth trying to do well. And so, if I were minded to welcome any great accession to our trade, it should not be from any reason of a higher wage, but because it was a trade which was useful in a very great and in a very high degree; which every honest tradesman could make more serviceable to mankind in his single strength; which was difficult to do well and possible to do better every year; which called for scrupulous thought on the part of all who practised it, and hence became a perpetual education to their nobler natures; and which, pay it as you please, in the large majority of the best cases will still be underpaid. For surely at this time of the day in the nineteenth century, there is nothing that an honest man should fear more timorously than getting and spending more than he deserves.

BOOKS WHICH HAVE
INFLUENCED ME

THE EDITOR [1] has somewhat insidiously laid a trap for his correspondents, the question put appearing at first so innocent, truly cutting so deep. It is not, indeed, until after some reconnaissance and review that the writer awakes to find himself engaged upon something in the nature of autobiography, or, perhaps worse, upon a chapter in the life of that little, beautiful brother whom we once all had, and whom we have all lost and mourned, the man we ought to have been, the man we hoped to be. But when word has been passed (even to an editor), it should, if possible, be kept; and if sometimes I am wise and say too little, and sometimes weak and say too much, the blame must lie at the door of the person who entrapped me.

The most influential books, and the truest in their influence, are works of fiction. They do not pin the reader to a dogma which he must afterwards discover to be inexact; they do not teach him a lesson which he must afterwards unlearn. They repeat, they rearrange, they clarify the lessons of life; they disengage us from ourselves, they constrain us to the acquaintance of others; and they show us the web of experience, not as

1. Of the *British Weekly*.

we can see it for ourselves, but with a singular change—that monstrous, consuming *ego* of ours being, for the nonce, struck out. To be so, they must be reasonably true to the human comedy; and any work that is so serves the turn of instruction. But the course of our education is answered best by those poems and romances where we breathe a magnanimous atmosphere of thought and meet generous and pious characters. Shakespeare has served me best. Few living friends have had upon me an influence so strong for good as Hamlet or Rosalind. The last character, already well beloved in the reading, I had the good fortune to see, I must think, in an impressionable hour, played by Mrs. Scott Siddons. Nothing has ever more moved, more delighted, more refreshed me; nor has the influence quite passed away. Kent's brief speech over the dying Lear had a great effect upon my mind, and was the burthen of my reflections for long, so profoundly, so touchingly generous did it appear in sense, so overpowering in expression. Perhaps my dearest and best friend outside of Shakespeare is D'Artagnan—the elderly D'Artagnan of the *Vicomte de Bragelonne*. I know not a more human soul, nor, in his way, a finer; I shall be very sorry for the man who is so much of a pedant in morals that he cannot learn from the Captain of Musketeers. Lastly, I must name the *Pilgrim's Progress*, a book that breathes of every beautiful and valuable emotion.

But of works of art little can be said; their influence is profound and silent, like the influence of nature; they mould by contact; we drink them up like water, and are bettered, yet know not how. It is in books more specifically didactic that we can follow out the effect, and distinguish and weigh and compare. A book which has been very influential upon me fell early into my hands, and so may stand first, though I think its influence was only sensible later on, and perhaps still keeps growing, for it is a book not easily outlived; the *Essais* of Montaigne. That temperate and genial picture of life is a great gift to place in the hands of persons of to-day; they will find in these smiling pages a magazine of heroism and wisdom, all of an antique strain; they will have their "linen decencies" and excited orthodoxies fluttered, and will (if they have any gift of reading) perceive that these have not been fluttered without some excuse and ground of reason; and (again if they have any gift of reading) they will end by seeing that this old gentleman was in a dozen ways a finer fellow, and held in a dozen ways a nobler view of life than they or their contemporaries.

The next book, in order of time, to influence me, was the New Testament, and in particular the Gospel according to St. Matthew. I believe it would startle and move any one if they could make a certain effort of imagination and read it freshly like a book, not droningly and dully like a portion of the Bible. Any would then be able to see in it those truths which we are all courteously supposed to know and all modestly refrain from applying. But upon this subject it is perhaps better to be silent.

I come next to Whitman's *Leaves of Grass,* a book of singular service, a book which tumbled the world upside down for me, blew into space a thousand cobwebs of genteel and ethical illusion, and, having thus shaken my tabernacle of lies, set me back again upon a strong foundation of all the original and manly virtues. But it is, once more, only a book for those who have the gift of reading. I will be very frank—I believe it is so with all good books except, perhaps, fiction. The average man lives, and must live, so wholly in convention, that gunpowder charges of the truth are more apt to discompose than to invigorate his creed. Either he cries out upon blasphemy and indecency, and crouches the closer round that little idol of part-truths and part-conveniences which is the contemporary deity, or he is convinced by what is new, forgets what is old, and becomes truly blasphemous and indecent himself. New truth is only useful to supplement the old; rough truth is only wanted to expand, not to destroy, our civil and often elegant conventions. He who cannot judge had better stick to fiction and the daily papers. There he will get little harm, and, in the first at least, some good.

Close upon the back of my discovery of Whitman, I came under the influence of Herbert Spencer. No more persuasive rabbi exists, and few better. How much of his vast structure will bear the touch of time, how much is clay and how much brass, it were too curious to inquire. But his words, if dry, are always manly and honest; there dwells in his pages a spirit of highly abstract joy, plucked naked like an algebraic symbol but still joyful; and the reader will find there a *caput-mortuum* of piety, with little indeed of its loveliness, but with most of its essentials; and these two qualities make him a wholesome, as his intellectual vigour makes him a bracing, writer. I should be much of a hound if I lost my gratitude to Herbert Spencer.

Goethe's Life, by Lewes, had a great importance for me when it first fell into my hands—a strange instance of the partiality of man's good and man's evil. I know no one whom I less admire than Goethe; he seems a very epitome of the sins of genius, breaking open the doors of private life and wantonly wounding friends, in that crowning offence of *Werther*, and in his own character a mere pen-and-ink Napoleon, conscious of the rights and duties of superior talents as a Spanish inquisitor was conscious of the rights and duties of his office. And yet in his fine devotion to his art, in his honest and serviceable friendship for Schiller, what lessons are contained! Biography, usually so false to its office, does here for once perform for us some of the work of fiction, reminding us, that is, of the truly mingled tissue of man's nature, and how huge faults and shining virtues cohabit and persevere in the same character. History serves us well to this effect, but in the originals not in the pages of the popular epitomiser, who is bound, by the very nature of his task, to make us feel the difference of epochs instead of the essential identity of man, and even in the originals only to those who can recognise their own human virtues and defects in strange forms often inverted, and under strange names often interchanged. Martial is a poet of no good repute and it gives a man new thoughts to read his works dispassionately, and find in this unseemly jester's serious passages the images of a kind, wise, and self-respecting gentleman. It is customary, I suppose, in reading Martial, to leave out these pleasant verses; I never heard of them, at least, until I found them for myself; and this partiality is one among a thousand things that help to build up our distorted and hysterical conception of the great Roman Empire.

This brings us by a natural transition to a very noble book—the *Meditations* of Marcus Aurelius. The dispassionate gravity, the noble forgetfulness of self, the tenderness of others, that are there expressed and were practised on so great a scale in the life of its writer, make this book a book quite by itself. No one can read it and not be moved. Yet it scarcely or rarely appeals to the feelings—those very mobile, those not very trusty parts of man. Its address lies further back: its lesson comes more deeply home; when you have read, you carry with you a memory of the man himself; it is as though you had touched a loyal hand, looked into brave eyes, and made a noble friend; there is another bond on you thenceforward, binding you to life and to the love of virtue.

Wordsworth should perhaps come next. Every one has been influenced by Wordsworth, and it is hard to tell precisely how. A certain innocence, a rugged austerity of joy, a sight of the stars, "the

silence that is in the lonely hills," something of
the cold thrill of dawn, cling to his work and give
it a particular address to what is best in us. I do
not know that you learn a lesson; you need not—
Mill did not—agree with any one of his beliefs;
and yet the spell is cast. Such are the best
teachers: a dogma learned is only a new error—
the old one was perhaps as good; but a spirit
communicated is a perpetual possession. These
best teachers climb beyond teaching to the plane
of art; it is themselves, and what is best in themselves, that they communicate.

I should never forgive myself if I forget *The
Egoist*. It is art, if you like, but it belongs purely
to didactic art, and from all the novels I have
read (and I have read thousands) stands in a
place by itself. Here is a Nathan for the modern
David; here is a book to send the blood into
men's faces. Satire, the angry picture of human
faults, is not great art; we can all be angry with
our neighbour; what we want is to be shown, not
his defects, of which we are too conscious, but
his merits, to which we are too blind. And *The
Egoist* is a satire; so much must be allowed; but
it is a satire of a singular quality, which tells you
nothing of that obvious mote, which is engaged
from first to last with that invisible beam. It is
yourself that is hunted down; these are your own
faults that are dragged into the day and numbered, with lingering relish, with cruel cunning
and precision. A young friend of Mr. Meredith's
(as I have the story) came to him in an agony.
"This is too bad of you," he cried. "Willoughby

is me!" "No, my dear fellow," said the author; "he is all of us." I have read *The Egoist* five or six times myself, and I mean to read it again; for I am like the young friend of the anecdote—I think Willoughby an unmanly but a very serviceable exposure of myself.

I suppose, when I am done, I shall find that I have forgotten much that was most influential, as I see already I have forgotten Thoreau, and Hazlitt whose paper "On the Spirit of Obligations" was a turning-point in my life, and Pen whose little book of aphorisms had a brief but strong effect on me, and Mitford's *Tales of Old Japan*, wherein I learned for the first time the proper attitude of any rational man to his country's laws—a secret found, and kept, in the Asiatic islands. That I should commemorate all is more than I can hope or the Editor could ask. It will be more to the point, after having said so much upon improving books, to say a word or two about the improvable reader. The gift of reading, as I have called it, is not very common, nor very generally understood. It consists, first of all, in a vast intellectual endowment—a free grace, I find I must call it—by which a man rises to understand that he is not punctually right, nor those from whom he differs absolutely wrong. He may hold dogmas; he may hold them passionately; and he may know that others hold them but coldly, or hold them differently, or hold them not at all. Well, if he has the gift of reading, these others will be full of meat for him. They will see the other side of propositions and the other side of virtues. He need not change his dogma for that, but he may change his reading of that dogma, and he must supplement and correct his deductions from it. A human truth, which is always very much a lie, hides as much of life as it displays. It is men who hold another truth, or, as it seems to us, perhaps, a dangerous lie, who can extend our restricted field of knowledge, and rouse our drowsy consciences. Something that seems quite new, or that seems insolently false or very dangerous, is the test of a reader. If he tries to see what it means, what truth excuses it, he has the gift, and let him read. If he is merely hurt, or offended, or exclaims upon his author's folly, he had better take to the daily papers; he will never be a reader.

And here, with the aptest illustrative force, after I have laid down my part-truth, I must step in with its opposite. For, after all, we are vessels of a very limited content. Not all men can read all books; it is only in a chosen few that any man will find his appointed food; and the fittest lessons are the most palatable, and make themselves welcome to the mind. A writer learns this early, and it is his chief support; he goes on unafraid, laying down the law; and he is sure at heart that most of what he says is demonstrably false, and much of a mingled strain, and some hurtful, and very little good for service; but he is sure besides that when his words fall into the hands of any genuine reader, they will be weighed and winnowed, and only that which suits will be assimilated; and when they fall into the hands of one who cannot intelligently read, they come there quite silent and inarticulate, falling upon deaf ears, and his secret is kept as if he had not written.

WALT WHITMAN

OF LATE YEARS the name of Walt Whitman has been a good deal bandied about in books and magazines. It has become familiar both in good and ill repute. His works have been largely bespattered with praise by his admirers, and cruelly mauled and mangled by irreverent enemies. Now, whether his poetry is good or bad as poetry, is a matter that may admit of a difference of opinion without alienating those who differ. We could not keep the peace with a man who should put forward claims to taste and yet depreciate the choruses in *Samson Agonistes*; but, I think, we may shake hands with one who sees no more in Walt Whitman's volume, from a literary point of view, than a farrago of incompetent essays in a wrong direction. That may not be at all our own opinion. We may think that, when a work contains many unforgettable phrases, it cannot be altogether devoid of literary merit. We may even see passages of a high poetry here and there among its eccentric contents. But when all is said, Walt Whitman is neither a Milton nor a Shakespeare; to appreciate his works is not a condition necessary to salvation; and I would not disinherit a son upon the question, nor even think much the worse of a critic, for I should always have an idea what he meant.

What Whitman has to say is another affair

from how he says it. It is not possible to acquit
anyone of defective intelligence, or else stiff
prejudice, who is not interested by Whitman's
matter and the spirit it represents. Not as a poet,
but as what we must call (for lack of a more exact
expression) a prophet, he occupies a curious and
prominent position. Whether he may greatly influence the future or not, he is a notable symptom
of the present. As a sign of the times, it would
be hard to find his parallel. I should hazard a
large wager, for instance, that he was not unacquainted with the works of Herbert Spencer;
and yet where, in all the history books, shall we
lay our hands on two more incongruous contemporaries? Mr. Spencer so decorous—I had
almost said, so dandy—in dissent; and Whitman, like a large shaggy dog, just unchained,
scouring the beaches of the world and baying at
the moon. And when was an echo more curiously
like a satire, than when Mr. Spencer found his
Synthetic Philosophy reverberated from the other
shores of the Atlantic in the "barbaric yawp"
of Whitman?

I

Whitman, it cannot be too soon explained,
writes up to a system. He was a theoriser about
society before he was a poet. He first perceived
something wanting, and then sat down squarely
to supply the want. The reader, running over his
works, will find that he takes nearly as much
pleasure in critically expounding his theory of
poetry as in making poems. This is as far as it

can be from the case of the spontaneous village minstrel dear to elegy, who has no theory whatever, although sometimes he may have fully as much poetry as Whitman. The whole of Whitman's work is deliberate and preconceived. A man born into a society comparatively new, full of conflicting elements and interests, could not fail, if he had any thoughts at all, to reflect upon the tendencies around him. He saw much good and evil on all sides, not yet settled down into some more or less unjust compromise as in older nations, but still in the act of settlement. And he could not but wonder what it would turn out; whether the compromise would be very just or very much the reverse, and give great or little scope for healthy human energies. From idle wonder to active speculation is but a step; and he seems to have been early struck with the inefficacy of literature and its extreme unsuitability to the conditions. What he calls "Feudal Literature" could have little living action on the tumult of American democracy; what he calls the "Literature of Wo," meaning the whole tribe of Werther and Byron, could have no action for good in any time or place. Both propositions, if art had none but a direct moral influence, would be true enough; and as this seems to be Whitman's view, they were true enough for him. He conceived the idea of a Literature which was to inhere in the life of the present; which was to be, first, human, and next, American; which was to be brave and cheerful as per contract; to give culture in a popular and poetical presentment; and, in so doing, catch and stereotype some democratic ideal of humanity which should be equally natural to all grades of wealth and education, and suited, in one of his favourite phrases, to "the average man." To the formation of some such literature as this his poems are to be regarded as so many contributions, one sometimes explaining, sometimes superseding, the other: and the whole together not so much a finished work as a body of suggestive hints. He does not profess to have built the castle, but he pretends he has traced the lines of the foundation. He has not made the poetry, but he flatters himself he has done something towards making the poets.

His notion of the poetic function is ambitious, and coincides roughly with what Schopenhauer has laid down as the province of the metaphysician. The poet is to gather together for men, and set in order, the materials of their existence. He is "The Answerer;" he is to find some way of speaking about life that shall satisfy, if only for the moment, man's enduring astonishment at his own position. And besides having an answer ready, it is he who shall provoke the question. He must shake people out of their indifference, and force them to make some election in this world, instead of sliding dully forward in a dream. Life is a business we are all apt to mismanage; either living recklessly from day to day, or suffering ourselves to be gulled out of our moments by the inanities of custom. We should despise a man who gave as little activity and forethought to the conduct of any other business.

But in this, which is the one thing of all others, since it contains them all, we cannot see the forest for the trees. One brief impression obliterates another. There is something stupefying in the recurrence of unimportant things. And it is only on rare provocations that we rise to take an outlook beyond daily concerns, and comprehend the narrow limits and great possibilities of our existence. It is the duty of the poet to induce such moments of clear sight. He is the declared enemy of all living by reflex action, of all that is done betwixt sleep and waking, of all the pleasureless pleasurings and imaginary duties in which we coin away our hearts and fritter invaluable years. He has to electrify his readers into an instant unflagging activity, founded on a wide and eager observation of the world, and make them direct their ways by a superior prudence, which has little or nothing in common with the maxims of the copy-book. That many of us lead such lives as they would heartily disown after two hours' serious reflection on the subject is, I am afraid, a true, and, I am sure, a very galling thought. The Enchanted Ground of dead-alive respectability is next, upon the map, to the Beulah of considerate virtue. But there they all slumber and take their rest in the middle of God's beautiful and wonderful universe; the drowsy heads have nodded together in the same position since first their fathers fell asleep; and not even the sounds of the last trumpet can wake them to a single active thought. The poet has a hard task before

him to stir up such fellows to a sense of their
own and other people's principles in life.

And it happens that literature is, in some ways,
but an indifferent means to such an end. Language is but a poor bull's-eye lantern wherewith
to show off the vast cathedral of the world; and
yet a particular thing once said in words is so
definite and memorable, that it makes us forget
the absence of the many which remain unexpressed; like a bright window in a distant view,
which dazzles and confuses our sight of its surroundings. There are not words enough in all
Shakespeare to express the merest fraction of a
man's experience in an hour. The speed of the
eyesight and the hearing, and the continual industry of the mind, produce, in ten minutes, what
it would require a laborious volume to shadow
forth by comparisons and roundabout approaches.
If verbal logic were sufficient, life would be as
plain sailing as a piece of Euclid. But, as a matter
of fact, we make a travesty of the simplest process
of thought when we put it into words; for the
words are all coloured and forsworn, apply in-
accurately, and bring with them, from former
uses, ideas of praise and blame that have nothing
to do with the question in hand. So we must
always see to it nearly, that we judge by the realities of life and not by the partial terms that
represent them in man's speech; and at times of
choice, we must leave words upon one side, and
act upon those brute convictions, unexpressed
and perhaps inexpressible, which cannot be flour-

ished in an argument, but which are truly the sum and fruit of our experience. Words are for communication, not for judgment. This is what every thoughtful man knows for himself, for only fools and silly schoolmasters push definitions over far into the domain of conduct; and the majority of women, not learned in these scholastic refinements, live all-of-a-piece and unconsciously, as a tree grows, without caring to put a name upon their acts or motives. Hence, a new difficulty for Whitman's scrupulous and argumentative poet; he must do more than waken up the sleepers to his words; he must persuade them to look over the book and at life with their own eyes.

This side of truth is very present to Whitman; it is this that he means when he tells us that "To glance with an eye confounds the learning of all times." But he is not unready. He is never weary of descanting on the undebatable conviction that is forced upon our minds by the presence of other men, of animals, or of inanimate things. To glance with an eye, were it only at a chair or a park railing, is by far a more persuasive process, and brings us to a far more exact conclusion, than to read the works of all the logicians extant. If both, by a large allowance, may be said to end in certainty, the certainty in the one case transcends the others to an incalculable degree. If people see a lion, they run away; if they only apprehend a deduction, they keep wandering round in an experimental humour. Now, how is the poet to convince like

nature, and not like books? Is there no actual
piece of nature that he can show the man to his
face, as he might show him a tree if they were
walking together? Yes, there is one: the man's
own thoughts. In fact, if the poet is to speak effi-
caciously, he must say what is already in his
hearer's mind. That, alone, the hearer will believe;
that, alone, he will be able to apply intelligently
to the facts of life. Any conviction, even if it be
a whole system or a whole religion, must pass into
the condition of common-place, or postulate, before it becomes fully operative. Strange excursions
and high-flying theories may interest, but they
cannot rule behaviour. Our faith is not the highest truth that we perceive, but the highest that
we have been able to assimilate into the very
texture and method of our thinking. It is not,
therefore, by flashing before a man's eyes the
weapons of dialectic; it is not by induction, deduction, or construction; it is not by forcing him
on from one stage of reasoning to another, that
the man will be effectually renewed. He cannot
be made to believe anything; but he can be made
to see that he has always believed it. And this
is the practical canon. It is when the reader cries,
"Oh, I know!" and is, perhaps half irritated to see
how nearly the author has forestalled his own
thoughts, that he is on the way to what is called
in theology a Saving Faith.

Here we have the key to Whitman's attitude.
To give a certain unity of ideal to the average
population of America—to gather their activities
about some conception of humanity that shall

be central and normal, if only for the moment—
the poet must portray that population as it is.
Like human law, human poetry is simply declaratory. If any ideal is possible, it must be already
in the thoughts of the people; and, by the same
reason, in the thoughts of the poet, who is one
of them. And hence Whitman's own formula:
"The poet is individual—he is complete in himself: the others are as good as he; only he sees
it, and they do not." To show them how good
they are, the poet must study his fellow-country-
men and himself somewhat like a traveller on the
hunt for his book of travels. There is a sense, of
course, in which all true books are books of travel;
and all genuine poets must run their risk of being
charged with the traveller's exaggeration; for to
whom are such books more surprising than to
those whose own life is faithfully and smartly pic-
tured? But this danger is all upon one side; and
you may judiciously flatter the portrait without
any likelihood of the sitter's disowning it for a
faithful likeness. And so Whitman has reasoned:
that by drawing at first hand from himself and
his neighbours, accepting without shame the inconsistencies and brutalities that go to make up
man, and yet treating the whole in a high, magnanimous spirit, he would make sure of belief,
and at the same time encourage people forward
by the means of praise.

II

We are accustomed nowadays to a great deal
of puling over the circumstances in which we are

placed. The great refinement of many poetical gentlemen has rendered them practically unfit for the jostling and ugliness of life, and they record their unfitness at considerable length. The bold and awful poetry of Job's complaint produces too many flimsy imitators; for there is always something consolatory in grandeur, but the symphony transposed for the piano becomes hysterically sad. This literature of woe, as Whitman calls it, this *Maladie de René,* as we like to call it in Europe, is in many ways a most humiliating and sickly phenomenon. Young gentlemen with three or four hundred a year of private means look down from a pinnacle of doleful experience on all the grown and hearty men who have dared to say a good word for life since the beginning of the world. There is no prophet but the melancholy Jacques, and the blue devils dance on all our literary wires.

It would be a poor service to spread culture, if this be its result, among the comparatively innocent and cheerful ranks of men. When our little poets have to be sent to look at the ploughman and learn wisdom, we must be careful how we tamper with our ploughmen. Where a man in not the best of circumstances preserves composure of mind, and relishes ale and tobacco, and his wife and children, in the intervals of dull and unremunerative labour; where a man in this predicament can afford a lesson by the way to what are called his intellectual superiors, there is plainly something to be lost, as well as something to be gained, by teaching him to think differently. It is better to leave him as he is than to teach him whining. It is better that he should go without the cheerful lights of culture, if cheerless doubt and paralysing sentimentalism are to be the consequence. Let us, by all means, fight against that hide-bound stolidity of sensation and sluggishness of mind which blurs and decolorises for poor natures the wonderful pageant of consciousness; let us teach people, as much as we can, to enjoy, and they will learn for themselves to sympathise; but let us see to it, above all, that we give these lessons in a brave, vivacious note, and build the man up in courage while we demolish its substitute, indifference.

Whitman is alive to all this. He sees that, if the poet is to be of any help, he must testify to the liveableness of life. His poems, he tells us, are to be "hymns of the praise of things." They are to make for a certain high joy in living, or what he calls himself "a brave delight fit for freedom's athletes." And he has no difficulty in introducing his optimism: it fitted readily enough to his system; for the average man is truly a courageous person and truly fond of living. One of Whitman's remarks upon this head is worth quotation, as he is there perfectly successful, and does precisely what he designs to do throughout: takes ordinary and even commonplace circumstances; throws them out, by a happy turn of thinking, into significance and something like beauty; and tacks a hopeful moral lesson to the end.

"The passionate tenacity of hunters, woodmen, early risers, cultivators of gardens and orchards and fields," he says, "the love of healthy women for the manly form, seafaring persons, drivers of horses, the passion for light and the open air,—all is an old unvaried sign of the unfailing perception of beauty, and of a residence of the poetic in outdoor people."

There seems to me something truly original in this choice of trite examples. You will remark how adroitly Whitman begins, hunters and woodmen being confessedly romantic. And one thing more. If he had said "the love of healthy men for the female form," he would have said almost a silliness; for the thing has never been dissembled out of delicacy, and is so obvious as to be a public nuisance. But by reversing it, he tells us something not unlike news; something that sounds quite freshly in words; and, if the reader be a man, gives him a moment of great self-satisfaction and spiritual aggrandisement. In many different authors you may find passages more remarkable for grammar, but few of a more ingenious turn, and none that could be more to the point in our connection. The tenacity of many ordinary people in ordinary pursuits is a sort of standing challenge to everybody else. If one man can grow absorbed in delving his garden, others may grow absorbed and happy over something else. Not to be upsides in this with any groom or gardener, is to be very meanly organised. A man should be ashamed to take his food if he has not alchemy enough in his stomach to turn some of it into intense and enjoyable occupation.

Whitman tries to reinforce this cheerfulness

by keeping up a sort of outdoor atmosphere of sentiment. His book, he tells us, should be read "among the cooling influences of external nature;" and this recommendation, like that other famous one which Hawthorne prefixed to his collected tales, is in itself a character of the work. Every one who has been upon a walking or a boating tour, living in the open air, with the body in constant exercise and the mind in fallow, knows true ease and quiet. The irritating action of the brain is set at rest; we think in a plain, unfeverish temper; little things seem big enough, and great things no longer portentous; and the world is smilingly accepted as it is. This is the spirit that Whitman inculcates and parades. He thinks very ill of the atmosphere of parlours and libraries. Wisdom keeps school outdoors. And he has the art to recommend this attitude of mind by simply pluming himself upon it as a virtue; so that the reader, to keep the advantage over his author which most readers enjoy, is tricked into professing the same view. And this spirit, as it is his chief lesson, is the greatest charm of his work. Thence, in spite of an uneven and emphatic key of expression, something trenchant and straightforward, something simple and surprising, distinguishes his poems. He has sayings that come home to one like the Bible. We fall upon Whitman, after the works of so many men who write better, with a sense of relief from strain, with a sense of touching nature, as when one passes out of the flaring, noisy thoroughfares of a great city into what he himself has called, with unexcelled imaginative justice of language, "the huge and thoughtful night." And his book in consequence, whatever may be the final judgment of its merit, whatever may be its influence on the future, should be in the hands of all parents and guardians as a specific for the distressing malady of being seventeen years old. Green-sickness yields to his treatment as to a charm of magic; and the youth, after a short course of reading, ceases to carry the universe upon his shoulders.

III

Whitman is not one of those who can be deceived by familiarity. He considers it just as wonderful that there are myriads of stars, as that one man should rise from the dead. He declares "a hair on the back of his hand just as curious as any special revelation." His whole life is to him what it was to Sir Thomas Browne, one perpetual miracle. Everything is strange, everything unaccountable, everything beautiful; from a bug to the moon, from the sight of the eyes to the appetite for food. He makes it his business to see things as if he saw them for the first time, and professes astonishment on principle. But he has no leaning towards mythology; avows his contempt for what he calls "unregenerate poetry;" and does not mean by nature.

"The smooth walks, trimmed hedges, butterflies, posies, and nightingales of the English poets, but the whole orb, with its geologic history, the

Kosmos, carrying fire and snow, that rolls through the illimitable areas, light as a feather though weighing billions of tons."

Nor is this exhaustive; for in his character of idealist all impressions, all thoughts, trees and people, love and faith, astronomy, history, and religion, enter upon equal terms into his notion of the universe. He is not against religion; not, indeed, against any religion. He wishes to drag with a larger net, to make a more comprehensive synthesis, than any or than all of them put together. In feeling after the central type of man, he must embrace all eccentricities; his cosmology must subsume all cosmologies, and the feelings that gave birth to them; his statements of facts must include all religion and all irreligion, Christ and Boodha, God and the devil. The world as it is, and the whole world as it is, physical, and spiritual, and historical, with its good and bad, with its manifold inconsistencies, is what he wishes to set forth, in strong, picturesque, and popular lineaments, for the understanding of the average man. One of his favourite endeavours is to get the whole matter in a nutshell; to knock the four corners of the universe, one after another, about his reader's ears; to hurry him, in breathless phrases, hither and thither, back and forward, in time and space; to focus all this about his own momentary personality; and then, drawing the ground from under his feet, as if by some cataclysm of nature, to plunge him into the unfathomable abyss sown with enormous suns and systems, and among the inconceivable numbers and magnitudes and velocities of the heavenly bodies. So that he concludes by striking into us some sense of that disproportion of things which Shelley has illuminated by the ironical flash of those eight words: The desire of the moth for the star.

The same truth, but to what a different purpose! Whitman's moth is mightily at his ease about all the planets in heaven, and cannot think too highly of our sublunary tapers. The universe is so large that imagination flags in the effort to conceive it; but here, in the meantime, is the world under our feet, a very warm and habitable corner. "The earth, that is sufficient; I do not want the constellations any nearer," he remarks. And again: "Let your soul stand cool and composed," says he, "before a million universes." It is the language of a transcendental common sense, such as Thoreau held and sometimes uttered. But Whitman, who has a somewhat vulgar inclination for technical talk and the jargon of philosophy, is not content with a few pregnant hints; he must put the dots upon his i's; he must corroborate the songs of Apollo by some of the darkest talk of human metaphysic. He tells his disciples that they must be ready "to confront the growing arrogance of Realism." Each person is, for himself, the keystone and the occasion of this universal edifice. "Nothing, not God," he says, "is greater to one than oneself is;" a statement with an irreligious smack at the first sight; but like most startling sayings, a manifest truism on a second. He will give effect to his own

111

character without apology; he sees "that the elementary laws never apologise." "I reckon," he adds, with quaint colloquial arrogance, "I reckon I behave no prouder than the level I plant my house by, after all." The level follows the law of its being; so, unrelentingly, will he; everything, every person, is good in his own place and way; God is the maker of all, and all are in one design. For he believes in God, and that with a sort of blasphemous security. "No array of terms," quoth he, "no array of terms can say how much at peace I am about God and about death." There certainly never was a prophet who carried things with a higher hand; he gives us less a body of dogmas than a series of proclamations by the grace of God; and language, you will observe, positively fails him to express how far he stands above the highest human doubts and trepidations.

But next in order of truths to a person's sublime conviction of himself, comes the attraction of one person for another, and all that we mean by the word love:—

> "The dear love of man for his comrade—the
> attraction of friend for friend,
> Of the well-married husband and wife, of
> children and parents,
> Of city for city and land for land."

The solitude of the most sublime idealist is broken in upon by other people's faces; he sees a look in their eyes that corresponds to something in his own heart; there comes a tone in their voices which convicts him of a startling weakness for his fellow-creatures. While he is hymning the *ego* and commercing with God and the universe, a woman goes below his window; and at the turn of her skirt, or the colour of her eyes, Icarus is recalled from heaven by the run. Love is so startlingly real that it takes rank upon an equal footing of reality with the consciousness of personal existence. We are as heartily persuaded of the identity of those we love as of our own identity. And so sympathy pairs with self-assertion, the two gerents of human life on earth; and Whitman's ideal man must not only be strong, free, and self-reliant in himself, but his freedom must be bounded and his strength perfected by the most intimate, eager, and long-suffering love for others. To some extent this is taking away with the left hand what has been so generously given with the right. Morality has been ceremoniously extruded from the door only to be brought in again by the window. We are told, on one page, to do as we please; and on the next we are sharply upbraided for not having done as the author pleases. We are first assured that we are the finest fellows in the world in our own right; and then it appears that we are only fine fellows in so far as we practise a most quixotic code of morals. The disciple who saw himself in clear ether a moment before is plunged down again among the fogs and complications of duty. And this is all the more overwhelming because Whitman insists not only on love between sex and sex, and between friends of the same sex, but in

113

the field of the less intense political sympathies; and his ideal man must not only be a generous friend but a conscientious voter into the bargain.

His method somewhat lessens the difficulty. He is not, the reader will remember, to tell us how good we ought to be, but to remind us how good we are. He is to encourage us to be free and kind, by proving that we are free and kind already. He passes our corporate life under review, to show that it is upheld by the very virtues of which he makes himself the advocate. "There is no object so soft," he says somewhere in his big plain way, "there is no object so soft but it makes a hub for the wheel'd universe." Rightly understood, it is on the softest of all objects, the sympathetic heart, that the wheel of society turns easily and securely as on a perfect axle. There is no room, of course, for doubt or discussion about conduct, where every one is to follow the law of his being with exact compliance. Whitman hates doubt, deprecates discussion, and discourages to his utmost the craving, carping sensibilities of the conscience. We are to imitate, to use one of his absurd and happy phrases, "the satisfaction and aplomb of animals." If he preaches a sort of ranting Christianity in morals, a fit consequent to the ranting optimism of his cosmology, it is because he declares it to be the original deliverance of the human heart; or at least, for he would be honestly historical in method, of the human heart as at present Christianised. His is a morality without a prohibition; his policy is one of encouragement all round. A man must be a born hero to come

114

up to Whitman's standard in the practice of any of the positive virtues; but of a negative virtue, such as temperance or chastity, he has so little to say, that the reader need not be surprised if he drops a word or two upon the wrong side. He would lay down nothing that would be a clog; he would prescribe nothing that cannot be done ruddily, in a heat. The great point is to get people under way. To the faithful Whitmanite this would be justified by the belief that God made all, and that all was good; the prophet, in this doctrine, has only to cry "Tally-ho," and mankind will break into a gallop on the road to El Dorado. Perhaps, to another class of minds, it may look like the result of the somewhat cynical reflection that you will not make a kind man out of one who is unkind by any precepts under heaven; tempered by the belief, that in natural circumstances, the large majority is well disposed. Thence it would follow, that if you can only get every one to feel more warmly and act more courageously, the balance of results will be for good.

So far, you see, the doctrine is pretty coherent as a doctrine; as a picture of man's life it is incomplete and misleading, although eminently cheerful. This he is himself the first to acknowledge; for if he is prophetic in anything, it is in his noble disregard of consistency. "Do I contradict myself?" he asks somewhere; and then pat comes the answer, the best answer ever given in print, worthy of a sage, or rather of a woman: "Very well, then, I contradict myself!" with this addition, not so feminine and perhaps not altogether so satisfactory: "I am large—I contain multitudes." Life, as a matter of fact, partakes largely of the nature of tragedy. The gospel according to Whitman, even if it be not so logical, has this advantage over the gospel according to Pangloss, that it does not utterly disregard the existence of temporal evil. Whitman accepts the fact of disease and wretchedness like an honest man; and instead of trying to qualify it in the interest of his optimism, sets himself to spur people up to be helpful. He expresses a conviction, indeed, that all will be made up to the victims in the end; that "what is untried and afterward" will fail no one, not even "the old man who has lived without purpose and feels it with bitterness worse than gall." But this is not to palliate our sense of what is hard or melancholy in the present. Pangloss, smarting under one of the worst things that ever was supposed to come from America, consoled himself with the reflection that it was the price we have to pay for cochineal. And with that murderous parody, logical optimism and the praises of the best of possible words went irrevocably out of season, and have been no more heard of in the mouths of reasonable men. Whitman spares us all allusions to the cochineal; he treats evil and sorrow in a spirit almost as of welcome; as an old sea-dog might have welcomed the sight of the enemy's topsails off the Spanish Main. There, at least, he seems to say, is something obvious to be done. I do not know many better things in literature than the brief pictures—brief and vivid like things seen by lightning,—with which he tries to stir up the world's heart upon the side of mercy. He braces us, on the one hand, with examples of heroic duty and helpfulness; on the other, he touches us with pitiful instances of people needing help. He knows how to make the heart beat at a brave story; to inflame us with just resentment over the hunted slave; to stop our mouths for shame when he tells of the drunken prostitute. For all the afflicted, all the weak, all the wicked, a good word is said in a spirit which I can only call one of ultra-Christianity; and however wild, however contradictory it may be in parts, this at least may be said for his book, as it may be said of the Christian Gospels, that no one will read it, however respectable, but he gets a knock upon his conscience; no one however fallen, but he finds a kindly and supporting welcome.

IV

Nor has he been content with merely blowing the trumpet for the battle of well-doing; he has given to his precepts the authority of his own brave example. Naturally a grave, believing man, with little or no sense of humour, he has succeeded as well in life as in his printed performances. The spirit that was in him has come forth most eloquently in his actions. Many who have only read his poetry have been tempted to set him down as an ass, or even as a charlatan; but I never met anyone who had known him personally who did not profess a solid affection and respect for the man's character. He practises as he professes;

he feels deeply that Christian love for all men, that toleration, that cheerful delight in serving others, which he often celebrates in literature with a doubtful measure of success. And perhaps, out of all his writings, the best and the most human and convincing passages are to be found in "these soil'd and creas'd little livraisons, each composed of a sheet or two of paper, folded small to carry in the pocket, and fastened with a pin," which he scribbled during the war by the bedsides of the wounded or in the excitement of great events. They are hardly literature in the formal meaning of the word; he has left his jottings for the most part as he made them; a homely detail, a word from the lips of a dying soldier, a business memorandum, the copy of a letter—short, straightforward to the point, with none of the trappings of composition; but they breathe a profound sentiment, they give us a vivid look at one of the sides of life, and they make us acquainted with the man whom it is an honour to love.

Whitman's intense Americanism, his unlimited belief in the future of these States (as, with reverential capitals, he loves to call them), made the war a period of great trial to his soul. The new virtue, Unionism, of which he is the sole inventor, seemed to have fallen into premature unpopularity. All that he loved, hoped, or hated, hung in the balance. And the game of war was not only momentous to him in its issues; it sublimated his spirit by its heroic displays, and tortured him intimately by the spectacle of its horrors. It was a theatre, it was a place of education, it was like a season of religious revival. He watched Lincoln going daily to his work; he studied and fraternised with young soldiery passing to the front; above all, he walked the hospitals, reading the Bible, distributing clean clothes, or apples, or tobacco; a patient, helpful, reverend man, full of kind speeches.

His memoranda of this period are almost bewildering to read. From one point of view they seem those of a district visitor; from another, they look like the formless jottings of an artist in the picturesque. More than one woman, on whom I tried the experiment, immediately claimed the writer for a fellow-woman. More than one literary purist might identify him as a shoddy newspaper correspondent without the necessary faculty of style. And yet the story touches home; and if you are of the order of mankind, you will certainly find your eyes fill with tears, of which you have no reason to be ashamed. There is only one way to characterise a work of this order, and that is to quote. Here is a passage from a letter to a mother, unknown to Whitman, whose son died in hospital:—

"Frank, as far as I saw, had everything requisite in surgical treatment, nursing, etc. He had watches much of the time. He was so good and well-behaved, and affectionate, I myself like him very much. I was in the habit of coming in afternoons and sitting by him, and he liked to have me—liked to put out his arm and lay his hand on my knee—would keep it so a long while. Toward the last he was more restless and flighty at night

—often fancied himself with his regiment—by his talk sometimes seem'd as if his feelings were hurt by being blamed by his officers for something he was entirely innocent of—said 'I never in my life was thought capable of such a thing, and never was.' At other times he would fancy himself talking as it seem'd to children or such like, his relatives, I suppose, and giving them good advice; would talk to them a long while. All the time he was out of his head not one single bad word or thought, or idea escaped him. It was remark'd that many a man's conversation in his senses was not half so good as Frank's delirium.

"He was perfectly willing to die—he had become very weak, and had suffer'd a good deal, and was perfectly resign'd, poor boy. I do not know his past life, but I feel as if it must have been good. At any rate what I saw of him here, under the most trying circumstances, with a painful wound, and among strangers, I can say that he behaved so brave, so composed, and so sweet and affectionate, it could not be surpassed. And now, like many other noble and good men, after serving his country as a soldier, he had yielded up his young life at the very outset in her service. Such things are gloomy—yet there is a text, 'God doeth all things well,' the meaning of which, after due time, appears to the soul.

"I thought perhaps a few words, though from a stranger, about your son, from one who was with him at the last, might be worth while, for I loved the young man, though I but saw him immediately to lose him."

It is easy enough to pick holes in the grammar of this letter, but what are we to say of its profound goodness and tenderness? It is written as though he had the mother's face before his eyes, and saw her wincing in the flesh at every word. And what, again, are we to say of its sober truthfulness, not exaggerating, not running to phrases, not seeking to make a hero out of what was only an ordinary but good and brave young man? Literary reticence is not Whitman's stronghold; and this reticence is not literary but humane; it is not that of a good artist but that of a good man. He knew that what the mother wished to hear about was Frank; and he told her about her Frank as he was.

V

Something should be said of Whitman's style, for style is of the essence of thinking. And where a man is so critically deliberate as our author, and goes solemnly about his poetry for an ulterior end, every indication is worth notice. He has chosen a rough, unrhymed, lyrical verse; sometimes instinct with a fine processional movement; often so rugged and careless that it can only be described by saying that he has not taken the trouble to write prose. I believe myself that it was selected principally because it was easy to write, although not without recollections of the marching measures of some of the prose in our English Old Testament. According to Whitman, on the other hand, "the time has arrived to essentially break down the barrier of form between Prose and

Poetry . . . for the most cogent purposes of those great inland states, and for Texas, and California, and Oregon;"—a statement which is among the happiest achievements of American humour. He calls his verses "recitatives," in easily followed allusion to a musical form. "Easily-written, loose-fingered chords," he cries, "I feel the thrum of your climax and close." Too often, I fear, he is the only one who can perceive the rhythm; and in spite of Mr. Swinburne, a great part of his work considered as verses is poor bald stuff. Considered, not as verse, but as speech, a great part of it is full of strange and admirable merits. The right detail is seized; the right word, bold and trenchant, is thrust into its place. Whitman has small regard to literary decencies, and is totally free from literary timidities. He is neither afraid of being slangy nor of being dull; nor, let me add, of being ridiculous. The result is a most surprising compound of plain grandeur, sentimental affectation, and downright nonsense. It would be useless to follow his detractors and give instances of how bad he can be at his worst; and perhaps it would be not much wiser to give extracted specimens of how happily he can write when he is at his best. These come in to most advantage in their own place; owing something, it may be, to the offset of their curious surroundings. And one thing is certain, that no one can appreciate Whitman's excellences until he has grown accustomed to his faults. Until you are content to pick poetry out of his pages almost as you must pick it out of a Greek play in Bohn's translation, your gravity will be continually upset, your ears perpetually disappointed, and the whole book will be no more to you than a particularly flagrant production by the Poet Close.

A writer of this uncertain quality was, perhaps, unfortunate in taking for thesis the beauty of the world as it now is, not only on the hill-tops but in the factory; not only by the harbour full of stately ships, but in the magazine of the hopelessly prosaic hatter. To show beauty in common things is the work of the rarest tact. It is not to be done by the wishing. It is easy to posit as a theory, but to bring it home to men's minds is the problem of literature, and is only accomplished by rare talent, and in comparatively rare instances. To bid the whole world stand and deliver, with a dogma in one's right hand by way of pistol; to cover reams of paper in a galloping, headstrong vein; to cry louder and louder over everything as it comes up, and make no distinction in one's enthusiasm over the most incomparable matters; to prove one's entire want of sympathy for the jaded, literary palate, by calling, not a spade a spade, but a hatter a hatter, in a lyrical apostrophe;—this, in spite of all the airs of inspiration, is not the way to do it. It may be very wrong, and very wounding to a respectable branch of industry, but the word "hatter" cannot be used seriously in emotional verse; not to understand this, is to have no literary tact; and I would, for his own sake, that this were the only inadmissible expression with which Whitman had bedecked his pages. The book teems with similar comicalities; and, to the reader who is determined to take it from that side only, presents a perfect carnival of fun.

A good deal of this is the result of theory playing its usual vile trick upon the artist. It is because he is a Democrat that Whitman must have in the hatter. If you may say Admiral, he reasons, why may you not say Hatter? One man is as good as another, and it is the business of the "great poet" to show poetry in the life of the one as well as the other. A most incontrovertible sentiment surely, and one which nobody would think of controverting, where—and here is the point— where any beauty has been shown. But how, where that is not the case? where the hatter is simply introduced, as God made him and as his fellow-men have miscalled him, at the crisis of a high-flown rhapsody? And what are we to say, where a man of Whitman's notable capacity for putting things in a bright, picturesque, and novel way, simply gives up the attempt, and indulges, with apparent exultation, in an inventory of trades or implements, with no more colour or coherence than so many index-words out of a dictionary? I do not know that we can say anything, but that it is a prodigiously amusing exhibition for a line or so. The worst of it is, that Whitman must have known better. The man is a great critic, and, so far as I can make out, a good one; and how much criticism does it require to know that capitulation is not description, or that fingering on a dumb keyboard, with whatever show of sentiment and execution, is not at

124

all the same thing as discoursing music? I wish I could believe he was quite honest with us; but, indeed, who was ever quite honest who wrote a book for a purpose? It is a flight beyond the reach of human magnanimity.

One other point, where his means failed him, must be touched upon, however shortly. In his desire to accept all facts loyally and simply, it fell within his programme to speak at some length and with some plainness on what is, for I really do not know what reason, the most delicate of subjects. Seeing in that one of the most serious and interesting parts of life, he was aggrieved that it should be looked upon as ridiculous or shameful. No one speaks of maternity with his tongue in his cheek; and Whitman made a bold push to set the sanctity of fatherhood beside the sanctity of motherhood, and introduce this also among the things that can be spoken of without either a blush or a wink. But the Philistines have been too strong; and, to say truth, Whitman has rather played the fool. We may be thoroughly conscious that his end is improving; that it would be a good thing if a window were opened on these close privacies of life; that on this subject, as on all others, he now and then lets fall a pregnant saying. But we are not satisfied. We feel that he was not the man for so difficult an enterprise. He loses our sympathy in the character of a poet by attracting too much of our attention in that of a Bull in a China Shop. And where, by a little more art, we might have been solemnised ourselves, it is too often Whitman alone who is solemn in the face of an audience somewhat indecorously amused.

VI

Lastly, as most important, after all, to human beings in our disputable state, what is that higher prudence which was to be the aim and issue of these deliberate productions?

Whitman is too clever to slip into a succinct formula. If he could have adequately said his say in a single proverb, it is to be presumed he would not have put himself to the trouble of writing several volumes. It was his programme to state as much as he could of the world with all its contradictions, and leave the upshot with God who planned it. What he has made of the world and the world's meanings is to be found at large in his poems. These altogether give his answers to the problems of belief and conduct; in many ways righteous and high-spirited, in some ways loose and contradictory. And yet there are two passages from the preface to the *Leaves of Grass* which do pretty well condense his teaching on all essential points, and yet preserve a measure of his spirit.

"This is what you shall do," he says in the one, "love the earth, and sun, and animals, despise riches, give alms to every one that asks, stand up for the stupid and crazy, devote your income and labour to others, hate tyrants, argue not concerning God, have patience and indulgence towards the people, take off your hat to nothing known or unknown, or to any man or number of men; go freely with powerful uneducated persons, and with the young, and mothers of families, read these leaves (his own works) in the open air every season of every year of your life; re-examine all you have been told at school or church, or in any book, and dismiss whatever insults your own soul."

"The prudence of the greatest poet," he adds in the other—and the greatest poet is, of course, himself—"knows that the young man who composedly perilled his life and lost it, has done exceedingly well for himself; while the man who has not perilled his life, and retains it to old age in riches and ease, has perhaps achieved nothing for himself worth mentioning; and that only that person has no great prudence to learn, who has learned to prefer real long-lived things, and favours body and soul the same, and perceives the indirect surely following the direct, and what evil or good he does leaping onward and waiting to meet him again, and who in his spirit, in any emergency whatever, neither hurries nor avoids death."

There is much that is Christian in these extracts, startingly Christian. Any reader who bears in mind Whitman's own advice and "dismisses whatever insults his own soul" will find plenty that is bracing, brightening, and chastening to reward him for a little patience at first. It seems hardly possible that any being should get evil from so healthy a book as the *Leaves of Grass*, which is simply comical wherever it falls short of nobility; but if there be any such, who cannot both take and leave, who cannot let a single opportunity pass by without some unworthy and unmanly thought, I should have as great difficulty, and neither more nor less, in recommending the works of Whitman as in lending them Shakespeare, or letting them go abroad outside of the grounds of a private asylum.

HENRY DAVID THOREAU
HIS CHARACTER AND OPINIONS

I

THOREAU'S thin, penetrating, big-nosed face, even a bad woodcut, conveys some hint of the limitations of his mind and character. With his almost acid sharpness of insight, with his almost animal dexterity in act, there went none of that large, unconscious geniality of the world's heroes. He was not easy, not ample, not urbane, not even kind; his enjoyment was hardly smiling, or the smile was not broad enough to be convincing; he had no waste lands nor kitchen-midden in his nature, but was all improved and sharpened to a point. "He was bred to no profession," says Emerson; "he never married; he lived alone; he never went to church; he never voted; he refused to pay a tax to the State; he ate no flesh, he drank no wine, he never knew the use of tobacco; and, though a naturalist, he used neither trap nor gun. When asked at dinner what dish he preferred, he answered, "the nearest." So many negative superiorities began to smack a little of the prig. From his later works he was in the habit of cutting out the humorous passages, under the impression that they were beneath the dignity of his moral muse; and there we see the prig stand public and confessed. It was "much easier," says Emerson acutely, much easier for Thoreau to say *no* than *yes*; and that is a characteristic which depicts the man. It is a useful accomplishment to be able to say *no*, but surely it is the essence of amiability to prefer to say *yes* where it is possible. There is something wanting in the man who does not hate himself whenever he is constrained to say no. And there was a great deal wanting in this born dissenter. He was almost shockingly devoid of weaknesses; he had not enough of them to be truly polar with humanity; whether you call him demi-god or demi-man, he was at least not altogether one of us, for he was not touched with a feeling of our infirmities. The world's heroes have room for all positive qualities, even those which are disreputable, in the capacious theatre of their dispositions. Such can live many lives; while a Thoreau can live but one, and that only with perpetual foresight.

He was no ascetic, rather an Epicurean of the nobler sort; and he had this one great merit, that he succeeded so far as to be happy. "I love my fate to the core and rind," he wrote once; and even while he lay dying, here is what he dictated (for it seems he was already too feeble to control the pen): "You ask particularly after my health. I *suppose* that I have not many months to live, but of course know nothing about it. I may say that I am enjoying existence as much as ever, and regret nothing." It is not given to all to bear so clear a testimony to the sweetness of their fate, nor to any without courage and wisdom; for this world in itself is but a painful and uneasy place of residence, and lasting happiness, at least to the self-conscious, comes only from within. Now Thoreau's content and ecstasy in living was, we may say, like a plant that he had watered and tended with womanish solicitude; for there is apt to be something unmanly, something almost dastardly, in a life that does not move with dash and freedom, and that fears the bracing contact of the world. In one word, Thoreau was a skulker. He did not wish virtue to go out of him among his fellow-men, but slunk into a corner to hoard it for himself. He left all for the sake of certain virtuous self-indulgences. It is true that his tastes were noble; that his ruling passion was to keep himself unspotted from the world; and that his luxuries were all of the same healthy order as cold tubs and early rising. But a man may be both coldly cruel in the pursuit of goodness, and morbid even in the pursuit of health. I cannot lay my hands on the passage in which he explains his abstinence from tea and coffee, but I am sure I have the meaning correctly. It is this: He thought it bad economy and worthy of no true virtuoso to spoil the natural rapture of the morning with such muddy stimulants; let him but see the sun rise and he was already sufficiently inspirited for the labours of the day. That may be reason good enough to abstain from tea; but when we go on to find the same man, on the same or similar grounds, abstain from nearly everything that his neighbours innocently and pleasurably use, and from the rubs and trials of

131

human society itself into the bargain, we recognise that valetudinarian healthfulness which is more delicate than sickness itself. We need have no respect for a state of artificial training. True health is to be able to do without it. Shakespeare, we can imagine, might begin the day upon a quart of ale, and yet enjoy the sunrise to the full as much as Thoreau, and commemorate his enjoyment in vastly better verses. A man who must separate himself from his neighbours' habits in order to be happy, is in much the same case with one who requires to take opium for the same purpose. What we want to see is one who can breast into the world, do a man's work, and still preserve his first and pure enjoyment of existence.

Thoreau's faculties were of a piece with his moral shyness; for they were all delicacies. He could guide himself about the woods on the darkest night by the touch of his feet. He could pick up at once an exact dozen of pencils, by the feeling, pace distances with accuracy, and gauge cubic contents by the eye. His smell was so dainty that he could perceive the fœtor of dwelling-houses as he passed them by at night; his palate so unsophisticated that, like a child, he disliked the taste of wine—or perhaps, living in America, had never tasted any that was good; and his knowledge of nature was so complete and curious that he could have told the time of year, within a day or so, by the aspect of the plants. In his dealings with animals he was the original of Hawthorne's Donatello. He pulled the woodchuck out of its hole by the tail; the hunted fox came

to him for protection; wild squirrels have been
seen to nestle in his waistcoat; he would thrust
his arm into a pool and bring forth a bright, pant-
ing fish, lying undismayed in the palm of his
hand. There were few things that he could not
do. He could make a house, a boat, a pencil, or
a book. He was a surveyor, a scholar, a natural
historian. He could run, walk, climb, skate, swim,
and manage a boat. The smallest occasion served
to display his physical accomplishment; and a
manufacturer, from merely observing his dexterity
with the window of a railway carriage, offered him
a situation on the spot. "The only fruit of much
living," he observes, "is the ability to do some
slight thing better." But such was the exactitude
of his senses, so alive was he in every fibre, that it
seems as if the maxim should be changed in his
case, for he could do most things with unusual
perfection. And perhaps he had an approving eye
to himself when he wrote: "Though the youth at
last grows indifferent, the laws of the universe
are not indifferent, *but are for ever on the side of
the most sensitive.*"

II

Thoreau had decided, it would seem, from the
very first to lead a life of self-improvement: the
needle did not tremble as with richer natures, but
pointed steadily north; and as he saw duty and
inclination in one, he turned all his strength in
that direction. He was met upon the threshold by
a common difficulty. In this world, in spite of its
many agreeable features, even the most sensitive

must undergo some drudgery to live. It is not possible to devote your time to study and meditation without what are quaintly but happily denominated private means; these absent, a man must contrive to earn his bread by some service to the public such as the public cares to pay him for; or, as Thoreau loved to put it, Apollo must serve Admetus. This was to Thoreau even a sourer necessity than it is to most; there was a love of freedom, a strain of the wild man, in his nature, that rebelled with violence against the yoke of custom; and he was so eager to cultivate himself and to be happy in his own society, that he could consent with difficulty even to the interruptions of friendship. "*Such are my engagements to myself* that I dare not promise," he once wrote in answer to an invitation; and the italics are his own. Marcus Aurelius found time to study virtue, and between whiles to conduct the imperial affairs of Rome; but Thoreau is so busy improving himself, that he must think twice about a morning call. And now imagine him condemned for eight hours a day to some uncongenial and unmeaning business! He shrank from the very look of the mechanical in life; all should, if possible, be sweetly spontaneous and swimmingly progressive. Thus he learned to make lead pencils, and, when he had gained the best certificate and his friends began to congratulate him on his establishment in life, calmly announced that he should never make another. "Why should I?" said he; "I would not do again what I have done once." For when a thing has once been done as well as it wants to be, it is of no further interest to the self-improver. Yet in after years, and when it became needful to support his family, he returned patiently to this mechanical art—a step more than worthy of himself.

The pencils seem to have been Apollo's first experiment in the service of Admetus; but others followed. "I have thoroughly tried school-keeping," he writes, "and found that my expenses were in proportion, or rather out of proportion, to my income; for I was obliged to dress and train, not to say think and believe, accordingly, and I lost my time into the bargain. As I did not teach for the benefit of my fellow-men, but simply for a livelihood, this was a failure. I have tried trade, but found that it would take ten years to get under way in that, and that then I should probably be on my way to the devil." Nothing, indeed, can surpass his scorn for all so-called business. Upon that subject gall squirts from him at a touch. "The whole enterprise of this nation is not illustrated by a thought," he writes; "it is not warmed by a sentiment; there is nothing in it for which a man should lay down his life, nor even his gloves." And again; "if our merchants did not most of them fail, and the banks too, my faith in the old laws of this world would be staggered. The statement that ninety-six in a hundred doing such business surely break down is perhaps the sweetest fact that statistics have revealed." The wish was probably father to the figures; but there is something enlivening in a hatred of so genuine a brand, hot as Corsican revenge, and sneering like Voltaire.

Pencils, school-keeping, and trade being thus discarded one after another, Thoreau, with a stroke of strategy, turned the position. He saw his way to get board and lodging for practically nothing; and Admetus never got less work out of any servant since the world began. It was his ambition to be an oriental philosopher; but he was always a very Yankee sort of oriental. Even in the peculiar attitude in which he stood to money, his system of personal economics, as we may call it, he displayed a vast amount of truly down-East calculation, and he adopted poverty like a piece of business. Yet his system is based on one or two ideas which, I believe, come naturally to all thoughtful youths, and are only pounded out of them by city uncles. Indeed, something essentially youthful distinguishes all Thoreau's knock-down blows at current opinion. Like the posers of a child, they leave the orthodox in a kind of speechless agony. These know the thing is nonsense. They are sure there must be an answer, yet somehow cannot find it. So it is with his system of economy. He cuts through the subject on so new a plane that the accepted arguments apply no longer; after you have been boxing for years on a polite, gladiatorial convention, here is an assailant who does not scruple to hit below the belt.

"The cost of a thing," says he, "is *the amount of what I will call life* which is required to be

exchanged for it, immediately or in the long run."
I have been accustomed to put it to myself, perhaps more clearly, that the price we have to pay
for money is paid in liberty. Between these two
ways of it, at least, the reader will probably not
fail to find a third definition of his own; and it
follows, on one or other, that a man may pay too
dearly for his livelihood, by giving, in Thoreau's
terms, his whole life for it, or, in mine, bartering
for it the whole of his available liberty, and becoming a slave till death. There are two questions
to be considered—the quality of what we buy,
and the price we have to pay for it. Do you want
a thousand a year, two thousand a year, or a ten
thousand a year livelihood? and can you afford
the one you want? It is a matter of taste; it is not
in the least degree a question of duty, though
commonly supposed so. But there is no authority
for that view anywhere. It is nowhere in the
Bible. It is true that we might do a vast amount
of good if we were wealthy, but it is also highly
improbable; not many do; and the art of growing
rich is not only quite distinct from that of doing
good, but the practice of the one does not at all
train a man for practising the other. "Money
might be of great service to me," writes Thoreau;
"but the difficulty now is that I do not improve
my opportunities, and therefore I am not prepared to have my opportunities increased." It is
a mere illusion that, above a certain income, the
personal desires will be satisfied and leave a wider
margin for the generous impulse. It is as difficult

to be generous, or anything else, except perhaps a member of Parliament, on thirty thousand as on two hundred a year.

Now Thoreau's tastes were well defined. He loved to be free, to be master of his times, and seasons, to indulge the mind rather than the body; he preferred long rambles to rich dinners, his own reflections to the consideration of society, and an easy, calm, unfettered, active life among green trees to dull toiling at the counter of a bank. And such being his inclination, he determined to gratify it. A poor man must save off something; he determined to save off his livelihood. "When a man has attained those things which are necessary to life," he writes, "there is another alternative than to obtain the superfluities; *he may adventure on life now*, his vacation from humbler toil having commenced." Thoreau would get shelter, some kind of covering for his body, and necessary daily bread; even these he should get as cheaply as possible; and then, his vacation from humbler toil having commenced, devote himself to oriental philosophers, the study of nature, and the work of self-improvement.

Prudence, which bids us all go to the ant for wisdom and hoard against the day of sickness, was not a favourite with Thoreau. He preferred that other, whose name is so much misappropriated: Faith. When he had secured the necessaries of the moment, he would not reckon up possible accidents or torment himself with trouble for the future. He had no toleration for the man "who ventures to live only by the aid of the mutual insurance company, which has promised to bury him decently." He would trust himself a little to the world. "We may safely trust a good deal more than we do," says he. "How much is not done by us! or what if we had been taken sick?" And then, with a stab of satire, he describes contemporary mankind in a phrase: "All the day long on the alert, at night we unwillingly say our prayers and commit ourselves to uncertainties." It is not likely that the public will be much affected by Thoreau, when they blink the direct injunctions of the religion they profess; and yet, whether we will or no we make the same hazardous ventures; we back our own health and the honesty of our neighbours for all that we are worth; and it is chilling to think how many must lose their wager.

In 1845, twenty-eight years old, an age by which the liveliest have usually declined into some conformity with the world, Thoreau, with a capital of something less than five pounds and a borrowed axe, walked forth into the woods by Walden Pond, and began his new experiment in life. He built himself a dwelling, and returned the axe, he says with characteristic and workman-like pride, sharper than when he borrowed it; he reclaimed a patch, where he cultivated beans, peas, potatoes, and sweet corn; he had his bread to bake, his farm to dig, and for the matter of six weeks in the summer he worked at surveying, carpentry, or some other of his numerous dexterities, for hire. For more than five years, this was all that he required to do for his support, and he had the winter and most of the summer at his entire disposal. For six weeks of occupation, a little cooking, and a little gentle hygienic gardening, the man, you may say, has as good as stolen his livelihood. Or we must rather allow that he had done far better; for the thief himself is continually and busily occupied; and even one born to inherit a million will have more calls upon his time than Thoreau. Well might he say, "What old people tell you you cannot do, you try and find you can." And how surprising is his conclusion: "I am convinced that *to maintain oneself on this earth is not a hardship, but a pastime,* if we will live simply and wisely; *as the pursuits of simpler nations are still the sports of the more artificial.*"

When he had enough of that kind of life, he showed the same simplicity in giving it up as in beginning it. There are some who could have done the one, but, vanity forbidding, not the other; and that is perhaps the story of the hermits; but Thoreau made no fetish of his own example, and did what he wanted squarely. And five years is long enough for an experiment and to prove the success of transcendental Yankeeism. It is not his frugality which is worthy of note; for, to begin with, that was inborn, and therefore inimitable by others who are differently constituted; and again, it was no new thing, but has often been equalled by poor Scotch students at the universities. The point is the sanity of his view of life, and the insight with which he recognised the position of money, and thought out for himself the problem of riches and a liveli-

hood. Apart from his eccentricities, he had perceived, and was acting on, a truth of universal
application. For money enters in two different
characters into the scheme of life. A certain
amount, varying with the number and empire of
our desires, is a true necessary to each one of us
in the present order of society; but beyond that
amount, money is a commodity to be bought or
not to be bought, a luxury in which we may either
indulge or stint ourselves, like any other. And
there are many luxuries that we may legitimately
prefer to it, such as a grateful conscience, a
country life, or the woman of our inclination.
Trite, flat, and obvious as this conclusion may
appear, we have only to look round us in society
to see how scantily it has been recognised; and
perhaps even ourselves, after a little reflection,
may decide to spend a trifle less for money, and
indulge ourselves a trifle more in the article of
freedom.

III

"To have done anything by which you earned
money merely," says Thoreau, "is to be" (have
been, he means) "idle and worse." There are
two passages in his letters, both, oddly enough,
relating to firewood, which must be brought together to be rightly understood. So taken, they
contain between them the marrow of all good
sense on the subject of work in its relation to
something broader than mere livelihood. Here is
the first: "I suppose I have burned up a good-
sized tree to-night—and for what? I settled with

Mr. Tarbell for it the other day; but that wasn't the final settlement. I got off cheaply from him. At last one will say: 'Let us see, how much wood did you burn, sir?' And I shall shudder to think that the next question will be, 'What did you do while you were warm?'" Even after we have settled with Admetus in the person of Mr. Tarbell, there comes, you see, a further question. It is not enough to have earned our livelihood. Either the earning itself should have been serviceable to mankind, or something else must follow. To live is sometimes very difficult, but it is never meritorious in itself; and we must have a reason to allege to our own conscience why we should continue to exist upon this crowded earth. If Thoreau had simply dwelt in his house at Walden, a lover of trees, birds, and fishes, and the open air and virtue, a reader of wise books, an idle, selfish self-improver, he would have managed to cheat Admetus, but, to cling to metaphor, the devil would have had him in the end. Those who can avoid toil altogether and dwell in the Arcadia of private means, and even those who can, by abstinence, reduce the necessary amount of it to some six weeks a year, having the more liberty, have only the higher moral obligation to be up and doing in the interest of man.

The second passage is this: "There is a far more important and warming heat, commonly lost, which precedes the burning of the wood. It is the smoke of industry, which is incense. I have been so thoroughly warmed in body and spirit, that when at length my fuel was housed, I came

near selling it to the ashman, as if I had extracted
all its heat." Industry is, in itself and when
properly chosen, delightful and profitable to the
worker; and when your toil has been a pleasure,
you have not, as Thoreau says, "earned money
merely," but money, health, delight, and moral
profit, all in one. "We must heap up a great pile
of doing for a small diameter of being," he says
in another place; and then exclaims, "How admirably the artist is made to accomplish his self-
culture by devotion to his art!" We may escape
uncongenial toil, only to devote ourselves to that
which is congenial. It is only to transact some
higher business that even Apollo dare play the
truant from Admetus. We must all work for the
sake of work; we must all work, as Thoreau says
again, in any "absorbing pursuit—it does not
much matter what, so it be honest;" but the most
profitable work is that which combines into one
continued effort the largest proportion of the
powers and desires of a man's nature; that into
which he will plunge with ardour, and from
which he will desist with reluctance; in which he
will know the weariness of fatigue, but not that of
satiety; and which will be ever fresh, pleasing,
and stimulating to his taste. Such work holds a
man together, braced at all points; it does not
suffer him to doze or wander; it keeps him actively conscious of himself, yet raised among
superior interests; it gives him the profit of industry with the pleasures of a pastime. This is
what his art should be to the true artist, and that
to a degree unknown in other and less intimate

pursuits. For other professions stand apart from the human business of life; but an art has its seat at the centre of the artist's doings and sufferings, deals directly with his experiences, teaches him the lessons of his own fortunes and mishaps, and becomes a part of his biography. So says Goethe:

> "Spät erklingt was früh erklang;
> Glück und Unglück wird Gesang."

Now Thoreau's art was literature; and it was one of which he had conceived most ambitiously. He loved and believed in good books. He said well, "Life is not habitually seen from any common platform so truly and unexaggerated as in the light of literature." But the literature he loved was of the heroic order. "Books, not which afford us a cowering enjoyment, but in which each thought is of unusual daring; such as an idle man cannot read, and a timid one would not be entertained by, which even make us dangerous to existing institutions—such I call good books." He did not think them easy to be read! "The heroic books," he says, "even if printed in the character of our mother-tongue, will always be in a language dead to degenerate times; and we must laboriously seek the meaning of each word and line, conjecturing a larger sense than common use permits out of what wisdom and valour and generosity we have." Nor does he suppose that such books are easily written. "Great prose, of equal elevation, commands our respect more than great verse," says he, "since it implies a more permanent and level height, a life more pervaded with the grandeur of the thought. The poet often only makes an irruption, like the Parthian, and is off again, shooting while he retreats; but the prose writer has conquered like a Roman and settled colonies." We may ask ourselves, almost with dismay, whether such works exist at all but in the imagination of the student. For the bulk of the best of books is apt to be made up with ballast; and those in which energy of thought is combined with any stateliness of utterance may be almost counted on the fingers. Looking round in English for a book that should answer Thoreau's two demands of a style like poetry and sense that shall be both original and inspiriting, I come to Milton's *Areopagitica*, and can name no other instance for the moment. Two things at least are plain: that if a man will condescend to nothing more commonplace in the way of reading, he must not look to have a large library; and that if he proposes himself to write in a similar vein, he will find his work cut out for him.

Thoreau composed seemingly while he walked, or at least exercise and composition were with him intimately connected; for we are told that "the length of his walk uniformly made the length of his writing." He speaks in one place of "plainness and vigour, the ornaments of style," which is rather too paradoxical to be comprehensively true. In another he remarks: "As for style of writing, if one has anything to say it drops from him simply as a stone falls to the ground." We must conjecture a very large sense indeed for

145

the phrase "if one has anything to say." When truth flows from a man, fittingly clothed in style and without conscious effort, it is because the effort has been made and the work practically completed before he sat down to write. It is only out of fulness of thinking that expression drops perfect like a ripe fruit; and when Thoreau wrote so nonchalantly at his desk, it was because he had been vigorously active during his walk. For neither clearness, compression, nor beauty of language, come to any living creature till after a busy and a prolonged acquaintance with the subject on hand. Easy writers are those who, like Walter Scott, choose to remain contented with a less degree of perfection than is legitimately within the compass of their powers. We hear of Shakespeare and his clean manuscript; but in the face of the evidence of the style itself and of the various editions of *Hamlet* this merely proves that Messrs. Hemming and Condell were unacquainted with the common enough phenomenon called a fair copy. He who would recast a tragedy already given to the world must frequently and earnestly have revised details in the study. Thoreau himself, and in spite of his protestations, is an instance of even extreme research in one direction; and his effort after heroic utterance is proved not only by the occasional finish, but by the determined exaggeration of his style. "I trust you realize what an exaggerator I am—that I lay myself out to exaggerate," he writes. And again, hinting at the explanation: "Who that has heard a strain of music feared lest he should speak extravagantly any more for ever?" And yet once more, in his essay on Carlyle, and this time with his meaning well in hand: "No truth, we think, was ever expressed but with this sort of emphasis, that for the time there seemed to be no other." Thus Thoreau was an exaggerative and a parabolical writer, not because he loved the literature of the East, but from a desire that people should understand and realise what he was writing. He was near the truth upon the general question; but in his own particular method, it appears to me, he wandered. Literature is not less a conventional art than painting or sculpture; and it is the least striking, as it is the most comprehensive of the three. To hear a strain of music, to see a beautiful woman, a river, a great city, or a starry night, is to make man despair of his Lilliputian arts in language. Now, to gain that emphasis which seems denied to us by the very nature of the medium, the proper method of literature is by selection, which is a kind of negative exaggeration. It is the right of the literary artist, as Thoreau was on the point of seeing, to leave out whatever does not suit his purpose. Thus we extract the pure gold; and thus the well-written story of a noble life becomes, by its very omissions, more thrilling to the reader. But to go beyond this, like Thoreau, and to exaggerate directly, is to leave the saner classical tradition, and to put the reader on his guard. And when you write the whole for the half, you do not express your thought more forcibly, but only express a different thought which is not yours.

Thoreau's true subject was the pursuit of self-improvement combined with an unfriendly criticism of life as it goes on in our societies; it is there that he best displays the freshness and surprising trenchancy of his intellect; it is there that his style becomes plain and vigorous, and therefore, according to his own formula, ornamental. Yet he did not care to follow this vein singly, but must drop into it by the way in books of a different purport. *Walden, or Life in the Woods, A Week on the Concord and Merrimack Rivers, The Maine Woods,*—such are the titles he affects. He was probably reminded by his delicate critical perception that the true business of literature is with narrative; in reasoned narrative, and there alone, that art enjoys all its advantages, and suffers least from its defects. Dry precept and disembodied disquisition, as they can only be read with an effort of abstraction, can never convey a perfectly complete or a perfectly natural impression. Truth, even in literature, must be clothed with flesh and blood, or it cannot tell its whole story to the reader. Hence the effect of anecdote on simple minds; and hence good biographies and works of high, imaginative art, are not only far more entertaining, but far more edifying, than books of theory or precept. Now Thoreau could not clothe his opinions in the garment of art, for that was not his talent; but he sought to gain the same elbow-room for himself, and to afford a similar relief to his readers, by mingling his thoughts with a record of experience.

Again, he was a lover of nature. The quality

which we should call mystery in a painting, and which belongs so particularly to the aspect of the external world and to its influence upon our feelings, was one which he was never weary of attempting to reproduce in his books. The seeming significance of nature's appearances, their unchanging strangeness to the senses, and the thrilling response which they waken in the mind of man, continued to surprise and stimulate his spirits. It appeared to him, I think, that if we could only write near enough to the facts, and yet with no pedestrian calm, but ardently, we might transfer the glamour of reality direct upon our pages; and that, if it were once thus captured and expressed, a new and instructive relation might appear between men's thought and the phenomena of nature. This was the eagle that he pursued all his life long, like a schoolboy with a butterfly net. Hear him to a friend: "Let me suggest a theme for you—to state to yourself precisely and completely what that walk over the mountains amounted to for you, returning to this essay again and again until you are satisfied that all that was important in your experience is in it. Don't suppose that you can tell it precisely the first dozen times you try, but at 'em again; especially when, after a sufficient pause, you suspect that you are touching the heart or summit of the matter, reiterate your blows there, and account for the mountain to yourself. Not that the story need be long, but it will take a long while to make it short." Such was the method, not consistent for a man whose meanings were to "drop from him as a stone falls to the ground." Perhaps the most successful work that Thoreau ever accomplished in this direction is to be found in the passages relating to fish in the *Week*. These are remarkable for a vivid truth of impression and a happy suitability of language, not frequently surpassed.

Whatever Thoreau tried to do was tried in fair, square prose, with sentences solidly built, and no help from bastard rhythms. Moreover, there is a progression—I cannot call it a progress—in his work towards a more and more strictly prosaic level, until at last he sinks into the bathos of the prosy. Emerson mentions having once remarked to Thoreau: "Who would not like to write something which all can read, like *Robinson Crusoe*? and who does not see with regret that his page is not solid with a right materialistic treatment which delights everybody?" I must say in passing that it is not the right materialistic treatment which delights the world in *Robinson*, but the romantic and philosophic interest of the fable. The same treatment does quite the reverse of delighting us when it is applied, in *Colonel Jack*, to the management of a plantation. But I cannot help suspecting Thoreau to have been influenced either by this identical remark or by some other closely similar in meaning. He began to fall more and more into a detailed materialistic treatment; he went into the business doggedly, as one who should make a guide-book; he not only chronicled what had been important in his own experience, but whatever might have been important in the experience of anybody else; not only what had affected him, but all that he saw or heard. His ardour had grown less, or perhaps it was inconsistent with a right materialistic treatment to display such emotions as he felt; and, to complete the eventful change, he chose, from a sense of moral dignity, to gut these later works of the saving quality of humour. He was not one of those authors who have learned, in his own words, "to leave out their dulness." He inflicts his full quantity upon the reader in such books as *Cape Cod*, or *The Yankee in Canada*. Of the latter he confessed that he had not managed to get much of himself into it. Heaven knows he had not, nor yet much of Canada, we may hope. "Nothing," he says somewhere, "can shock a brave man but dulness." Well, there are few spots more shocking to the brave than the pages of *The Yankee in Canada*.

There are but three books of his that will be read with much pleasure: the *Week*, *Walden*, and the collected letters. As to his poetry, Emerson's word shall suffice for us, it is so accurate and so prettily said: "The thyme and marjoram are not yet honey." In this, as in his prose, he relied greatly on the goodwill of the reader, and wrote throughout in faith. It was an exercise of faith to suppose that many would understand the sense of his best work, or that any could be exhilarated by the dreary chronicling of his worst. "But," as he says, "the gods do not hear any rude or discordant sound, as we learn from the echo; and I know that the nature towards which

I launch these sounds is so rich that it will modulate anew and wonderfully improve my rudest strain."

IV

"What means the fact," he cries, "that a soul which has lost all hope for itself can inspire in another listening soul such an infinite confidence in it, even while it is expressing its despair?" The question is an echo and an illustration of the words last quoted; and it forms the key-note of his thoughts on friendship. No one else, to my knowledge, has spoken in so high and just a spirit of the kindly relations; and I doubt whether it be a drawback that these lessons should come from one in many ways so unfitted to be a teacher in this branch. The very coldness and egoism of his own intercourse gave him a clearer insight into the intellectual basis of our warm, mutual tolerations; and testimony to their worth comes with added force from one who was solitary and disobliging, and of whom a friend remarked, with equal wit and wisdom, "I love Henry, but I cannot like him."

He can hardly be persuaded to make any distinction between love and friendship; in such rarefied and freezing air, upon the mountain-tops of meditation, had he taught himself to breathe. He was, indeed, too accurate an observer not to have remarked that "there exists already a natural disinterestedness and liberality" between men and women; yet, he thought, "friendship is no respecter of sex." Perhaps there is a sense in which the words are true; but they were spoken in ignorance; and perhaps we shall have put the matter most correctly, if we call love a foundation for a nearer and freer degree of friendship than can be possible without it. For there are delicacies, eternal between persons of the same sex, which are melted and disappear in the warmth of love.

To both, if they are to be right, he attributes the same nature and condition. "We are not what we are," says he, "nor do we treat or esteem each other for such, but for what we are capable of being." "A friend is one who incessantly pays us the compliment of expecting all the virtues from us, and who can appreciate them in us." "The friend asks no return but that his friend will religiously accept and wear and not disgrace his apotheosis of him." "It is the merit and preservation of friendship that it takes place on a level higher than the actual characters of the parties would seem to warrant." This is to put friendship on a pedestal indeed; and yet the root of the matter is there; and the last sentence, in particular, is like a light in a dark place, and makes many mysteries plain. We are different with different friends; yet if we look closely we shall find that every such relation reposes on some particular apotheosis of oneself; with each friend, although we could not distinguish it in words from any other, we have at least one special reputation to preserve: and it is thus that we run, when mortified, to our friend or the woman that we love, not to hear ourselves called better, but to be better men in point of fact. We seek this society to flatter ourselves with our own good conduct. And hence any falsehood in the relation, any incomplete or perverted understanding, will spoil even the pleasure of these visits. Thus says Thoreau again: "Only lovers know the value of truth." And yet again: "They ask for words and deeds, when a true relation is word and deed."

But it follows that since they are neither of them so good as the other hopes, and each is, in a very honest manner, playing a part above his powers, such an intercourse must often be disappointing to both. "We may bid farewell sooner than complain," says Thoreau, "for our complaint is too well grounded to be uttered." "We have not so good a right to hate any as our friend."

> "It were treason to our love
> And a sin to God above,
> One iota to abate
> Of a pure, impartial hate."

Love is not blind, nor yet forgiving. "O yes, believe me," as the song says, "Love has eyes!" The nearer the intimacy, the more cuttingly do we feel the unworthiness of those we love; and because we love one, and would die for that love tomorrow, you have not forgotten, and you never will forgive, that friend's misconduct. If you want a person's faults, go to those who love him. They will not tell you, but they know. And herein lies the magnanimous courage of love, that it endures this knowledge without change.

It required a cold, distant personality like that

of Thoreau, perhaps, to recognise and certainly
to utter this truth; for a more human love makes
it a point of honour not to acknowledge those
faults of which it is most conscious. But his point
of view is both high and dry. He has no illusions;
he does not give way to love any more than to
hatred, but preserves them both with care like
valuable curiosities. A more bald-headed picture
of life, if I may so express myself, has seldom
been presented. He is an egoist; he does not remember, or does not think it worth while to remark, that, in these near intimacies, we are
ninety-nine times disappointed in our beggarly
selves for once that we are disappointed in our
friend; that it is we who seem most frequently un-
deserving of the love that unites us; and that it
is by our friend's conduct that we are continually
rebuked and yet strengthened for a fresh en-
deavour. Thoreau is dry, priggish, and selfish. It is
profit he is after in these intimacies; moral profit,
certainly, but still profit to himself. If you will be
the sort of friend I want, he remarks naïvely,
"my education cannot dispense with your society." His education! as though a friend were a
dictionary. And with all this, not one word about
pleasure, or laughter, or kisses, or any quality of
flesh and blood. It was not inappropriate, surely,
that he had such close relations with the fish. We
can understand the friend already quoted, when
he cried: "As for taking his arm, I would as soon
think of taking the arm of an elm-tree!"

As a matter of fact he experienced but a broken
enjoyment in his intimacies. He says he has been

perpetually on the brink of the sort of intercourse he wanted, and yet never completely attained it. And what else had he to expect when he would not, in a happy phrase of Carlyle's, "nestle down into it"? Truly, so it will be always if you only stroll in to see a cricket match; and even then not simply for the pleasure of the thing, but with some afterthought of self-improvement, as though you had come to the cricket match to bet. It was his theory that people saw each other too frequently, so that their curiosity was not properly whetted, nor had they anything fresh to communicate; but friendship must be something else than a society for mutual improvement—indeed, it must only be that by the way, and to some extent unconsciously; and if Thoreau had been a man instead of a manner of elm-tree, he would have felt that he saw his friends too seldom, and have reaped benefits unknown to his philosophy from a more sustained and easy intercourse. We might remind him of his own words about love: "We should have no reserve; we should give the whole of ourselves to that business. But commonly men have not imagination enough to be thus employed about a human being, but must be coopering a barrel, forsooth." Ay, or reading oriental philosophers. It is not the nature of the rival occupation, it is the fact that you suffer it to be a rival, that renders loving intimacy impossible. Nothing is given for nothing in this world; there can be no true love, even on your own side, without devotion; devotion is the exercise of love, by which it grows; but if you will give enough of that, if you will pay the price in a sufficient "amount of what you call life," why then, indeed, whether with wife or comrade, you may have months and even years of such easy, natural, pleasurable, and yet improving intercourse as shall make time a moment and kindness a delight.

The secret of his retirement lies not in misanthropy, of which he had no tincture, but part in his engrossing design of self-improvement and part in the real deficiencies of social intercourse. He was not so much difficult about his fellow human beings as he could not tolerate the terms of their association. He could take to a man for any genuine qualities, as we see by his admirable sketch of the Canadian woodcutter in *Walden*; but he would not consent, in his own words, to "feebly fabulate and paddle in the social slush." It seemed to him, I think, that society is precisely the reverse of friendship, in that it takes place on a lower level than the characters of any of the parties would warrant us to expect. The society talk of even the most brilliant man is of greatly less account than what you will get from him in (as the French say) a little committee. And Thoreau wanted geniality; he had not enough of the superficial, even at command; he could not swoop into a parlour and, in the naval phrase, "cut out" a human being from that dreary port; nor had he inclination for the task. I suspect he loved books and nature as well and near as warmly as he loved his fellow-creatures,—a melancholy, lean degeneration of the human character.

"As for the dispute about solitude and society,"

he thus sums up: "Any comparison is impertinent. It is an idling down on the plain at the base of the mountain instead of climbing steadily to its top. Of course you will be glad of all the society you can get to go up with? Will you go to glory with me? is the burden of the song. It is not that we love to be alone, but that we love to soar, and when we do soar the company grows thinner and thinner till there is none at all. It is either the tribune on the plain, a sermon on the mount, or a very private ecstasy still higher up. Use all the society that will abet you." But surely it is no very extravagant opinion that it is better to give than to receive, to serve than to use our companions; and above all, where there is no question of service upon either side, that it is good to enjoy their company like a natural man. It is curious and in some ways dispiriting that a writer may be always best corrected out of his own mouth; and so, to conclude, here is another passage from Thoreau which seems aimed directly at himself: "Do not be too moral; you may cheat yourself out of much life so. . . . *All fables, indeed, have their morals; but the innocent enjoy the story.*"

V

"The only obligation," says he, "which I have a right to assume is to do at any time what I think right." "Why should we ever go abroad, even across the way, to ask a neighbour's advice?" "There is a nearer neighbour within, who is incessantly telling us how we should behave. *But we wait for the neighbour without to tell us of some false, easier way.*" "The greater part of what my neighbours call good I believe in my soul to be bad." To be what we are, and to become what we are capable of becoming, is the only end of life. It is "when we fall behind ourselves" that "we are cursed with duties and the neglect of duties." "I love the wild," he says, "not less than the good." And again: "The life of a good man will hardly improve us more than the life of a freebooter, for the inevitable laws appear as plainly in the infringement as in the observance, and" (mark this) *"our lives are sustained by a nearly equal expense of virtue of some kind."* Even although he were a prig, it will be owned he could announce a startling doctrine. "As for doing good," he writes elsewhere, "that is one of the professions that are full. Moreover, I have tried it fairly, and, strange as it may seem, am satisfied that it does not agree with my constitution. Probably I should not conscientiously and deliberately forsake my particular calling to do the good which society demands of me, to save the universe from annihilation; and I believe that a like but infinitely greater steadfastness elsewhere is all that now preserves it. If you should ever be betrayed into any of these philanthropies, do not let your left hand know what your right hand does, for it is not worth knowing." Elsewhere he returns upon the subject, and explains his meaning thus: "If I ever *did* a man any good in their sense, of course it was something exceptional and insignificant compared with the good or evil I am constantly doing by being what I am."

There is a rude nobility, like that of a barbarian king, in this unshaken confidence in himself and indifference to the wants, thoughts, or sufferings of others. In his whole works I find no trace of pity. This was partly the result of theory, for he held the world too mysterious to be criticised, and asks conclusively: "What right have I to grieve who have not ceased to wonder?" But it sprang still more from constitutional indifference and superiority; and he grew up healthy, composed, and unconscious from life's horrors, like a green bay-tree from a field of battle. It was from this lack in himself that he failed to do justice to the spirit of Christ; for while he could glean more meaning from individual precepts than any score of Christians, yet he conceived life in such a different hope, and viewed it with such contrary emotions, that the sense and purport of the doctrine as a whole seems to have passed him by or left him unimpressed. He could understand the idealism of the Christian view, but he was himself so unaffectedly unhuman that he did not recognise the human intention and essence of that teaching. Hence he complained that Christ did not leave us a rule that was proper and sufficient for this world, not having conceived the nature of the rule that was laid down; for things of that character that are sufficiently unacceptable become positively non-existent to the mind. But perhaps we shall best appreciate the defect in

Thoreau by seeing it supplied in the case of
Whitman. For the one, I feel confident, is the
disciple of the other; it is what Thoreau clearly
whispered that Whitman so uproariously bawls; it
is the same doctrine, but with how immense a
difference! the same argument, but used to what
a new conclusion! Thoreau had plenty of humour
until he tutored himself out of it, and so forfeited
that best birthright of a sensible man; Whitman,
in that respect, seems to have been sent into the
world naked and unashamed; and yet by a strange
consummation, it is the theory of the former that
is arid, abstract, and claustral. Of these two phi-
losophies so nearly identical at bottom, the one
pursues Self-improvement—a churlish, mangy
dog; the other is up with the morning, in the best
of health, and following the nymph Happiness,
buxom, blithe, and debonair. Happiness, at least,
is not solitary; it joys to communicate; it loves
others, for it depends on them for its existence;
it sanctions and encourages to all delights that are
not unkind in themselves; if it lived to a thousand, it would not make excision of a single
humorous passage; and while the self-improver
dwindles towards the prig, and, if he be not of
an excellent constitution, may even grow de-
formed into an Obermann, the very name and
appearance of a happy man breathe of good-
nature, and help the rest of us to live.

In the case of Thoreau, so great a show of
doctrine demands some outcome in the field of
action. If nothing were to be done but build a
shanty beside Walden Pond, we have heard al-

together too much of these declarations of independence. That the man wrote some books is nothing to the purpose, for the same has been done in a suburban villa. That he kept himself happy is perhaps a sufficient excuse, but it is disappointing to the reader. We may be unjust, but when a man despises commerce and philanthropy alike, and has views of good so soaring that he must take himself apart from mankind for their cultivation, we will not be content without some striking act. It was not Thoreau's fault if he were not martyred; had the occasion come, he would have made a noble ending. As it is, he did once seek to interfere in the world's course: he made one practical appearance on the stage of affairs; and a strange one it was, and strangely characteristic of the nobility and eccentricity of the man. It was forced on him by his calm and radical opposition to negro slavery. "Voting for the right is doing nothing for it," he saw; "it is only expressing to men feebly your desire that it should prevail." For his part, he would not "for an instant recognise that political organisation for *his* government which is the *slave's* government also." "I do not hesitate to say," he adds, "that those who call themselves Abolitionists should at once effectually withdraw their support, both in person and property, from the government of Massachusetts." This is what he did: in 1843 he ceased to pay the poll-tax. The highway-tax he paid, for he said he was as desirous to be a good neighbour as to be a bad subject; but no more poll-tax to the State of Massachusetts. Thoreau had now seceded, and was a polity unto himself; or, as he explains it with admirable sense, "In fact, I quietly declare war with the State after my fashion, though I will still make what use and get what advantage of her I can, as is usual in such cases." He was put in prison; but that was a part of his design. "Under a government which imprisons any unjustly, the true place for a just man is also a prison. I know this well, that if one thousand, if one hundred, if ten men whom I could name—ay, if *one* HONEST man, in this State of Massachusetts, *ceasing to hold slaves*, were actually to withdraw from this copartnership, and be locked up in the county gaol therefor, it would be the abolition of slavery in America. For it matters not how small the beginning may seem to be; what is once well done is done for ever." Such was his theory of civil disobedience.

And the upshot? A friend paid the tax for him; continued year by year to pay it in the sequel; and Thoreau was free to walk the woods unmolested. It was a *fiasco*, but to me it does not seem laughable; even those who joined in the laughter at the moment would be insensibly affected by this quaint instance of a good man's horror for injustice. We may compute the worth of that one night's imprisonment as outweighing half a hundred voters at some subsequent election: and if Thoreau had possessed as great a power of persuasion as (let us say) Falstaff, if he had counted a party however small, if his example had been followed by a hundred or by thirty of his fellows, I cannot but believe it would have greatly pre-

cipitated the era of freedom and justice. We feel
the misdeeds of our country with so little fervour,
for we are not witnesses to the suffering they
cause; but when we see them wake an active horror in our fellow-men, when we see a neighbour
prefer to lie in prison rather than be so much as
passively implicated in their perpetration, even
the dullest of us will begin to realise them with a
quicker pulse.

Not for from twenty years later, when Captain
John Brown was taken at Harper's Ferry, Thoreau
was the first to come forward in his defence. The
committees wrote to him unanimously that his
action was premature. "I did not send to you for
advice," said he, "but to announce that I was to
speak." I have used the word "defence;" in truth
he did not seek to defend him, even declared it
would be better for the good cause that he should
die; but he praised his action as I think Brown
would have liked to hear it praised.

Thus this singularly eccentric and independent
mind, wedded to a character of so much strength,
singleness, and purity, pursued its own path of
self-improvement for more than half a century,
part gymnosophist, part backwoodsman; and thus
did it come twice, though in a subaltern attitude,
into the field of political history.

NOTE.—For many facts in the above essay, among
which I may mention the incident of the squirrel, I am
indebted to *Thoreau: His Life and Aims,* by H. A. Page,
or, as is well known, Dr. Japp.

"A PENNY PLAIN AND TWOPENCE COLOURED"

THESE WORDS will be familiar to all students of Skelt's Juvenile Drama. That national monument, after having changed its name to Park's, to Webb's, to Redington's, and last of all to Pollock's, has now become, for the most part, a memory. Some of its pillars, like Stonehenge, are still afoot, the rest clean vanished. It may be the Museum numbers a full set; and Mr. Ionides perhaps, or else her gracious Majesty, may boast their great collections; but to the plain private person they are become, like Raphaels, unattainable. I have, at different times, possessed *Aladdin, The Red Rover, The Blind Boy, The Old Oak Chest, The Wood Dæmon, Jack Sheppard, The Miller and his Men, Der Freischütz, The Smuggler, The Forest of Bondy, Robin Hood, The Waterman, Richard I., My Poll and my Partner Joe, The Inchcape Bell* (imperfect), and *Three-Fingered Jack, the Terror of Jamaica*; and I have assisted others in the illumination of *The Maid of the Inn* and *The Battle of Waterloo*. In this roll-call of stirring names you read the evidences of a happy childhood; and though not half of them are still to be procured of any living stationer, in the mind of their once happy owner all survive, kaleidoscopes of changing pictures, echoes of the past.

There stands, I fancy, to this day (but now

165

how fallen!) a certain stationer's shop at a corner of the wide thoroughfare that joins the city of my childhood with the sea. When, upon any Saturday, we made a party to behold the ships, we passed that corner; and since in those days I loved a ship as a man loves Burgundy or daybreak, this of itself had been enough to hallow it. But there was more than that. In the Leith Walk window, all the year round, there stood displayed a theatre in working order, with a "forest set," a "combat," and a few "robbers carousing" in the slides; and below and about, dearer tenfold to me! the plays themselves, those budgets of romance, lay tumbled one upon another. Long and often have I lingered there with empty pockets. One figure, we shall say, was visible in the first plate of characters, bearded, pistol in hand, or drawing to his ear the clothyard arrow; I would spell the name: was it Macaire, or Long Tom Coffin, or Grindoff, 2d dress? O, how I would long to see the rest! how—if the name by chance were hidden—I would wonder in what play he figured, and what immortal legend justified his attitude and strange apparel! And then to go within, to announce yourself as an intending purchaser, and, closely watched, be suffered to undo those bundles and breathlessly devour those pages of gesticulating villains, epileptic combats, bosky forests, palaces and war-ships, frowning fortresses and prison vaults—it was a giddy joy. That shop, which was dark and smelt of Bibles, was a loadstone rock for all that bore the name of boy. They could not pass it by, nor, having entered, leave it.

166

It was a place besieged; the shopmen, like the Jews rebuilding Salem, had a double task. They kept us at the stick's end, frowned us down, snatched each play out of our hand ere we were trusted with another; and, incredible as it may sound, used to demand of us upon our entrance, like banditti, if we came with money or with empty hand. Old Mr. Smith himself, worn out with my eternal vacillation, once swept the treasures from before me, with the cry: "I do not believe, child, that you are an intending purchaser at all!" These were the dragons of the garden; but for such joys of paradise we could have faced the Terror of Jamaica himself. Every sheet we fingered was another lightning glance into obscure, delicious story; it was like wallowing in the raw stuff of story-books. I know nothing to compare with it save now and then in dreams, when I am privileged to read in certain unwrit stories of adventure, from which I awake to find the world all vanity. The *crux* of Buridan's donkey was as nothing to the uncertainty of the boy as he handled and lingered and doated on these bundles of delight; there was a physical pleasure in the sight and touch of them which he would jealously prolong; and when at length the deed was done, the play selected, and the impatient shopman had brushed the rest into the gray portfolio, and the boy was forth again, a little late for dinner, the lamps springing into light in the blue winter's even, and *The Miller*, or *The Rover*, or some kindred drama clutched against his side— on what gay feet he ran, and how he laughed aloud in exultation! I can hear that laughter still. Out of all the years of my life, I can recall but one home-coming to compare with these, and that was on the night when I brought back with me the *Arabian Entertainments* in the fat, old, double-columned volume with the prints. I was just well into the story of the Hunchback, I remember, when my clergyman-grandfather (a man we counted pretty stiff) came in behind me. I grew blind with terror. But instead of ordering the book away, he said he envied me. Ah, well he might!

The purchase and the first half-hour at home, that was the summit. Thenceforth the interest declined by little and little. The fable, as set forth in the play-book, proved to be not worthy of the scenes and characters: what fable would not? Such passages as: "Scene 6. The Hermitage. Night set scene. Place back of scene 1, No. 2, at back of stage and hermitage, Fig. 2, out of set piece, R. H. in a slanting direction"—such passages, I say, though very practical, are hardly to be called good reading. Indeed, as literature, these dramas did not much appeal to me. I forget the very outline of the plots. Of *The Blind Boy*, beyond the fact that he was a most injured prince and once, I think, abducted, I know nothing. And *The Old Oak Chest*, what was it all about? that proscript (1st dress), that prodigious number of banditti, that old woman with the broom, and the magnificent kitchen in the third act (was it in the third?)—they are all fallen in a deliquium, swim faintly in my brain, and mix and vanish.

I cannot deny that joy attended the illumination; nor can I quite forget that child who, wilfully foregoing pleasure, stoops to "twopence coloured." With crimson lake (hark to the sound of it—crimson lake!—the horns of elf-land are not richer on the ear)—with crimson lake and Prussian blue a certain purple is to be compounded which, for cloaks especially, Titian could not equal. The latter colour with gamboge, a hated name although an exquisite pigment, supplied a green of such a savoury greenness that to-day my heart regrets it. Nor can I recall without a tender weakness the very aspect of the water where I dipped my brush. Yes, there was pleasure in the painting. But when all was painted, it is needless to deny it, all was spoiled. You might, indeed, set up a scene or two to look at; but to cut the figures out was simply sacrilege; nor could any child twice court the tedium, the worry, and the long-drawn disenchantment of an actual performance. Two days after the purchase the honey had been sucked. Parents used to complain; they thought I wearied of my play. It was not so: no more than a person can be said to have wearied of his dinner when he leaves the bones and dishes; I had got the marrow of it and said grace.

Then was the time to turn to the back of the playbook and to study that enticing double file of names, where poetry, for the true child of Skelt, reigned happy and glorious like her Majesty the Queen. Much as I have travelled in these realms of gold, I have yet seen, upon that map or abstract,

names of El Dorados that still haunt the ear of
memory, and are still but names. *The Floating
Beacon*—why was that denied me? or *The Wreck
Ashore*? *Sixteen-String Jack* whom I did not even
guess to be a highwayman, troubled me awake
and haunted my slumbers; and there is one se-
quence of three from that enchanted calender
that I still at times recall, like a loved verse of
poetry: *Lodoiska, Silver Palace, Echo of West-
minster Bridge*. Names, bare names, are surely
more to children than we poor, grown-up, obliterated fools remember.

The name of Skelt itself has always seemed a
part and parcel of the charm of his productions.
It may be different with the rose, but the attraction of this paper drama sensibly declined when
Webb had crept into the rubric: a poor cuckoo,
flaunting in Skelt's nest. And now we have
reached Pollock, sounding deeper gulfs. Indeed,
this name of Skelt appears so stagey and piratic,
that I will adopt it boldly to design these qualities. Skeltery, then, is a quality of much art. It
is even to be found, with reverence be it said,
among the works of nature. The stagey is its
generic name; but it is an old, insular, home-bred
staginess, not French, domestically British; not of
to-day, but smacking of O. Smith, Fitzball, and
the great age of melodrama: a peculiar fragrance
haunting it; uttering its unimportant message in
a tone of voice that has the charm of fresh antiquity. I will not insist upon the art of Skelt's
purveyors. These wonderful characters that once
so thrilled our soul with their bold attitude, array

of deadly engines and incomparable costume, to-day look somewhat pallidly; the extreme hard favour of the heroine strikes me, I had almost said with pain; the villain's scowl no longer thrills me like a trumpet; and the scenes themselves, those once unparalleled landscapes, seem the efforts of a prentice hand. So much of fault we find; but on the other side the impartial critic rejoices to remark the presence of a great unity of gusto; of those direct clap-trap appeals, which a man is dead and buriable when he fails to answer; of the footlight glamour, the ready-made, bare-faced, transpontine picturesque, a thing not one with cold reality, but how much dearer to the mind!

The scenery of Skeltdom—or, shall we say, the kingdom of Transpontus?—had a prevailing character. Whether it set forth Poland as in *The Blind Boy*, or Bohemia with *The Miller and his Men*, or Italy with *The Old Oak Chest*, still it was Transpontus. A botanist could tell it by the plants. The hollyhock was all pervasive, running wild in deserts; the dock was common, and the bending reed; and overshadowing these were poplar, palm, potato tree, and *Quercus Skeltica* —brave growths. The caves were all embowelled in the Surreyside formation; the soil was all betrodden by the light pump of T. P. Cooke. Skelt, to be sure, had yet another, an oriental string: he held the gorgeous east in fee; and in the new quarter of Hyères, say, in the garden of the Hotel des Iles d'Or, you may behold these blessed visions realised. But on these I will not dwell;

171

they were an outwork; it was in the occidental scenery that Skelt was all himself. It had a strong flavour of England; it was a sort of indigestion of England and drop-scenes, and I am bound to say was charming. How the roads wander, how the castle sits upon the hill, how the sun eradiates from behind the cloud, and how the congregated clouds themselves uproll, as stiff as bolsters! Here is the cottage interior, the usual first flat, with the cloak upon the nail, the rosaries of onions, the gun and powder-horn and corner-cupboard; here is the inn (this drama must be nautical, I foresee Captain Luff and Bold Bob Bowsprit) with the red curtain, pipes, spittoons, and eight-day clock; and there again is that impressive dungeon with the chains, which was so dull to colour. England, the hedgerow elms, the thin brick houses, windmills, glimpses of the navigable Thames—England, when at last I came to visit it, was only Skelt made evident: to cross the border was, for the Scotsman, to come home to Skelt; there was the inn-sign and there the horse-trough, all foreshadowed in the faithful Skelt. If, at the ripe age of fourteen years, I bought a certain cudgel, got a friend to load it, and thenceforward walked the tame ways of the earth my own ideal, radiating pure romance—still I was but a puppet in the hand of Skelt; the original of that regretted bludgeon, and surely the antitype of all the bludgeon kind, greatly improved from Cruikshank, had adorned the hand of Jonathan Wild, pl. 1. "This is mastering me," as Whitman cries, upon some lesser provocation. What am I? what are life, art, letters, the world, but what my Skelt has made them? He stamped himself upon my immaturity. The world was plain before I knew him, a poor penny world; but soon it was all coloured with romance. If I go to the theatre to see a good old melodrama, 'tis but Skelt a little faded. If I visit a bold scene in nature, Skelt would have been bolder; there had been certainly a castle on that mountain, and the hollow tree—that set piece—I seem to miss it in the foreground. Indeed, out of this cut-and-dry, dull, swaggering, obtrusive, and infantile art, I seem to have learned the very spirit of my life's enjoyment; met there the shadows of the characters I was to read about and love in a late future; got the romance of *Der Freischütz* long ere I was to hear of Weber or the mighty Formes; acquired a gallery of scenes and characters with which, in the silent theatre of the brain, I might enact all novels and romances; and took from these rude cuts an enduring and transforming pleasure. Reader—and yourself?

A word of moral: it appears that B. Pollock, late J. Redington, No. 73 Hoxton Street, not only publishes twenty-three of these old stage favourites, but owns the necessary plates and displays a modest readiness to issue other thirty-three. If you love art, folly, or the bright eyes of children, speed to Pollock's, or to Clarke's of Garrick Street. In Pollock's list of *publicanda* I perceive a pair of my ancient aspirations: *Wreck Ashore* and *Sixteen-String Jack*; and I cherish the belief that when these shall see once more the light of day, B. Pollock will remember this apologist. But, indeed, I have a dream at times that is not all a dream. I seem to myself to wander in a ghostly street—E. W., I think, the postal district —close below the fool's-cap of St. Paul's, and yet within easy hearing of the echo of the Abbey bridge. There is a dim shop, low in the roof and smelling strong of glue and footlights, I find myself in quaking treaty with great Skelt himself, the aboriginal, all dusty from the tomb. I buy, with what a choking heart—I buy them all, all but the pantomimes; I pay my mental money, and go forth; and lo! the packets are dust.

JOHN KNOX AND HIS RELATIONS
TO WOMEN

1   THE CONTROVERSY ABOUT FEMALE RULE

WHEN first the idea became widely spread
among men that the Word of God, instead of
being truly the foundation of all existing institutions, was rather a stone which the builders had
rejected, it was but natural that the consequent
havoc among received opinions should be accompanied by the generation of many new and lively
hopes for the future. Somewhat as in the early
days of the French Revolution, men must have
looked for an immediate and universal improvement in their condition. Christianity, up to that
time, had been somewhat of a failure politically.
The reason was now obvious, the capital flaw was
detected, the sickness of the body politic traced
at last to its efficient cause. It was only necessary
to put the Bible thoroughly into practice, to set
themselves strenuously to realise in life the Holy
Commonwealth, and all abuses and iniquities
would surely pass away. Thus, in a pageant played
at Geneva in the year 1523, the world was represented as a sick man at the end of his wits for
help, to whom his doctor recommends Lutheran
specifics.[1]

1. Gaberel's *Eglise de Genève*, i. 88.

175

The Reformers themselves had set their affections in a different world, and professed to look for the finished result of their endeavours on the other side of death. They took no interest in politics as such; they even condemned political action as Antichristian: notably, Luther in the case of the Peasants' War. And yet, as the purely religious question was inseparably complicated with political difficulties, and they had to make opposition, from day to day, against principalities and powers, they were led, one after another, and again and again, to leave the sphere which was more strictly their own, and meddle, for good and evil, with the affairs of State. Not much was to be expected from interference in such a spirit. Whenever a minister found himself galled or hindered, he would be inclined to suppose some contravention of the Bible. Whenever Christian liberty was restrained (and Christian liberty for each individual would be about coextensive with what he wished to do), it was obvious that the State was Antichristian. The great thing, and the one thing, was to push the Gospel and the Reformers' own interpretation of it. Whatever helped was good; whatever hindered was evil; and if this simple classification proved inapplicable over the whole field, it was no business of his to stop and reconcile incongruities. He had more pressing concerns on hand; he had to save souls; he had to be about his Father's business. This short-sighted view resulted in a doctrine that was actually Jesuitical in application. They had no serious ideas upon politics, and they were ready, nay, they seemed almost bound, to adopt and support whichever ensured for the moment the greatest benefit to the souls of their fellow-men. They were dishonest in all sincerity. Thus La-bitte, in the introduction to a book[2] in which he supposes the hypocritical democracy of the Catholics under the League, steps aside for a moment to stigmatise the hypocritical democracy of the Protestants. And nowhere was this expediency in political questions more apparent than about the question of female sovereignty. So much was this the case that one James Thomasius, of Leipsic, wrote a little paper[3] about the religious partialities of those who took part in the controversy, in which some of these learned disputants cut a very sorry figure.

Now Knox had been from the first a man well hated; and it is somewhat characteristic of his luck that he figures here in the very forefront of the list of partial scribes who trimmed their doctrine with the wind in all good conscience, and were political weathercocks out of conviction. Not only has Thomasius mentioned him, but Bayle has taken the hint from Thomasius, and dedicated a long note to the matter at the end of his article on the Scotch Reformer. This is a little less than fair. If anyone among the evangelists of that period showed more serious political sense than another, it was assuredly Knox; and even in this very matter of female rule, although

2. *La Démocratie chez les Prédicateurs de la Ligue.*
3. *Historia affectuum se immiscentium controversiæ de gynacocratia.* It is in his collected prefaces, Leipsic, 1683.

177

I do not suppose anyone nowadays will feel inclined to endorse his sentiments, I confess I can make great allowance for his conduct. The controversy, besides, has an interest of its own, in view of later controversies.

John Knox, from 1556 to 1559, was resident in Geneva, as minister, jointly with Goodman, of a little church of English refugees. He and his congregation were banished from England by one woman, Mary Tudor, and proscribed in Scotland by another, the Regent Mary of Guise. The coincidence was tempting: here were many abuses centring about one abuse; here was Christ's Gospel persecuted in the two kingdoms by one anomalous power. He had not far to go to find the idea that female government was anomalous. It was an age, indeed, in which women, capable and incapable, played a conspicuous part upon the stage of European history; and yet their rule, whatever may have been the opinion of here and there a wise man and enthusiast, was regarded as an anomaly by the great bulk of their contemporaries. It was defended as an anomaly. It, and all that accompanied and sanctioned it, was set aside as a single exception; and no one thought of reasoning down from queens and extending their privileges to ordinary women. Great ladies, as we know, had the privilege of entering into monasteries and cloisters, otherwise forbidden to their sex. As with one thing, so with another. Thus, Margaret of Navarre wrote books with great acclamation, and no one, seemingly, saw fit to call her conduct in question; but Mademoiselle de Gournay, Montaigne's adopted daughter, was in controversy with the world as to whether a woman might be an author without incongruity. Thus, too, we have Théodore Agrippa d'Aubigné writing to his daughters about the learned women of his century, and cautioning them, in conclusion, that the study of letters was unsuited to ladies of a middling station, and should be reserved for princesses.[4] And once more, if we desire to see the same principle carried to ludicrous extreme, we shall find that Reverend Father in God the Abbot of Brantôme, claiming, on the authority of some lord of his acquaintance, a privilege, or rather a duty, of free love for great princesses, and carefully excluding other ladies from the same gallant dispensation.[5] One sees the spirit in which these immunities were granted; and how they were but the natural consequence of that awe for courts and kings that made the last writer tell us, with simple wonder, how Catherine de Medici would "laugh her fill just like another" over the humours of pantaloons and zanies. And such servility was, of all things, what would touch most nearly the republican spirit of Knox. It was not difficult for him to set aside this weak scruple of loyalty. The lantern of his analysis did not always shine with a very serviceable light; but he had the virtue, at least, to carry it into many places of fictitious holiness, and was not abashed by the tinsel divinity that hedged kings and queens from his contemporaries.

4. *Œuvres de d'Aubigné*, i. 449.
5. *Dames Illustres*, pp. 358-360.

And so he could put the proposition in the form already mentioned: there was Christ's Gospel persecuted in the two kingdoms, by one anomalous power; plainly, then, the "regiment of women" was Antichristian. Early in 1558 he communicated this discovery to the world, by publishing at Geneva his notorious book—*The First Blast of the Trumpet against the Monstrous Regiment of Women*.[6]

As a whole, it is a dull performance; but the preface, as is usual with Knox, is both interesting and morally fine. Knox was not one of those who are humble in the hour of triumph; he was aggressive even when things were at their worst. He had a grim reliance in himself, or rather in his mission; if he were not sure that he was a great man, he was at least sure that he was one set apart to do great things. And he judged simply that whatever passed in his mind, whatever moved him to flee from persecution instead of constantly facing it out, or, as here, to publish and withhold his name from the title-page of a critical work, would not fail to be of interest, perhaps of benefit, to the world. There may be something more finely sensitive in the modern humour, that tends more and more to withdraw a man's personality from the lessons he inculcates or the cause that he has espoused; but there is a loss herewith of wholesome responsibility; and when we find in the works of Knox, as in the Epistles of Paul, the man himself standing

6. Works of John Knox, iv. 349.

nakedly forward, courting and anticipating criticism, putting his character, as it were, in pledge for the sincerity of his doctrine, we had best waive the question of delicacy, and make our acknowledgments for a lesson of courage, not unnecessary in these days of anonymous criticism, and much light, otherwise unattainable, on the spirit in which great movements were initiated and carried forward. Knox's personal revelations are always interesting; and, in the case of the "First Blast," as I have said, there is no exception to the rule. He begins by stating the solemn responsibility of all who are watchmen over God's flock; and all are watchmen (he goes on to explain, with that fine breadth of spirit that characterises him even when, as here, he shows himself most narrow), all are watchmen "whose eyes God doth open, and whose conscience he pricketh to admonish the ungodly." And with the full consciousness of this great duty before him, he set himself to answer the scruples of timorous or worldly-minded people. How can a man repent, he asks, unless the nature of his transgression is made plain to him? "And therefore I say," he continues, "that of necessity it is that this monstriferous empire of women (which among all enormities that this day do abound upon the face of the whole earth, is most detestable and damnable) be openly and plainly declared to the world, to the end that some may repent and be saved." To those who think the doctrine useless, because it cannot be expected to amend those princes whom it would dispossess if once ac-

181

cepted, he makes answer in a strain that shows him at his greatest. After having instanced how the rumour of Christ's censures found its way to Herod in his own court, "even so," he continues, "may the sound of our weak trumpet, by the support of some wind (blow it from the south, or blow it from the north, it is of no matter), come to the ears of the chief offenders. *But whether it do or not, yet dare we not cease to blow as God will give strength. For we are debtors to more than to princes, to wit, to the great multitude of our brethren,* of whom, no doubt, a great number have heretofore offended by error and ignorance."

It is for the multitude, then, he writes; he does not greatly hope that his trumpet will be audible in palaces, or that crowned women will submissively discrown themselves at his appeal; what he does hope, in plain English, is to encourage and justify rebellion; and we shall see, before we have done, that he can put his purpose into words as roundly as I can put it for him. This he sees to be a matter of much hazard; he is not "altogether so brutish and insensible, but that he has laid his account what the finishing of the work may cost." He knows that he will find many adversaries, since "to the most part of men, lawful and godly appeareth whatsoever antiquity hath received." He looks for opposition, "not only of the ignorant multitude, but of the wise, politic, and quiet spirits of the earth." He will be called foolish, curious, despiteful, and a sower of sedition; and one day, perhaps, for all he is now nameless, he may be attainted of treason. Yet he has "determined to obey God, notwithstanding that the world shall rage thereat." Finally, he makes some excuse for the anonymous appearance of this first instalment: it is his purpose thrice to blow the trumpet in this matter, if God so permit; twice he intends to do it without name; but at the last blast to take the odium upon himself, that all others may be purged.

Thus he ends the preface, and enters upon his argument with a secondary title: "The First Blast to awake Women degenerate." We are in the land of assertion without delay. That a woman should bear rule, superiority, dominion or empire over any realm, nation, or city, he tells us, is repugnant to nature, contumely to God, and a subversion of good order. Women are weak, frail, impatient, feeble, and foolish. God has denied to woman wisdom to consider, or providence to foresee, what is profitable to a commonwealth. Women have been ever lightly esteemed; they have been denied the tutory of their own sons, and subjected to the unquestionable sway of their husbands; and surely it is irrational to give the greater where the less has been withheld, and suffer a woman to reign supreme over a great kingdom who would be allowed no authority by her own fireside. He appeals to the Bible; but though he makes much of the first transgression and certain strong texts in Genesis and Paul's Epistles, he does not appeal with entire success. The cases of Deborah and Huldah can be brought into no sort of harmony with his thesis. Indeed, I may say that, logically, he left his bones there; and that it is but the phantom of an argument that he parades thenceforward to the end. Well was it for Knox that he succeeded no better; it is under this very ambiguity about Deborah that we shall find him fain to creep for shelter before he is done with the regiment of women. After having thus exhausted Scripture, and formulated its teaching in the somewhat blasphemous maxim that the man is placed above the woman, even as God above the angels, he goes on triumphantly to adduce the testimonies of Tertullian, Augustine, Ambrose, Basil, Chrysostom, and the Pandects; and having gathered this little cloud of witnesses about him, like pursuivants about a herald, he solemnly proclaims all reigning women to be traitoresses and rebels against God; discharges all men thenceforward from holding any office under such monstrous regiment, and calls upon all the lieges with one consent to "*study to repress the inordinate pride and tyranny*" of *queens*. If this is not treasonable teaching, one would be glad to know what is; and yet, as if he feared he had not made the case plain enough against himself, he goes on to deduce the startling corollary that all oaths of allegiance must be incontinently broken. If it was sin thus to have sworn even in ignorance, it were obstinate sin to continue to respect them after fuller knowledge. Then comes the peroration, in which he cries aloud against the cruelties of that cursed Jezebel of England—that horrible monster Jezebel of England; and after having predicted sudden destruction to her rule and to the rule of all crowned

women, and warned all men that if they presume
to defend the same when any "noble heart" shall
be raised up to vindicate the liberty of his country, they shall not fail to perish themselves in the
rain, he concludes with a last rhetorical flourish:
"And therefore let all men be advertised, for THE
TRUMPET HATH ONCE BLOWN."

The capitals are his own. In writing, he probably felt the want of some such reverberation of
the pulpit under strong hands as he was wont to
emphasise his spoken utterances withal; there
would seem to him a want of passion in the
orderly lines of type; and I suppose we may take
the capitals as a mere substitute for the great
voice with which he would have given it forth,
had we heard it from his own lips. Indeed, as it
is, in this little strain of rhetoric about the trumpet, this current allusion to the fall of Jericho,
that alone distinguishes his bitter and hasty production, he was probably right, according to all
artistic canon, thus to support and accentuate in
conclusion the sustained metaphor of a hostile
proclamation. It is curious, by the way, to note
how favourite an image the trumpet was with the
reformer. He returns to it again and again; it is
the Alpha and Omega of his rhetoric; it is to him
what a ship is to the stage sailor; and one would
almost fancy he had begun the world as a trum-
peter's apprentice. The partiality is surely characteristic. All his life long he was blowing sum-
monses before various Jerichos, some of which
fell duly, but not all. Wherever he appears in
history his speech is loud, angry, and hostile;

there is no peace in his life, and little tenderness;
he is always sounding hopefully to the front for
some rough enterprise. And as his voice had something of the trumpet's hardness, it had something
also of the trumpet's warlike inspiration. So
Randolph, possibly fresh from the sound of the
Reformer's preaching, writes of him to Cecil:—
"Where your honour exhorteth us to stoutness,
I assure you the voice of one man is able, in an
hour, to put more life in us than six hundred
trumpets continually blustering in our ears." [7]

Thus was the proclamation made. Nor was it
long in wakening all the echoes of Europe. What
success might have attended it, had the question
decided been a purely abstract question, it is
difficult to say. As it was, it was to stand or fall,
not by logic, but by political needs and sympathies. Thus, in France, his doctrine was to have
some future, because Protestants suffered there
under the feeble and treacherous regency of
Catherine de Medici; and thus it was to have
no future anywhere else, because the Protestant
interest was bound up with the prosperity of
Queen Elizabeth. This stumbling-block lay at the
very threshold of the matter; and Knox, in the
text of the "First Blast," had set everybody the
wrong example and gone to the ground himself.
He finds occasion to regret "the blood of innocent Lady Jane Dudley." But Lady Jane Dudley,
or Lady Jane Grey, as we call her, was a would-be
traitoress and rebel against God, to use his own
expressions. If, therefore, political and religious

7. M'Crie's *Life of Knox*, ii. 41.

sympathy led Knox himself into so grave a partiality, what was he to expect from his disciples? If the trumpet gave so ambiguous a sound, who could heartily prepare himself for the battle? The question whether Lady Jane Dudley was an innocent martyr, or a traitoress against God, whose inordinate pride and tyranny had been effectually repressed, was thus left altogether in the wind; and it was not, perhaps, wonderful if many of Knox's readers concluded that all right and wrong in the matter turned upon the degree of the sovereign's orthodoxy and possible helpfulness to the Reformation. He should have been the more careful of such an ambiguity of meaning, as he must have known well the lukewarm indifference and dishonesty of his fellow-reformers in political matters. He had already, in 1556 or 1557, talked the matter over with his great master, Calvin, in "a private conversation;" and the interview[8] must have been truly distasteful to both parties. Calvin, indeed, went a far way with him in theory, and owned that the "government of women was a deviation from the original and proper order of nature, to be ranked, no less than slavery, among the punishments consequent upon the fall of man." But, in practice, their two roads separated. For the Man of Geneva saw difficulties in the way of the Scripture proof in the cases of Deborah and Huldah, and in the prophecy of Isaiah that queens should be the nursing mothers of the Church. And as the Bible was not decisive,

8. Described by Calvin in a letter to Cecil, Knox's Works, vol. iv.

he thought the subject should be let alone, because, "by custom and public consent and long practice, it has been established that realms and principalities may descend to females by hereditary right, and would not be lawful to unsettle governments which are ordained by the peculiar providence of God." I imagine Knox's ears must have burned during this interview. Think of him listening dutifully to all this—how it would not do to meddle with anointed kings—how there was a peculiar providence in these great affairs; and then think of his own peroration, and the "noble heart" whom he looks for "to vindicate the liberty of his country;" or his answer to Queen Mary, when she asked him who he was, to interfere with the affairs of Scotland:—"Madam, a subject born within the same!" Indeed, the two doctors who differed at this private conversation represented, at the moment, two principles of enormous import in the subsequent history of Europe. In Calvin we have represented that passive obedience, that toleration of injustice and absurdity, that holding back of the hand from political affairs as from something unclean, which lost France, if we are to believe M. Michelet, for the Reformation; a spirit necessarily fatal in the long run to the existence of any sect that may profess it; a suicidal doctrine that survives among us to this day in narrow views of personal duty, and the low political morality of many virtuous men. In Knox, on the other hand, we see foreshadowed the whole Puritan Revolution and the scaffold of Charles I.

There is little doubt in my mind that this interview was what caused Knox to print this book without a name.[9] It was a dangerous thing to contradict the Man of Geneva, and doubly so, surely, when one had had the advantage of correction from him in a private conversation; and Knox had his little flock of English refugees to consider. If they had fallen into bad odour at Geneva, where else was there left to flee to? It was printed, as I said, in 1558; and, by a singular *mal-à-propos*, in that same year Mary died, and Elizabeth succeeded to the throne of England. And just as the accession of Catholic Queen Mary had condemned female rule in the eyes of Knox, the accession of Protestant Queen Elizabeth justified it in the eyes of his colleagues. Female rule ceases to be an anomaly, not because Elizabeth can "reply to eight ambassadors in one day in their different languages," but because she represents for the moment the political future of the Reformation. The exiles troop back to England with songs of praise in their mouths. The bright occidental star, of which we have all read in the Preface to the Bible, has risen over the darkness of Europe. There is a thrill of hope through the persecuted Churches of the Continent. Calvin writes to Cecil, washing his hands of Knox and his political heresies. The sale of the "First Blast" is prohibited in Geneva; and along

9. It was anonymously published, but no one seems to have been in doubt about its authorship; he might as well have set his name to it, for all the good he got by holding it back.

with it the bold book of Knox's colleague, Goodman—a book dear to Milton—where female rule
was briefly characterised as a "monster in nature
and disorder among men." [10] Any who may ever
have doubted, or been for a moment led away by
Knox or Goodman, or their own wicked imagina-
tions, are now more than convinced. They have
seen the occidental star. Aylmer, with his eye set
greedily on a possible bishopric, and "the better
to obtain the favour of the new Queen," [11] sharp-
ens his pen to confound Knox by logic. What
need? He has been confounded by facts. "Thus
what had been to the refugees of Geneva as the
very word of God, no sooner were they back in
England than, behold! it was the word of the
devil." [12]

Now, what of the real sentiments of these loyal
subjects of Elizabeth? They professed a holy horror of Knox's position. Let us see if their own
would please a modern audience any better, or
was, in substance, greatly different.

John Aylmer, afterwards Bishop of London,
published an answer to Knox, under the title of
*An Harbour for Faithful and true Subjects against
the late Blown Blast, concerning the government
of Women.*[13] And certainly he was a thought
more acute, a thought less precipitate and simple,

10. Knox's Works, iv. 358.
11. Strype's *Aylmer*, p. 16.
12. It may interest the reader to know that these (so
says Thomasius) are the "ipsissima verba Schlusselburgii."
13. I am indebted for a sight of this book to the kindness of Mr. David Laing, the editor of Knox's Works.

than his adversary. He is not to be led away by such captious terms as *natural* and *unnatural*. It is obvious to him that a woman's disability to rule is not natural in the same sense in which it is a natural for a stone to fall or fire to burn. He is doubtful, on the whole, whether this disability be natural at all; nay, when he is laying it down that a woman should not be a priest, he shows some elementary conception of what many of us now hold to be the truth of the matter. "The bringing-up of women," he says, "is commonly such" that they cannot have the necessary qualifications, "for they are not brought up in learning in schools, nor trained in disputation." And even so, he can ask, "Are there not in England women, think you, that for learning and wisdom could tell their household and neighbours as good a tale as any Sir John there?" For all that, his advocacy is weak. If women's rule is not unnatural in a sense preclusive of its very existence, it is neither so convenient nor so profitable as the government of men. He holds England to be specially suitable for the government of women, because there the governor is more limited and restrained by the other members of the constitution than in other places; and this argument has kept his book from being altogether forgotten. It is only in hereditary monarchies that he will offer any defence of the anomaly. "If rulers were to be chosen by lot or suffrage, he would not that any women should stand in the election, but men only." The law of succession of crowns was a law to him, in the same sense as the law of evolution is a law to Mr. Herbert Spencer; and the one and the other counsels his readers, in a spirit suggestively alike, not to kick against the pricks or seek to be more wise than he who made them.[14] If God has put a female child into the direct line of inheritance, it is God's affair. His strength will be perfected in her weakness. He makes the Creator address the objectors in this not very flattering vein:—"I that could make Daniel, a sucking babe, to judge better than the wisest lawyers; a brute beast to reprehend the folly of the prophet; and poor fishers to confound the great clerks of the world—cannot I make a woman to be a good ruler over you?" This is the last word of his reasoning. Although he was not altogether without Puritanic leaven, shown particularly in what he says of the incomes of Bishops, yet it was rather loyalty to the old order of things than any generous belief in the capacity of women, that raised up for them this clerical champion. His courtly spirit contrasts singularly with the rude, bracing republicanism of Knox. "Thy knee shall bow," he says, "thy cap shall off, thy tongue shall speak reverently of thy sovereign." For himself, his tongue is even more than reverent. Nothing can stay the issue of his eloquent adulation. Again and again, "the remembrance of Elizabeth's virtues" carries him away; and he has to hark back again to find the scent of his argument. He is repressing his vehement adoration throughout, until, when the end comes, and he feels his business at an end, he can indulge

14. *Social Statics*, p. 64, etc.

himself to his heart's content in indiscriminate laudation of his royal mistress. It is humorous to think that this illustrious lady, whom he here praises, among many other excellences, for the simplicity of her attire and "marvellous meekness of her stomach," threatened him, years after, in no very meek terms, for a sermon against female vanity in dress, which she held as a reflection on herself.[15]

Whatever was wanting here in respect for women generally, there was no want of respect for the Queen; and one cannot very greatly wonder if these devoted servants looked askance, not upon Knox only, but on his little flock, as they came back to England tainted with disloyal doctrine. For them, as for him, the occidental star rose somewhat red and angry. As for poor Knox, his position was the saddest of all. For the juncture seemed to him of the highest importance; it was the nick of time, the floodwater of opportunity. Not only was there an opening for him in Scotland, a smouldering brand of civil liberty and religious enthusiasm which it should be for him to kindle into flame with his powerful breath; but he had his eye seemingly on an object of even higher worth. For now, when religious sympathy ran so high that it could be set against national aversion, he wished to begin the fusion together of England and Scotland, and to begin it at the sore place. If once the open wound were closed at the Border, the work would be half done. Ministers placed at Berwick and such places

15. Hallam's *Const. Hist. of England*, i. 225, note [m].

might seek their converts equally on either side of the march; old enemies would sit together to hear the gospel of peace, and forget the inherited jealousies of many generations in the enthusiasm of a common faith; or—let us say better—a common heresy. For people are not most conscious of brotherhood when they continue languidly together in one creed, but when, with some doubt, with some danger perhaps, and certainly not without reluctance, they violently break with the tradition of the past, and go forth from the sanctuary of their fathers to worship under the bare heaven. A new creed, like a new country, is an unhomely place of sojourn; but it makes men lean on one another and join hands. It was on this that Knox relied to begin the union of the English and the Scotch. And he had, perhaps, better means of judging than any even of his contemporaries. He knew the temper of both nations; and already during his two years' chaplaincy at Berwick, he had seen his scheme put to the proof. But whether practicable or not, the proposal does him much honour. That he should have sought to make a love-match of it between the two peoples, and tried to win their inclination towards a union instead of simply transferring them, like so many sheep, by a marriage, or testament, or private treaty, is thoroughly characteristic of what is best in the man. Nor was this all. He had, besides, to assure himself of English support, secret or avowed, for the reformation party in Scotland; a delicate affair, trenching upon treason. And so he had plenty to say to Cecil, plenty he did not care to "commit to paper neither yet to the knowledge of many." But his miserable publication had shut the doors of England in his face. Summoned to Edinburgh by the confederate lords, he waited at Dieppe, anxiously praying for leave to journey through England. The most dispiriting tidings reached him. His messengers, coming from so obnoxious a quarter, narrowly escape imprisonment. His old congregation are coldly received, and even begin to look back again to their place of exile with regret. "My First Blast," he writes ruefully, "has blown from me all my friends of England." And then he adds, with a snarl, "The Second Blast, I fear, shall sound somewhat more sharp, except men be more moderate than I hear they are." [16] But the threat is empty; there will never be a second blast—he has had enough of that trumpet. Nay, he begins to feel uneasily that, unless he is to be rendered useless for the rest of his life, unless he is to lose his right arm and go about his great work maimed and impotent, he must find some way of making his peace with England and the indignant Queen. The letter just quoted was written on the 6th of April, 1559; and on the 10th, after he had cooled his heels for four days more about the streets of Dieppe, he gave in altogether, and writes a letter of capitulation to Cecil. In this letter,[17] which he kept back until the 22nd, still hoping that things

16. Knox to Mrs. Locke, 6th April, 1559. Works, vi. 14.
17. Knox to Sir William Cecil, 10th April, 1559. Works, ii. 16, or vi. 15.

would come right of themselves, he censures the
great secretary for having "followed the world in
the way of perdition," characterises him as
"worthy of hell," and threatens him, if he be not
found simple, sincere, and fervent in the cause of
Christ's gospel, that he shall "taste of the same
cup that politic heads have drunken in before
him." This is all, I take it, out of respect for the
Reformer's own position; if he is going to be
humiliated, let others be humiliated first; like a
child who will not take his medicine until he has
made his nurse and his mother drink of it before
him. "But I have, say you, written a treasonable
book against the regimen and empire of women.
. . . The writing of that book I will not deny;
but to prove it treasonable I think it shall be
hard. . . . It is hinted that my book shall be
written against. If so be, sir, I greatly doubt they
shall rather hurt nor (than) mend the matter."
And here come the terms of capitulation; for he
does not surrender unconditionally, even in this
sore strait: "And yet if any," he goes on, "think
me enemy to the person, or yet to the regiment,
of her whom God hath now promoted, they are
utterly deceived in me, *for the miraculous work of
God, comforting His afflicted by means of an in-
firm vessel, I do acknowledge, and the power of
His most potent hand I will obey. More plainly
to speak, if Queen Elizabeth shall confess, that
the extraordinary dispensation of God's great
mercy maketh that lawful unto her which both
nature and God's law do deny to all women*, then
shall none in England be more willing to main-

196

tain her lawful authority than I shall be. But if (God's wondrous work set aside) she ground (as God forbid) the justness of her title upon consuetude, laws, or ordinances of men, then"— Then Knox will denounce her? Not so; he is more politic nowadays—then, he "greatly fears" that her ingratitude to God will not go long without punishment.

His letter to Elizabeth, written some few months later, was a mere amplification of the sentences quoted above. She must base her title entirely upon the extraordinary providence of God; but if she does this, "if thus, in God's presence, she humbles herself, so will he with tongue and pen justify her authority, as the Holy Ghost hath justified the same in Deborah, that blessed mother of Israel." [18] And so, you see, his consistency is preserved; he is merely applying the doctrine of the "First Blast." The argument goes thus: The regiment of women is, as before noted in our work, repugnant to nature, contumely to God, and a subversion of good order. It has nevertheless pleased God to raise up, as exceptions to this law, first Deborah, and afterward Elizabeth Tudor—whose regiment we shall proceed to celebrate.

There is no evidence as to how the Reformer's explanations were received, and indeed it is most probable that the letter was never shown to Elizabeth at all. For it was sent under cover of another to Cecil, and as it was not of a very courtly con-

18. Knox to Queen Elizabeth, July 20th, 1559. Works, vi. 47, or ii. 26.

ception throughout, and was, of all things, what would most excite the Queen's uneasy jealousy about her title, it is like enough that the secretary exercised his discretion (he had Knox's leave in this case, and did not always wait for that, it is reputed) to put the letter harmlessly away beside other valueless or unpresentable State Papers. I wonder very much if he did the same with another,[19] written two years later, after Mary had come into Scotland, in which Knox almost seeks to make Elizabeth an accomplice with him in the matter of the "First Blast." The Queen of Scotland is going to have that work refuted, he tells her; and "though it were but foolishness in him to prescribe unto her Majesty what is to be done," he would yet remind her that Mary is neither so much alarmed about her own security, nor so generously interested in Elizabeth's, "that she would take such pains, *unless her crafty counsel in so doing shot at a further mark*." There is something really ingenious in this letter; it showed Knox in the double capacity of the author of the "First Blast" and the faithful friend of Elizabeth; and he combines them there so naturally, that one would scarcely imagine the two to be incongruous.

Twenty days later he was defending his intemperate publication to another queen—his own queen, Mary Stuart. This was on the first of those three interviews which he has preserved for us with so much dramatic vigour in the picturesque

19. Knox to Queen Elizabeth, August 6th, 1561. Works, vi. 126.

pages of his history. After he had avowed the authorship in his usual haughty style, Mary asked: "You think, then, that I have no just authority?" The question was evaded. "Please your Majesty," he answered, "that learned men in all ages have had their judgments free, and most commonly disagreeing from the common judgment of the world; such also have they published by pen and tongue; and yet notwithstanding they themselves have lived in the common society with others, and have borne patiently with the errors and imperfections which they could not amend." Thus did "Plato the philosopher:" thus will do John Knox. "I have communicated my judgment to the world: if the realm finds no inconvenience from the regiment of a woman, that which they approve, shall I not further disallow than within my own breast; but shall be as well content to live under your Grace, as Paul was to live under Nero. And my hope is, that so long as ye defile not your hands with the blood of the saints of God, neither I nor my book shall hurt either you or your authority." All this is admirable in wisdom and moderation, and, except that he might have hit upon a comparison less offensive than that with Paul and Nero, hardly to be bettered. Having said thus much, he feels he needs say no more; and so, when he is further pressed, he closes that part of the discussion with an astonishing sally. If he has been content to let this matter sleep, he would recommend her Grace to follow his example with thankfulness of heart; it is grimly to be understood which of them has most to fear if the question should be re-awakened. So the talk wandered to other subjects. Only, when the Queen was summoned at last to dinner ("for it was afternoon") Knox made his salutation in this form of words: "I pray God, Madam, that you may be as much blessed within the Commonwealth of Scotland, if it be the pleasure of God, as ever Deborah was in the Commonwealth of Israel." [20] Deborah again.

But he was not yet done with the echoes of his own "First Blast." In 1571, when he was already near his end, the old controversy was taken up in one of a series of anonymous libels against the Reformer affixed, Sunday after Sunday, to the church door. The dilemma was fairly enough stated. Either his doctrine is false, in which case he is a "false doctor" and seditious; or, if it be true, why does he "avow and approve the contrare, I mean that regiment in the Queen of England's person; which he avoweth and approveth, not only praying for the maintenance of her estate, but also procuring her aid and support against his own native country?" Knox answered the libel, as his wont was, next Sunday, from the pulpit. He justified the "First Blast" with all the old arrogance; there is no drawing back there. The regiment of women is repugnant to nature, contumely to God, and a subversion of good order, as before. When he prays for the maintenance of Elizabeth's estate, he is only following the example of those prophets of God who warned and comforted the wicked kings of Israel;

20. Knox's Works, ii. 278-280.

or of Jeremiah, who bade the Jews pray for the prosperity of Nebuchadnezzar. As for the Queen's aid, there is no harm in that: *quia* (these are his own words) *quia omnia munda mundis:* because to the pure all things are pure. One thing, in conclusion, he "may not pretermit;" to give the lie in the throat to his accuser, where he charges him with seeking support against his native country. "What I have been to my country," said the old Reformer, "What I have been to my country, albeit this unthankful age will not know, yet the ages to come will be compelled to bear witness to the truth. And thus I cease, requiring of all men that have anything to oppone against me, that he may (they may) do it so plainly, as that I make myself and all my doings manifest to the world. For to me it seemeth a thing unreasonable, that, in this my decrepit age, I shall be compelled to fight against shadows, and howlets that dare not abide the light." [21]

Now, in this, which may be called his *Last Blast*, there is as sharp speaking as any in the "First Blast" itself. He is of the same opinion to the end, you see, although he has been obliged to cloak and garble that opinion for political ends. He has been tacking indeed, and he has indeed been seeking the favour of a queen; but what man ever sought a queen's favour with a more virtuous purpose, or with as little courtly policy? The question of consistency is delicate, and must be made plain. Knox never changed

21. Calderwood's *History of the Kirk of Scotland*, edition of the Woodrow Society, iii. 51-54.

his opinion about female rule, but lived to regret that he had published that opinion. Doubtless he had many thoughts so far out of the range of public sympathy, that he could only keep them to himself, and, in his own words, bear patiently with the errors and imperfections that he could not amend. For example, I make no doubt myself that, in his own heart, he did hold the shocking dogma attributed to him by more than one calumniator; and that, had the time been ripe, had there been aught to gain by it, instead of all to lose, he would have been the first to assert that Scotland was elective instead of hereditary— "elective as in the days of paganism," as one Thevet says in holy horror.[22] And yet, because the time was not ripe, I find no hint of such an idea in his collected works. Now, the regiment of women was another matter that he should have kept to himself; right or wrong, his opinion did not fit the moment; right or wrong, as Aylmer puts it, "the *Blast* was blown out of season." And this it was that he began to perceive after the accession of Elizabeth; not that he had been wrong, and that female rule was a good thing, for he had said from the first that "the felicity of some women in their empires" could not change the law of God and the nature of created things; not this, but that the regiment of women was one of those imperfections of society which must be borne with because yet they cannot be remedied. The thing had seemed so obvious to him, in his sense of unspeakable masculine superiority, and

22. Bayle's *Historical Dictionary*, art. Knox, remark G.

his fine contempt for what is only sanctioned by antiquity and common consent, he had imagined that, at the first hint, men would arise and shake off the debasing tyranny. He found himself wrong, and he showed that he could be moderate in his own fashion, and understood the spirit of true compromise. He came round to Calvin's position, in fact, but by a different way. And it derogates nothing from the merit of this wise attitude that it was the consequence of a change of interest. We are all taught by interest; and if the interest be not merely selfish, there is no wiser preceptor under heaven, and perhaps no sterner.

Such is the history of John Knox's connection with the controversy about female rule. In itself, this is obviously an incomplete study; not fully to be understood, without a knowledge of his private relations with the other sex, and what he thought of their position in domestic life. This shall be dealt with in another paper.

2 Private Life

To those who know Knox by hearsay only, I believe the matter of this paper will be somewhat astonishing. For the hard energy of the man in all public matters has possessed the imagination of the world; he remains for posterity in certain traditional phrases, brow-beating Queen Mary, or breaking beautiful carved work in abbeys and cathedrals, that had long smoked themselves out and were no more than sorry ruins, while he was still quietly teaching children in a country gentlemen's family. It does not consist with the common acceptation of his character to fancy him much moved, except with anger. And yet the language of passion came to his pen as readily, whether it was a passion of denunciation against some of the abuses that vexed his righteous spirit, or of yearning for the society of an absent friend. He was vehement in affection, as in doctrine. I will not deny that there may have been, along with his vehemence, something shifty, and for the moment only; that, like many men, and many Scotchmen, he saw the world and his own heart, not so much under any very steady, equable light, as by extreme flashes of passion, true for the moment, but not true in the long run. There does seem to me to be something of this traceable in the Reformer's utterances: precipitation and repentance, hardy speech and action somewhat circumspect, a strong tendency to see himself in a heroic light and to place a ready belief in the disposition of the moment. Withal he had considerable confidence in himself, and in the uprightness of his own disciplined emotions, underlying much sincere aspiration after spiritual humility. And it is this confidence that makes this intercourse with women so interesting to a modern. It would be easy, of course, to make fun of the whole affair, to picture him strutting vaingloriously among these inferior creatures, or compare a religious friendship in the sixteenth century with what was called, I think, a literary friendship in the eighteenth. But it is more just and profitable to recognise what there

is sterling and human underneath all his theo-
retical affectations of superiority. Women, he has
said in his "First Blast," are "weak, frail, impatient, feeble, and foolish;" and yet it does not
appear that he was himself any less dependent
than other men upon the sympathy and affection
of these weak, frail, impatient, feeble, and foolish
creatures; it seems even as if he had been rather
more dependent than most.

Of those who are to act influentially on their
fellows, we should expect always something large
and public in their way of life, something more or
less urbane and comprehensive in their sentiment
for others. We should not expect to see them
spend their sympathy in idyls, however beautiful. We should not seek them among those who,
if they have but a wife to their bosom, ask no
more of womankind, just as they ask no more
of their own sex, if they can find a friend or two
for their immediate need. They will be quick to
feel all the pleasures of our association—not the
great ones alone, but all. They will know not love
only, but all those other ways in which man and
woman mutually make each other happy—by
sympathy, by admiration, by the atmosphere they
bear about them down to the mere impersonal
pleasure of passing happy faces in the street. For,
through all this gradation, the difference of sex
makes it itself pleasurely felt. Down to the most
lukewarm courtesies of life, there is a special
chivalry due and a special pleasure received, when
the two sexes are brought ever so lightly into contact. We love our mothers otherwise than we love

our fathers; a sister is not as a brother to us; and friendship between man and woman, be it never so unalloyed and innocent, is not the same as friendship between man and man. Such friendship is not even possible for all. To conjoin tenderness for a woman that is not far short of passionate with such disinterestedness and beautiful gratuity of affection as there is between friends of the same sex, requires no ordinary disposition in the man. For either it would presuppose quite womanly of perception, and, as it were, a curiosity in shades of differing sentiment; or it would mean that he accepted the large, simple divisions of society: a strong and positive spirit robustly virtuous, who has chosen a better part coarsely, and holds to it steadfastly, with all its consequences of pain to himself and others; as one who should go straight before him on a journey, neither tempted by wayside flowers nor very scrupulous of small lives under foot. It was in virtue of this latter disposition that Knox was capable of those intimacies with women that embellished his life; and we find him preserved for us in old letters as a man of many women friends; a man of some expansion towards the other sex; a man ever ready to comfort weeping women, and to weep along with them.

Of such scraps and fragments of evidence as to his private life and more intimate thoughts as have survived to us from all the perils that environ written paper, an astonishingly large proportion is in the shape of letters to women of his familiarity. He was twice married, but that is not greatly to the purpose; for the Turk, who thinks even more meanly of women than John Knox, is none the less given to marrying. What is really significant is quite apart from marriage. For the man Knox was a true man, and woman, the *ewig-weibliche*, was as necessary to him, in spite of all low theories, as ever she was to Goethe. He came to her in a certain halo of his own, as the minister of truth, just as Goethe came to her in a glory of art; he made himself necessary to troubled hearts and minds exercised in the painful complications that naturally result from all changes in the world's way of thinking; and those whom he had thus helped became dear to him, and were made the chosen companions of his leisure if they were at hand, or encouraged and comforted by letter if they were afar.

It must not be forgotten that Knox had been a presbyter of the old Church, and that the many women whom we shall see gathering round him, as he goes through life, had probably been accustomed, while still in the communion of Rome, to rely much upon some chosen spiritual director, so that the intimacies of which I propose to offer some account while testifying to a good heart in the Reformer, testify also to a certain survival of the spirit of the confessional in the Reformed Church, and are not properly to be judged without this idea. There is no friendship so noble, but it is the product of the time; and a world of little finical observances, and little frail proprieties and fashions of the hour, go to make or to mar, to stint or to perfect, the union of spirits the most loving and the most tolerant of such interference. The trick of the country and the age steps in even between the mother and the child, counts out their caresses upon niggardly fingers, and says, in the voice of authority, that this one thing shall be a matter of confidence between them, and this other thing shall not. And thus it is that we must take into reckoning whatever tended to modify the social atmosphere in which Knox and his women friends met, and loved and trusted each other. To the man who had been their priest and was now their minister, women would be able to speak with a confidence quite impossible in these latter days; the women would be able to speak, and the man to hear. It was a beaten road just then; and I daresay we should be no less scandalised at their plain speech than they, if they could come back to earth, would be offended at our waltzes and worldly fashions. This, then, was the footing on which Knox stood with his many women friends. The reader will see, as he goes on, how much of the warmth, of interest, and of that happy mutual dependence which is the very gist of friendship, he contrived to ingraft upon this somewhat dry relationship of penitent and confessor.

It must be understood that we know nothing of his intercourse with women (as indeed we know little at all about his life) until he came to Berwick in 1549, when he was already in the forty-fifth year of his age. At the same time it is just possible that some of a little group at Edinburgh with whom he corresponded during his last absence, may have been friends of an older standing. Certainly they were, of all his female correspondents, the least personally favoured. He treats them throughout in a comprehensive sort of spirit that must at times have been a little wounding. Thus, he remits one of them to his former letters, "which I trust be common betwixt you and the rest of your sisters, for to me ye are all equal in Christ." [23] Another letter is a gem in this way. "Albeit" it begins, "albeit I have no particular matter to write to you, beloved sister, yet I could not refrain to write these few lines to you in declaration of my remembrance to you. True it is that I have many whom I bear in equal remembrance before God with you, to whom at present I write nothing, either for that I esteem them stronger than you, and therefore they need the less my rude labours, or else because they have not provoked me by their writing to recompense their remembrance." [24] His "sisters in Edinburgh" had evidently to "provoke" his attention pretty constantly; nearly all his letters are on the face of them answers to questions, and the answers are given with a certain crudity that I do not find repeated when he writes to those he really cares for. So when they consult him about women's apparel (a subject on which his opinion may be pretty correctly imagined by the ingenious reader for himself) he takes occasion to anticipate some of the most offensive matter of the "First Blast"

23. Works, v. 244.
24. Ibid. iv. 246.

in a style of real brutality.[25] It is not merely that
he tells them "the garments of women do declare
their weakness and inability to execute the office
of man," though that in itself is neither very wise
nor very opportune in such a correspondence one
would think; but if the reader will take the trouble to wade through the long, tedious sermon for
himself, he will see proof enough that Knox
neither loved, nor very deeply respected, the
women he was then addressing. In very truth,
I believe these Edinburgh sisters simply bored
him. He had a certain interest in them as his
children in the Lord; they were continually "pro-
voking him by their writing;" and, if they handed
his letters about, writing to them was as good a
form of publication as was then open to him in
Scotland. There is one letter, however, in this
budget, addressed to the wife of Clerk-Register
Mackgil, which is worthy of some further mention. The Clerk-Register had not opened his
heart, it would appear, to the preaching of the
gospel, and Mrs. Mackgil had written, seeking the
Reformer's prayers in his behalf. "Your husband,"
he answers, "is dear to me for that he is a man
indued with some good gifts, but more dear for
that he is your husband. Charity moveth me to
thirst his illumination, both for his comfort and
for the trouble which you sustain by his coldness,
which justly may be called infidelity." He wishes
her, however, not to hope too much; he can
promise that his prayers will be earnest, but not
that they will be effectual; it is possible that this

25. *Ibid.* iv. 225.

is to be her "cross" in life; that "her head, appointed by God for her comfort, should be her enemy." And if this be so, well, there is nothing for it; "with patience she must abide God's merciful deliverance," taking heed only that she does not "obey manifest iniquity for the pleasure of any mortal man." [26] I conceive this epistle would have given a very modified sort of pleasure to the Clerk-Register, had it chanced to fall into his hands. Compare its tenor—the dry resignation not without hope of merciful deliverance therein recommended—with these words from another letter, written but the year before to two married women of London: "Call first for grace by Jesus, and thereafter communicate with your faithful husbands, and then shall God, I doubt not, conduct your footsteps, and direct your counsels to His glory." [27] Here the husbands are put in a very high place; we can recognise here the same hand that has written for our instruction how the man is set above the woman, even as God above the angels. But the point of the distinction is plain. For Clerk-Register Mackgil was not a faithful husband; displayed, indeed, towards religion a "coldness which justly might be called infidelity." We shall see in more notable instances how much Knox's conception of the duty of wives varies according to the zeal and orthodoxy of the husband.

As I have said, he may possibly have made the acquaintance of Mrs. Mackgil, Mrs. Guthrie, or

26. *Ibid*. iv. 245.
27. *Ibid*. iv. 221.

some other, or all, of these Edinburgh friends
while he was still Douglas of Longniddry's private
tutor. But our certain knowledge begins in 1549.
He was then but newly escaped from his captivity
in France, after pulling an oar for nineteen
months on the benches of the galley *Nostre
Dame;* now up the rivers, holding steady intercourse with other Scottish prisoners in the castle
of Rouen; now out in the North Sea, raising his
sick head to catch a glimpse of the far-off steeples
of St. Andrews. And now he was sent down by
the English Privy Council as a preacher to Ber-
wick-upon-Tweed; somewhat shaken in health by
all his hardships full of pains and agues, and
tormented by gravel, that sorrow of great men;
altogether, what with his romantic story, his weak
health, and his great faculty of eloquence, a very
natural object for the sympathy of devout women.
At this happy juncture he fell into the company
of a Mrs. Elizabeth Bowes, wife of Richard
Bowes, of Aske, in Yorkshire, to whom she had
borne twelve children. She was a religious hypochondriac, a very weariful woman, full of doubts
and scruples, and giving no rest on earth either to
herself or to those whom she honoured with her
confidence. From the first time she heard Knox
preach she formed a high opinion of him, and
was solicitous ever after of his society.[28] Nor was
Knox unresponsive. "I have always delighted in
your company," he writes, "and when labours
would permit, you know I have not spared hours
to talk and commune with you." Often when

28. *Ibid.* vi. 514.

they had met in depression he reminds her, "God hath sent great comfort unto both." [29] We can gather from such letters as are yet extant how close and continuous was their intercourse. "I think it best you remain till the morrow," he writes once, "and so shall we commune at large at afternoon. This day you know to be the day of my study and prayer unto God; yet if your trouble be intolerable, or if you think my presence may release your pain, do as the Spirit shall move you. . . . Your messenger found me in bed, after a sore trouble and most dolorous night, and so dolour may complain to dolour when we two meet. . . . And this is more plain than ever I spoke, to let you know you have a companion in trouble." [30] Once we have the curtain raised for a moment, and can look at the two together for the length of a phrase. "After the writing of this preceding," writes Knox, "your brother and mine, Harrie Wycliffe, did advertise me by writing, that your adversary (the devil) took occasion to trouble you because that *I did start back from you rehearsing your infirmities. I remember myself so to have done, and that is my common consuetude when anything pierceth or toucheth my heart. Call to your mind what I did standing at the cupboard at Alnwick.* In very deed I thought that no creature had been tempted as I was; and when I heard proceed from your mouth the very same words that he troubles me with, I did wonder and from my heart lament your sore trou-

29. *Ibid.* iii. 338.
30. *Ibid.* iii. 352, 353.

ble, knowing in myself the dolour thereof." [31]
Now intercourse of so very close a description,
whether it be religious intercourse or not, is apt
to displease and disquiet a husband; and we
know incidentally from Knox himself that there
was some little scandal about his intimacy with
Mrs. Bowes. "The slander and fear of men," he
writes, "has impeded me to exercise my pen so
oft as I would; *yea, very shame hath holden me
from your company, when I was most surely persuaded that God had appointed me at that time
to comfort and feed your hungry and afflicted
soul. God in His infinite mercy,*" he goes on
"*remove not only from me all fear that tendeth
not to godliness, but from others suspicion to
judge of me otherwise than it becometh one
member to judge of another.*" [32] And this scandal,
such as it was, would not be allayed by the dissension in which Mrs. Bowes seemed to have
lived with her family upon the matter of religion,
and the countenance shown by Knox to her
resistance. Talking of these conflicts, and her
courage against "her own flesh and most inward
affections, yea, against some of her most natural
friends," he writes it, "to the praise of God, he
has wondered at the bold constancy which he
has found in her when his own heart was
faint." [33]

Now, perhaps in order to stop scandalous
mouths, perhaps out of a desire to bind the

31. *Ibid.* iii. 350.
32. *Ibid.* iii. 390, 391.
33. *Ibid.* iii. 142.

much-loved evangelist nearer to her in the only manner possible, Mrs. Bowes conceived the scheme of marrying him to her fifth daughter, Marjorie; and the Reformer seems to have fallen in with it readily enough. It seems to have been believed in the family that the whole matter had been originally made up between these two, with no very spontaneous inclination on the part of the bride.[34] Knox's idea of marriage, as I have said, was not the same for all men; but on the whole, it was not lofty. We have a curious letter of his, written at the request of Queen Mary, to the Earl of Argyle, on very delicate household matters; which, as he tells us, "was not well accepted by the said Earl." [35] We may suppose, however, that his own home was regulated in a similar spirit. I can fancy that for such a man, emotional, and with a need, now and again, to exercise parsimony in emotions not strictly needful, something a little mechanical, something hard and fast and clearly understood, would enter into his ideal of a home. There were storms enough without, and equability was to be desired at the fireside even at a sacrifice of deeper pleasures. So, from a wife, of all women, he would not ask much. One letter to her which has come down to us is, I had almost said, conspicuous for coldness.[36] He calls her, as he called other female correspondents, "dearly beloved sister;" the epistle is doctrinal, and nearly the half of it bears,

34. *Ibid*. iii. 378.
35. *Ibid*. ii. 379.
36. *Ibid*. iii. 394.

not upon her own case, but upon that of her mother. However, we know what Heine wrote in his wife's album; and there is, after all, one passage that may be held to intimate some tenderness, although even that admits of an amusingly opposite construction. "I think," he says, "I *think* this be the first letter I ever wrote to you." This, if we are to take it literally, may pair off with the "two *or three* children" whom Montaigne mentions having lost at nurse; the one is as eccentric in a lover as the other in a parent. Nevertheless, he displayed more energy in the course of his troubled wooing than might have been expected. The whole Bowes family, angry enough already at the influence he had obtained over the mother, set their faces obdurately against the match. And I daresay the opposition quickened his inclination. I find him writing to Mrs. Bowes that she need no further trouble herself about the marriage; it should now be his business altogether; it behoved him now to jeopard his life "for the comfort of his own flesh both fear and friendship of all earthly creature laid aside." [37] This is a wonderfully chivalrous utterance for a Reformer forty-eight years old; and it compares well with the leaden coquetries of Calvin, not much over thirty, taking this and that into consideration, weighing together dowries and religious qualifications and the instancy of friends, and exhibiting what M. Bungener calls "an honourable and Christian difficulty" of choice, in frigid indecisions and insincere proposals. But

37. *Ibid.* iii. 376.

Knox's next letter is in a humbler tone; he has not found the negotiation so easy as he fancied; he despairs of the marriage altogether, and talks of leaving England,—regards not "what country consumes his wicked carcass." "You shall understand," he says, "that this sixth of November, I spoke with Sir Robert Bowes" (the head of the family, his bride's uncle) "in the matter you know, according to your request; whose disdainful, yea, despiteful, words hath so pierced my heart that my life is bitter to me. I bear a good countenance with a sore troubled heart, because he that ought to consider matters with a deep judgment is become not only a despiser, but also a taunter of God's messengers—God be merciful unto him! Amongst others his most unpleasant words, while that I was about to have declared my heart in the whole matter, he said, 'Away with your rhetorical reasons! for I will not be persuaded with them.' God knows I did use no rhetoric nor coloured speech; but would have spoken the truth, and that in most simple manner. I am not a good orator in my own cause; but what he would not be content to hear of me, God shall declare to him one day to his displeasure, unless he repent." [38] Poor Knox, you see, is quite commoved. It has been a very unpleasant interview. And as it is the only sample that we have of how things went with him during his courtship, we may infer that the period was not as agreeable for Knox as it has been for some others.

38. *Ibid*. iii. 378.

However, when once they were married, I imagine he and Marjorie Bowes hit it off together
comfortably enough. The little we know of it
may be brought together in a very short space.
She bore him two sons. He seems to have kept
her pretty busy, and depended on her to some
degree in his work; so that when she fell ill, his
papers got at once into disorder.[39] Certainly she
sometimes wrote to his dictation; and, in this
capacity, he calls her "his left hand." [40] In June
1559, at the headiest moment of the Reformation in Scotland, he writes regretting the absence
of his helpful colleague, Goodman, "whose presence" (this is the not very grammatical form of
his lament) "whose presence I more thirst, than
she that is my own flesh." [41] And this, consider-
ing the source and the circumstances, may be
held as evidence of a very tender sentiment. He
tells us himself in his history, on the occasion of
a certain meeting at the Kirk of Field, that "he
was in no small heaviness by reason of the late
death of his dear bed-fellow, Marjorie Bowes." [42]
Calvin, condoling with him, speaks of her as "a
wife whose like is not to be found everywhere"
(that is very like Calvin), and again, as "the
most delightful of wives." We know what Calvin
thought desirable in a wife, "good humour, chastity, thrift, patience, and solicitude for her husband's health," and so we may suppose that the

39. *Ibid*. vi. 104.
40. *Ibid*. v. 5.
41. *Ibid*. vi. 27.
42. *Ibid*. ii. 138.

218

first Mrs. Knox fell not far short of this ideal.

The actual date of the marriage is uncertain; but by September 1566, at the latest, the Reformer was settled in Geneva with his wife. There is no fear either that he will be dull; even if the chaste, thrifty, patient Marjorie should not altogether occupy his mind, he need not go out of the house to seek more female sympathy; for behold! Mrs. Bowes is duly domesticated with the young couple. Dr. M'Crie imagined that Richard Bowes was now dead, and his widow, consequently, free to live where she would; and where could she go more naturally than to the house of a married daughter? This, however, is not the case. Richard Bowes did not die till at least two years later. It is impossible to believe that he approved of his wife's desertion, after so many years of marriage, after twelve children had been born to them; and accordingly we find in his will, dated 1558, no mention either of her or of Knox's wife.[43] This is plain sailing. It is easy enough to understand the anger of Bowes against this interloper, who had come into a quiet family, married the daughter in spite of the father's opposition, alienated the wife from the husband and the husband's religion, supported her in a long course of resistance and rebellion, and, after years of intimacy, already too close and tender for any jealous spirit to behold without resentment, carried her away with him at last to a foreign land. But it is not quite easy to understand how, except

43. Mr. Lang's preface to the sixth volume of Knox's Works, p. lxii.

out of sheer weariness and disgust, he was ever brought to agree to the arrangement. Nor is it easy to square the Reformer's conduct with his public teaching. We have, for instance, a letter addressed by him, Craig, and Spottiswood, to the Archbishop of Canterbury and York, anent "a wicked and rebellious woman," one Anne Good, spouse to "John Barron, a minister of Christ Jesus his evangel," who, "after great rebellion shown unto him, and divers admonitions given, as well by himself as by others in his name, that she should in no wise depart from this realm, nor from his house without his license, hath not less stubbornly and rebelliously departed, separated herself from his society, left his house, and withdrawn herself from this realm." [44] Perhaps some sort of license was extorted, as I have said, from Richard Bowes, weary with years of domestic dissension; but setting that aside, the words employed with so much righteous indignation by Knox, Craig, and Spottiswood to describe the conduct of that wicked and rebellious woman, Mrs. Barron, would describe nearly as exactly the conduct of the religious Mrs. Bowes. It is a little bewildering, until we recollect the distinction between faithful and unfaithful husbands; for Barron was "a minister of Christ Jesus his evangel," while Richard Bowes, besides being own brother to a despiser and taunter of God's messengers, is shrewdly suspected to have been "a bigoted adherent of the Roman Catholic faith," or, as

44. Works, vi. 534.

Knox himself would have expressed it, "a rotten Papist."

You would have thought that Knox was now pretty well supplied with female society. But we are not yet at the end of the roll. The last year of his sojourn in England had been spent principally in London, where he was resident as one of the chaplains of Edward the Sixth; and here he boasts, although a stranger, he had, by God's grace, found favour before many.[45] The godly women of the metropolis made much of him; once he writes to Mrs. Bowes that her last letter had found him closeted with three, and he and the three women were all in tears.[46] Out of all, however, he had chosen two. "God," he writes to them, *brought us in such familiar acquaintance, that your hearts were incensed and kindled with a special care over me, as a mother useth to be over her natural child;* and my heart was opened and compelled in your presence to be more plain than ever I was to any."[47] And out of the two even he had chosen one, Mrs. Anne Locke, wife to Mr. Harry Locke, merchant, nigh to Bow Court, Cheapside, in London, as the address runs. If one may venture to judge upon such imperfect evidence, this was the woman he loved best. I have a difficulty in quite forming to myself an idea of her character. She may have been one of the three tearful visitors before

45. *Ibid.* iv. 220.
46. *Ibid.* iii. 380.
47. *Ibid.* iv. 220.

alluded to; she may even have been that one of them who was so profoundly moved by some passages of Mrs. Bowes's letter, which the Reformer opened, and read aloud to them before they went. "O would to God," cried this impressionable matron, "would to God that I might speak to that person, for I perceive there are more tempted than I." [48] This *may* have been Mrs. Locke, as I say; but even if it were, we must not conclude from this one fact that she was such another as Mrs. Bowes. All the evidence tends the other way. She was a woman of understanding, plainly, who followed political events with interest, and to whom Knox thought it worth while to write, in detail, the history of his trials and successes. She was religious, but without that morbid perversity of spirit that made religions so heavy a burden for the poor-hearted Mrs. Bowes. More of her I do not find, save testimony to the profound affection that united her to the Reformer. So we find him writing to her from Geneva, in such terms as these:—"You write that your desire is earnest to see me. *Dear sister, if I should express the thirst and languor which I have had for your presence, I should appear to pass measure. . . . Yea, I weep and rejoice in remembrance of you;* but that would evanish by the comfort of your presence, which I assure you is so dear to me, that if the charge of this little flock here, gathered together in Christ's name, did not impede me, my coming should

48. *Ibid.* iii. 380.

prevent my letter." [49] I say that this was written
from Geneva; and yet you will observe that it is
no consideration for his wife or mother-in-law,
only the charge of his little flock, that keeps him
from setting out forthwith for London, to comfort himself with the dear presence of Mrs. Locke.
Remember that was a certain plausible enough
pretext for Mrs. Locke to come to Geneva—"the
most perfect school of Christ that ever was on
earth since the days of the Apostles"—for we
are now under the reign of that "horrible monster Jezebel of England," when a lady of good
orthodox sentiments was better out of London.
It was doubtful, however, whether this was to be.
She was detained in England, partly by circumstances unknown, "partly by empire of her head,"
Mr. Harry Locke, the Cheapside merchant. It is
somewhat humorous to see Knox struggling for
resignation, now that he has to do with a faithful
husband (for Mr. Harry Locke was faithful).
Had it been otherwise, "in my heart," he says, "I
could have wished—yea," here he breaks out,
"yea, and cannot cease to wish—that God would
guide you to this place." [50] And after all, he had
not long to wait, for, whether Mr. Harry Locke
died in the interval, or was wearied, he too, into
giving permission, five months after the date of
the letter just quoted, "Mrs. Anne Locke, Harry
her son, and Anne her daughter, and Katharine
her maid," arrived in that perfect school of

49. *Ibid*. iv. 238.
50. *Ibid*. iv. 240.

Christ, the Presbyterian paradise, Geneva. So now, and for the next two years, the cup of Knox's happiness was surely full. Of an afternoon, when the bells rang out for the sermon, the shops closed, and the good folk gathered to the churches, psalm-book in hand, we can imagine him drawing near to the English chapel in quite patriarchal fashion, with Mrs. Knox and Mrs. Bowes and Mrs. Locke, James his servant, Patrick his pupil, and a due following of children and maids. He might be alone at work all morning in his study, for he wrote much during these two years; but at night, you may be sure, there was a circle of admiring women, eager to hear the new paragraph, and not sparing of applause. And what work, among others, was he elaborating at this time, but the notorious "First Blast"? So that he may have rolled out in his big pulpit voice, how women were weak, frail, impatient, feeble, foolish, inconstant, variable, cruel, and lacking the spirit of counsel, and how men were above them, even as God is above the angels, in the ears of his own wife, and the two dearest friends he had on earth. But he had lost the sense of incongruity, and continued to despise in theory the sex he honoured so much in practice, of whom he chose his most intimate associates, and whose courage he was compelled to wonder at, when his own heart was faint.

We may say that such a man was not worthy of his fortune; and so, as he would not learn, he was taken away from that agreeable school, and his fellowship of women was broken up, not to be reunited. Called into Scotland to take at last that strange position in history which is his best claim to commemoration, he was followed thither by his wife and his mother-in-law. The wife soon died. The death of her daughter did not altogether separate Mrs. Bowes from Knox, but she seems to have come and gone between his house and England. In 1562, however, we find him characterised as "a sole man by reason of the absence of his mother-in-law, Mrs. Bowes," and a passport is got for her, her man, a maid, and "three horses, whereof two shall return," as well as liberty to take all her own money with her into Scotland. This looks like a definite arrangement; but whether she died at Edinburgh, or went back to England yet again, I cannot find. With that great family of hers, unless in leaving her husband she had quarrelled with them all, there must have been frequent occasion for her presence, one would think. Knox at least survived her; and we possess his epigraph to their long intimacy, given to the world by him in an appendix to his latest publication. I have said in a former paper that Knox was not shy of personal revelations in his published works. And the trick seems to have grown on him. To this last tract, a controversial onslaught on a Scottish Jesuit, he prefixed a prayer, not very pertinent to the matter in hand, and containing references to his family which were the occasion of some wit in his adversary's answer; and appended what seems equally irrelevant, one of his devout letters to Mrs. Bowes, with an explanatory preface. To say truth, I believe he had always felt uneasily that the circumstances of this intimacy were very capable of misconstruction; and now, when he was an old man, taking "his good night of all the faithful in both realms," and only desirous "that without any notable slander to the evangel of Jesus Christ, he might end his battle; for as the world was weary of him, so was he of it;"—in such a spirit it was not, perhaps, unnatural that he should return to this old story, and seek to put it right in the eyes of all men, ere he died. "Because that God," he says, "because that God now in his mercy hath put an end to the battle of my dear mother, Mistress Elizabeth Bowes, before that He put an end to my wretched life, I could not cease but declare to the world what was the cause of our great familiarity and long acquaintance; which was neither flesh nor blood, but a troubled conscience on her part, which never suffered her to rest but when she was in the company of the faithful, of whom (from the first hearing of the word at my mouth) she judged me to be one. . . . Her company to me was comfortable (yea, honourable and profitable, for she was to me and mine a mother), but yet it was not without some cross; for besides trouble and fashery of body sustained for her, my mind was seldom quiet, for doing somewhat for the comfort of her troubled conscience." [51] He had written to her years before, from his first exile at Dieppe, that "only God's hand" could withhold him from once more speaking with her face to

51. *Ibid.* vi. 513, 514.

face; and now, when God's hand has indeed interposed, when there lies between them, instead of the voyageable straits, that great gulf over which no man can pass, this is the spirit in which we can look back upon their long acquaintance. She was a religious hypochondriac, it appears, whom, not without some cross and fashery of mind and body, he was good enough to tend. He might have given a truer character of their friendship, had he thought less of his own standing in public estimation, and more of the dead woman. But he was in all things, as Burke said of his son in that ever memorable passage, a public creature. He wished that even into this private place of his affections posterity should follow him with a complete approval; and he was willing, in order that this might be so, to exhibit the defects of his lost friend, and tell the world what weariness he had sustained through her unhappy disposition. There is something here that reminds one of Rousseau.

I do not think he ever saw Mrs. Locke after he left Geneva; but his correspondence with her continued for three years. It may have continued longer, of course, but I think the last letters we possess read like the last that would be written. Perhaps Mrs. Locke was then remarried, for there is much obscurity over her subsequent history. For as long as their intimacy was kept up, at least, the human element remains in the Reformer's life. Here is one passage, for example, the most likeable utterance of Knox's that I can quote:—Mrs. Locke has been upbraiding him as a bad correspondent. "My remembrance of you," he answers, "is not so dead, but I trust it shall be fresh enough, albeit it be renewed by no outward token for one year. *Of nature, I am churlish; yet one thing I ashame not to affirm, that familiarity once thoroughly contracted was never yet broken on my default. The cause may be that I have rather need of all, than that any have need of me.* However it (*that*) be, it cannot be, as I say, the corporal absence of one year or two that can quench in my heart that familiar acquaintance in Christ Jesus, which half a year did engender, and almost two years did nourish and confirm. And therefore, whether I write or no, be assuredly persuaded that I have in you such memory as becometh the faithful to have of the faithful." [52] This is the truest touch of personal humility that I can remember to have seen in all the five volumes of the Reformer's collected works: it is no small honour to Mrs. Locke that his affection for her should have brought home to him this unwonted feeling of dependence upon others. Everything else in the course of the correspondence testifies to a good, sound, downright sort of friendship between the two, less ecstatic than it was at first, perhaps, but serviceable and very equal. He gives her ample details as to the progress of the work of reformation; sends her the sheets of the *Confession of Faith*, "in quairs," as he calls it; asks her to assist him with her prayers, to collect money for the good cause in

52. *Ibid*. vi. 11.

Scotland, and to send him books for himself—
books by Calvin especially, one on Isaiah, and
a new revised edition of the "Institutes." "I must
be bold on your liberality," he writes, "not only
in that, but in greater things as I shall need." [53]
On her part she applies to him for spiritual advice, not after the manner of the drooping Mrs.
Bowes, but in a more positive spirit—advice as
to practical points, advice as to the Church of
England, for instance, whose ritual he condemns
as a "mingle-mangle." [54] Just at the end she
ceases to write, sends him "a token, without writing." "I understand your impediment," he answers, "and therefore I cannot complain. Yet if
you understood the variety of my temptations, I
doubt not but you would have written somewhat." [55] One letter more, and then silence.

And I think the best of the Reformer died out
with that correspondence. It is after this, of
course, that he wrote that ungenerous description
of his intercourse with Mrs. Bowes. It is after
this, also, that we come to the unlovely episode of
his second marriage. He had been left a widower
at the age of fifty-three. Three years after it occurred apparently to yet another pious parent to
sacrifice a child upon the altar of his respect for
the Reformer. In January 1563, Randolph writes
to Cecil: "Your Honour will take it for a great
wonder when I shall write unto you that Mr.

53. *Ibid.* vi. 21, 101, 108, 130.
54. *Ibid.* vi. 83.
55. *Ibid.* vi. 129.

Knox shall marry a very near kinswoman of the Duke's, a Lord's daughter, a young lass not above sixteen years of age." [56] He adds that he fears he will be laughed at for reporting so mad a story. And yet it is true; and on Palm Sunday, 1564, Margaret Stewart, daughter of Andrew Lord Stewart of Ochiltree, aged seventeen, was duly united to John Knox, Minister of St. Giles's Kirk, Edinburgh, aged fifty-nine,—to the great disgust of Queen Mary from family pride, and I would fain hope of many others for more humane considerations. "In this," as Randolph says, "I wish he had done otherwise." The Consistory of Geneva, "that most perfect school of Christ that ever was on earth since the days of the Apostles," were wont to forbid marriages on the ground of too great a disproportion in age. I cannot help wondering whether the old Reformer's conscience did not uneasily remind him, now and again, of this good custom of his religious metropolis, as he thought of the two-and-forty years that separated him from his poor bride. Fitly enough, we hear nothing of the second Mrs. Knox until she appears at her husband's deathbed, eight years after. She bore him three daughters in the interval; and I suppose the poor child's martyrdom was made as easy for her as might be. She was "extremely attentive to him" at the end, we read; and he seems to have spoken to her with some confidence. Moreover, and this is very characteristic, he had copied out for her use a little volume of his own devotional letters to other women.

56. *Ibid.* vi. 532.

This is the end of the roll, unless we add to it Mrs. Adamson, who had delighted much in his company "by reason that she had a troubled conscience," and whose deathbed is commemorated at some length in the pages of his history.[57]

And now, looking back, it cannot be said that Knox's intercourse with women was quite of the highest sort. It is characteristic that we find him more alarmed for his own reputation than for the reputation of the women with whom he was familiar. There was a fatal preponderance of self in all his intimacies: many women came to learn from him, but he never condescended to become a learner in his turn. And so there is not anything idyllic in these intimacies of his; and they were never renovating to his spirit as they might have been. But I believe they were good enough for the women. I fancy the women knew what they were about when so many of them followed after Knox. It is not simply because a man is always fully persuaded that he knows the right from the wrong and sees his way plainly through the maze of life, great qualities as these are, that people will love and follow him, and write him letters full of their "earnest desire for him" when he is absent. It is not over a man, whose one characteristic is grim fixity of purpose, that the hearts of women are "incensed and kindled with a special care," as it were over their natural children. In the strong quiet patience of all his letters to the weariful Mrs. Bowes, we may perhaps see one cause of the fascination he possessed for these

57. *Ibid.* i. 246.

231

religious women. Here was one whom you could besiege all the year round with inconsistent scruples and complaints; you might write to him on Thursday that you were so elated it was plain the devil was deceiving you, and again on Friday that you were so depressed it was plain God had cast you off for ever; and he would read all this patiently and sympathetically, and give you an answer in the most reassuring polysyllables, and all divided into heads—who knows?—like a treatise on divinity. And then, those easy tears of his. There are some women who like to see men crying; and here was this great-voiced bearded man of God, who might be seen beating the solid pulpit every Sunday, and casting abroad his clamorous denunciations to the terror of all, and who on Monday would sit in their parlours by the hour, and weep with them over their manifold trials and temptations. Nowadays, he would have to drink a dish of tea with all these penitents. . . . It sounds a little vulgar, as the past will do if we look into it too closely. We could not let these great folk of old into our drawing-rooms. Queen Elizabeth would positively not be eligible for a housemaid. The old manners and the old customs go sinking from grade to grade, until, if some mighty emperor revisited the glimpses of the moon, he would not find anyone of his way of thinking, anyone he could strike hands with and talk to freely and without offence, save perhaps the porter at the end of the street, or the fellow with his elbows out who loafs all day before the public-house. So that this little note of vulgarity is not a thing to be dwelt upon; it is to be put away from us, as we recall the fashion of these old intimacies; so that we may only remember Knox as one who was very long-suffering with women, kind to them in his own way, loving them in his own way—and that not the worst way, if it was not the best—and once at least, if not twice, moved to his heart of hearts by a woman, and giving expression to the yearning he had for her society in words that none of us need to be ashamed to borrow.

And let us bear in mind always that the period I have gone over in this essay begins when the Reformer was already beyond the middle age, and already broken in bodily health; it had been the story of an old man's friendships. This it is that makes Knox enviable. Unknown until past forty, he had then before him five-and-thirty years of splendid and influential life, passed through uncommon hardships to an uncommon degree of power, lived in his own country as a sort of king, and did what he would with the sound of his voice out of the pulpit. And besides all this, such a following of faithful women! One would take the first forty years gladly, if one could be sure of the last thirty. Most of us, even if, by reason of great strength and the dignity of gray hairs, we retain some degree of public respect in the latter days of our existence, will find a falling away of friends, and a solitude making itself round about us day by day, until we are left alone with the hired sick-nurse. For the attraction of a man's character is apt to be outlived, like the attraction of his body; and the power to love grows feeble in its turn, as well as the power to inspire love in others. It is only with a few rare natures that friendship is added to friendship, love to love, and the man keeps growing richer in affection—richer, I mean, as a bank may be said to grow richer, both giving and receiving more—after his head is white and his back weary, and he prepares to go down into the dust of death.

SOME COLLEGE MEMORIES [1]

I AM ASKED to write something (it is not specifically stated what) to the profit and glory of my *Alma Mater;* and the fact is I seem to be in very nearly the same case with those who addressed me, for while I am willing enough to write something, I know not what to write. Only one point I see, that if I am to write at all, it should be of the University itself and my own days under its shadow; of the things that are still the same and of those that are already changed: such talk, in short, as would pass naturally between a student of to-day and one of yesterday, supposing them to meet and grow confidential.

The generations pass away swiftly enough on the high seas of life; more swiftly still in the little bubbling backwater of the quadrangle; so that we see there, on a scale startlingly diminished, the flight of time and the succession of men. I looked for my name the other day in last year's case-book of the Speculative. Naturally enough I looked for it near the end; it was not there, nor yet in the next column, so that I began to think it had been dropped at press; and when at last I found it, mounted on the shoulders of so many successors, and looking in that posture like the name of a man of ninety, I was conscious of some of the

1. Written for the "Book" of the Edinburgh University Union Fancy Fair.

235

dignity of years. This kind of dignity of temporal precession is likely, with prolonged life, to become more familiar, possibly less welcome; but I felt strongly then, it is strongly on me now, and I am the more emboldened to speak with my successors in the tone of a parent and a praiser of things past.

For, indeed, that which they attend is but a fallen University; it has doubtless some remains of good, for human institutions decline by gradual stages; but decline, in spite of all seeming embellishments, it does; and what is perhaps more singular, began to do so when I ceased to be a student. Thus, by an odd chance, I had the very last of the very best of *Alma Mater*; the same thing, I hear (which makes it the more strange), had previously happened to my father; and if they are good and do not die, something not at all unsimilar will be found in time to have befallen my successors of today. Of the specific points of change, of advantage in the past, of shortcoming in the present, I must own that, on a near examination, they look wondrous cloudy. The chief and far the most lamentable change is the absence of a certain lean, ugly, idle, unpopular student, whose presence was for me the gist and heart of the whole matter; whose changing humours, fine occasional purposes of good, flinching acceptance of evil, shiverings on wet, east-windy, morning journeys up to class, infinite yawnings during lecture and unquenchable gusto in the delights of truantry, made up the sunshine and shadow of my college life. You cannot fancy what you missed in missing him; his virtues, I make sure, are inconceivable to his successors, just as they were apparently concealed from his contemporaries, for I was practically alone in the pleasure I had in his society. Poor soul, I remember how much he was cast down at times, and how life (which had not yet begun) seemed to be already at an end, and hope quite dead, and misfortune and dishonour, like physical presences, dogging him as he went. And it may be worth while to add that these clouds rolled away in their season, and that all clouds roll away at last, and the troubles of youth in particular are things but of a moment. So this student, whom I have in my eye, took his full share of these concerns, and that very largely by his own fault; but he still clung to his fortune, and in the midst of much misconduct, kept on in his own way learning how to work; and at last, to his wonder, escaped out of the stage of studentship not openly shamed; leaving behind him the University of Edinburgh shorn of a good deal of its interest for myself.

But while he is (in more senses than one) the first person, he is by no means the only one whom I regret, or whom the students of to-day, if they knew what they had lost, would regret also. They have still Tait, to be sure—long may they have him!—and they have still Tait's classroom, cupola and all; but think of what a different place it was when this youth of mine (at least on roll days) would be present on the benches, and, at the near end of the platform, Lindsay senior[2] was airing his robust old age. It is possible my successors may have never even heard of Old Lindsay; but when he went, a link snapped with the last century. He had something of a rustic air, sturdy and fresh and plain; he spoke with a ripe east-country accent, which I used to admire; his reminiscences were all of journeys on foot or highways busy with post-chaises—a Scotland before steam; he had seen the coal fire on the Isle of May, and he regaled me with tales of my own grandfather. Thus he was for me a mirror of things perished; it was only in his memory that I could see the huge shock of flames of the May beacon stream to leeward, and the watchers, as they fed the fire, lay hold un-scorched of the windward bars of the furnace; it was only thus that I could see my grandfather driving swiftly in a gig along the seaboard road from Pittenweem to Crail, and for all his business hurry, drawing up to speak good-humouredly with those he met. And now, in his turn, Lindsay is gone also; inhabits only the memories of other men, till these shall follow him; and figures in my reminiscences as my grandfather figured in his.

To-day, again, they have Professor Butcher, and I hear he has a prodigious deal of Greek; and they have Professor Chrystal, who is a man filled with the mathematics. And doubtless these are set-offs. But they cannot change the fact that Professor Blackie has retired, and that Professor Kelland is dead. No man's education is complete

2. Professor Tait's laboratory assistant.

or truly liberal who knew not Kelland. There
were unutterable lessons in the mere sight of that
frail old clerical gentleman, lively as a boy, kind
like a fairy godfather, and keeping perfect order
in his class by the spell of that very kindness. I
have heard him drift into reminiscences in class
time, though not for long, and give us glimpses of
old-world life in out-of-the-way English parishes
when he was young; thus playing the same part
as Lindsay—the part of the surviving memory,
signalling out of the dark backward and abysm
of time the images of perished things. But it was
a part that scarce became him; he somehow
lacked the means: for all his silver hair and worn
face, he was not truly old; and he had too much
of the unrest and petulant fire of youth, and too
much unvincible innocence of mind, to play the
veteran well. The time to measure him best, to
taste (in the old phrase) his gracious nature, was
when he received his class at home. What a
pretty simplicity would he then show, trying to
amuse us like children with toys; and what an
engaging nervousness of manner, as fearing that
his efforts might not succeed! Truly he made us
all feel like children, and like children embar-
rassed, but at the same time filled with sympathy
for the conscientious, troubled elder-boy who was
working so hard to entertain us. A theorist has
held the view that there is no feature in man so
tell-tale as his spectacles; that the mouth may be
compressed and the brow smoothed artificially,
but the sheen of the barnacles is diagnostic. And
truly it must have been thus with Kelland; for as

I still fancy I behold him frisking actively about the platform, pointer in hand, that which I seem to see most clearly is the way his glasses glittered with affection. I never knew but one other man who had (if you will permit the phrase) so kind a spectacle; and that was Dr. Appleton. But the light in his case was tempered and passive; in Kelland's it danced, and changed, and flashed vivaciously among the students, like a perpetual challenge to goodwill.

I cannot say so much about Professor Blackie, for a good reason. Kelland's class I attended, once even gained there a certificate of merit, the only distinction of my University career. But although I am the holder of a certificate of attendance in the professor's own hand, I cannot remember to have been present in the Greek class above a dozen times. Professor Blackie was even kind enough to remark (more than once) while in the very act of writing the document above referred to, that he did not know my face. Indeed, I denied myself many opportunities; acting upon an extensive and highly rational system of truantry, which cost me a great deal of trouble to put in exercise—perhaps as much as would have taught me Greek—and sent me forth into the world and the profession of letters with the merest shadow of an education. But they say it is always a good thing to have taken pains, and that success is its own reward, whatever be its nature; so that, perhaps, even upon this I should plume myself, that no one ever played the truant with more deliberate care, and none ever had

more certificates for less education. One consequence, however, of my system is that I have
much less to say of Professor Blackie than I had
of Professor Kelland; and as he is still alive, and
will long, I hope, continue to be so, it will not
surprise you very much that I have no intention
of saying it.

Meanwhile, how many others have gone—Jenkin, Hodgson, and I know not who besides; and
of that tide of students that used to throng the
arch and blacken the quadrangle, how many are
scattered into the remotest parts of the earth, and
how many more have lain down beside their
fathers in their "resting-graves"! And again, how
many of these last have not found their way
there, all too early, through the stress of education! That was one thing, at least, from which my
truantry protected me. I am sorry indeed that I
have no Greek, but I should be sorrier still if I
were dead; nor do I know the name of that
branch of knowledge which is worth acquiring at
the price of a brain fever. There are many sordid
tragedies in the life of the student, above all if he
be poor, or drunken, or both; but nothing more
moves a wise man's pity than the case of the lad
who is in too much hurry to be learned. And so,
for the sake of a moral at the end, I will call up
one more figure, and have done. A student, ambitious of success by that hot, intemperate manner of study that now grows so common, read
night and day for an examination. As he went
on, the task became more easy to him, sleep was
more easily banished, his brain grew hot and clear

and more capacious, the necessary knowledge daily fuller and more orderly. It came to the eve of the trial and he watched all night in his high chamber, reviewing what he knew, and already secure of success. His window looked eastward, and being (as I said) high up, and the house itself standing on a hill, commanded a view over dwindling suburbs to a country horizon. At last my student drew up his blind, and still in quite a jocund humour, looked abroad. Day was breaking, the east was tinging with strange fires, the clouds breaking up for the coming of the sun; and at the sight, nameless terror seized upon his mind. He was sane, his senses were undisturbed; he saw clearly, and knew what he was seeing, and knew that it was normal; but he could neither bear to see it nor find the strength to look away, and fled in panic from his chamber into the enclosure of the street. In the cool air and silence, and among the sleeping houses, his strength was renewed. Nothing troubled him but the memory of what had passed, and an abject fear of its return.

> "Gallo canente, spes redit,
> Aegris salus refunditur,
> Lapsis fides revertitur,"

as they sang of old in Portugal in the Morning Office. But to him that good hour of cockcrow, and the changes of the dawn, had brought panic, and lasting doubt, and such terror as he still shook to think of. He dared not return to his lodging; he could not eat; he sat down, he rose up, he wandered; the city woke about him with its cheerful bustle, the sun climbed overhead; and still he grew but the more absorbed in the distress of his recollection and the fear of his past fear. At the appointed hour, he came to the door of the place of examination; but when he was asked, he had forgotten his name. Seeing him so disordered, they had not the heart to send him away, but gave him a paper and admitted him, still nameless, to the Hall. Vain kindness, vain efforts. He could only sit in a still growing horror, writing nothing, ignorant of all, his mind filled with a single memory of the breaking day and his own intolerable fear. And that same night he was tossing in a brain fever.

People are afraid of war and wounds and dentists, all with excellent reason; but these are not to be compared with such chaotic terrors of the mind as fell on this young man, and made him cover his eyes from the innocent morning. We all have by our bedsides the box of the Merchant Abudah, thank God, securely enough shut; but when a young man sacrifices sleep to labour, let him have a care, for he is playing with the lock.

A GOSSIP ON ROMANCE

IN ANYTHING fit to be called by the name of reading, the process itself should be absorbing and voluptuous; we should gloat over a book, be rapt clean out of ourselves, and rise from the perusal, our mind filled with the busiest, kaleidoscopic dance of images, incapable of sleep or of continuous thought. The words, if the book be eloquent, should run thenceforward in our ears like the noise of breakers, and the story, if it be a story, repeat itself in a thousand coloured pictures to the eye. It was for this last pleasure that we read so closely, and loved our books so dearly, in the bright, troubled period of boyhood. Eloquence and thought, character and conversation, were but obstacles to brush aside as we dug blithely after a certain sort of incident, like a pig for truffles. For my part, I liked a story to begin with an old wayside inn where, "towards the close of the year 17—," several gentlemen in three-cocked hats were playing bowls. A friend of mine preferred the Malabar coast in a storm, with a ship beating to windward, and a scowling fellow of Herculean proportions striding along the beach; he, to be sure, was a pirate. This was further afield than my home-keeping fancy loved to travel, and designed altogether for a larger canvas than the tales that I affected. Give me a highwayman and I was full to the brim; a Jacobite would do, but the highwayman was my favourite dish. I can still hear that merry clatter of the hoofs along the moonlit lane; night and the coming of day are still related in my mind with the doings of John Rann or Jerry Abershaw; and the words "post-chaise," the "great North road," "ostler," and "nag" still sound in my ears like poetry. One and all, at least, and each with his particular fancy, we read story-books in childhood, not for eloquence or character or thought, but for some quality of the brute incident. That quality was not mere bloodshed or wonder. Although each of these was welcome in its place, the charm for the sake of which we read depended on something different from either. My elders used to read novels aloud; and I can still remember four different passages which I heard, before I was ten, with the same keen and lasting pleasure.

One I discovered long afterwards to be the admirable opening of *What will he Do with It*: it was no wonder I was pleased with that. The other three still remain unidentified. One is a little vague; it was about a dark, tall house at night, and people groping on the stairs by the light that escaped from the open door of a sickroom. In another, a lover left a ball, and went walking in a cool, dewy park, whence he could watch the lighted windows and the figures of the dancers as they moved. This was the most sentimental impression I think I had yet received, for a child is somewhat deaf to the sentimental. In the last, a poet, who had been tragically wrangling with his wife, walked forth on the sea-beach on a tempestuous night and witnessed the horrors of a wreck.[1] Different as they are, all these early favourites have a common note—they have all a touch of the romantic.

Drama is the poetry of conduct, romance the poetry of circumstance. The pleasure that we take in life is of two sorts—the active and the passive. Now we are conscious of a great command over our destiny; anon we are lifted up by circumstance, as by a breaking wave, and dashed we knew not how into the future. Now we are pleased by our conduct, anon merely pleased by our surroundings. It would be hard to say which of these modes of satisfaction is the more effective, but the latter is surely the more constant. Conduct is three parts of life, they say; but I think they put it high. There is a vast deal in life and letters both which is not immoral, but simply a-moral; which either does not regard the human will at all, or deals with it in obvious and healthy relations; where the interest turns, not upon what a man shall choose to do, but on how he manages to do it; not on the passionate slips and hesitations of the conscience, but on the problems of the body and of the practical intelligence, in clean, open-air adventure, the shock of arms or the diplomacy of life. With such material as this it is impossible to build a play, for the serious theatre exists solely on moral grounds, and is a standing proof of the dissemination of the human

1. Since traced by many obliging correspondents to the gallery of Charles Kingsley.

conscience. But it is possible to build, upon this ground, the most joyous of verses, and the most lively, beautiful, and buoyant tales.

One thing in life calls for another; there is a fitness in events and places. The sight of a pleasant arbour puts it in our mind to sit there. One place suggests work, another idleness, a third early rising and long rambles in the dew. The effect of night, of any flowing water, of lighted cities, of the peep of day, of ships, of the open ocean, calls up in the mind an army of anonymous desires and pleasures. Something, we feel, should happen; we know not what, yet we proceed in quest of it. And many of the happiest hours of life fleet by us in this vain attendance on the genius of the place and moment. It is thus that tracts of young fir, and low rocks that reach into deep soundings, particularly torture and delight me. Something must have happened in such places, and perhaps ages back, to members of my race; and when I was a child I tried in vain to invent appropriate games for them, as I still try, just as vainly, to fit them with the proper story. Some places speak distinctly. Certain dank gardens cry aloud for a murder; certain old houses demand to be haunted; certain coasts are set apart for shipwreck. Other spots again seem to abide their destiny, suggestive and impenetrable, "miching mallecho." The inn at Burford Bridge, with its arbours and green garden and silent, eddying river—though it is known already as the place where Keats wrote some of his *Endymion* and Nelson parted from his Emma—still seems to wait the coming of the appropriate legend. Within these ivied walls, behind these old green shutters, some further business smoulders, waiting for its hour. The old Hawes Inn at the Queen's Ferry makes a similar call upon my fancy. There it stands, apart from the town, beside the pier, in a climate of its own, half inland, half marine—in front, the ferry bubbling with the tide and the guardship swinging to her anchor; behind, the old garden with the trees. Americans seek it already for the sake of Lovel and Oldbuck, who dined there at the beginning of the *Antiquary*. But you need not tell me—that is not all; there is some story, unrecorded or not yet complete, which must express the meaning of that inn more fully. So it is with names and faces; so it is with incidents that are idle and inconclusive in themselves, and yet seem like the beginning of some quaint romance, which the all-careless author leaves untold. How many of these romances have we not seen determine at their birth; how many people have met us with a look of meaning in their eye, and sunk at once into trivial acquaintances; to how many places have we not drawn near, with express intimations—"here my destiny awaits me"—and we have but dined there and passed on! I have lived both at the Hawes and Burford in a perpetual flutter, on the heels, as it seemed, of some adventure that should justify the place; but though the feeling had me to bed at night and called me again at morning in one unbroken round of pleasure and suspense, nothing befell me in either worth remark. The man or the hour had not yet come; but some day, I think, a boat shall put off from the Queen's Ferry, fraught with a dear cargo, and some frosty night a horseman, on a tragic errand, rattle with his whip upon the green shutters of the inn at Burford.[2]

Now, this is one of the natural appetites with which any lively literature has to count. The desire for knowledge, I had almost added the desire for meat, is not more deeply seated than this demand for fit and striking incident. The dullest of clowns tells, or tries to tell, himself a story, as the feeblest of children uses invention in his play; and even as the imaginative grown person, joining in the game, at once enriches it with many delightful circumstances, the great creative writer shows us the realisation and the apotheosis of the day-dreams of common men. His stories may be nourished with the realities of life, but their true mark is to satisfy the nameless longings of the reader, and to obey the ideal laws of the day-dream. The right kind of thing should fall out in the right kind of place; the right kind of thing should follow; and not only the characters talk aptly and think naturally, but all the circumstances in a tale answer one to another like notes in music. The threads of a story come from time to time together and make a picture in the web; the characters fall from time to time into some attitude to each other or to nature, which

2. Since the above was written I have tried to launch the boat with my own hands in *Kidnapped*. Some day, perhaps, I may try a rattle at the shutters.

stamps the story home like an illustration. Crusoe recoiling from the footprint, Achilles shouting over against the Trojans, Ulysses bending the great bow, Christian running with his fingers in his ears, these are each culminating moments in the legend, and each has been printed on the mind's eye for ever. Other things we may forget; we may forget the words, although they are beautiful; we may forget the author's comment, although perhaps it was ingenious and true; but these epoch-making scenes, which put the last mark of truth upon a story and fill up, at one blow, our capacity for sympathetic pleasure, we so adopt into the very bosom of our mind that neither time nor tide can efface or weaken the impression. This, then, is the plastic part of literature: to embody character, thought, or emotion in some act or attitude that shall be remarkably striking to the mind's eye. This is the highest and hardest thing to do in words; the thing which, once accomplished, equally delights the schoolboy and the sage, and makes, in its own right, the quality of epics. Compared with this, all other purposes in literature, except the purely lyrical or the purely philosophic, are bastard in nature, facile of execution, and feeble in result. It is one thing to write about the inn at Burford, or to describe scenery with the word-painters; it is quite another to seize on the heart of the suggestion and make a country famous with a legend. It is one thing to remark and to dissect, with the most cutting logic, the complications of life, and of the human spirit; it is quite another to give them body and blood in the story of Ajax or of Hamlet. The first is literature, but the second is something besides, for it is likewise art.

English people of the present day[3] are apt, I know not why, to look somewhat down on incident, and reserve their admiration for the clink of teaspoons and the accents of the curate. It is thought clever to write a novel with no story at all, or at least with a very dull one. Reduced even to the lowest terms, a certain interest can be communicated by the art of narrative; a sense of human kinship stirred; and a kind of monotonous fitness, comparable to the words and air of *Sandy's Mull*, preserved among the infinitesimal occurrences recorded. Some people work, in this manner, with even a strong touch. Mr. Trollope's inimitable clergyman naturally arise to the mind in this connection. But even Mr. Trollope does not confine himself to chronicling small beer. Mr. Crawley's collision with the Bishop's wife, Mr. Melnotte dallying in the deserted banquet-room, are typical incidents, epically conceived, fitly embodying a crisis. Or again look at Thackeray. If Rawdon Crawley's blow were not delivered, *Vanity Fair* would cease to be a work of art. That scene is the chief ganglion of the tale; and the discharge of energy from Rawdon's fist is the reward and consolation of the reader. The end of *Esmond* is a yet wider excursion from the author's customary fields; the scene at Castlewood is pure Dumas; the great and wily English borrower has

3. 1882.

here borrowed from the great, unblushing French thief; as usual, he has borrowed admirably well, and the breaking of the sword rounds off the best of all his books with a manly, martial note. But perhaps nothing can more strongly illustrate the necessity for marking incident than to compare the living fame of *Robinson Crusoe* with the discredit of *Clarissa Harlowe*. *Clarissa* is a book of a far more startling import, worked out, on a great canvas, with inimitable courage and unflagging art. It contains wit, character, passion, plot, conversations full of spirit and insight, letters sparkling with unstrained humanity; and if the death of the heroine be somewhat frigid and artificial, the last days of the hero strike the only note of what we now call Byronism, between the Elizabethans and Byron himself. And yet a little story of a shipwrecked sailor, with not a tenth part of the style nor a thousandth part of the wisdom, exploring none of the arcana of humanity and deprived of the perennial interest of love, goes on from edition to edition, ever young, while *Clarissa* lies upon the shelves unread. A friend of mine, a Welsh blacksmith, was twenty-five years old and could neither read nor write, when he heard a chapter of *Robinson* read aloud in a farm kitchen. Up to that moment he had sat content, huddled in his ignorance, but he left that farm another man. There were day-dreams, it appeared, divine day-dreams, written and printed and bound, and to be bought for money and enjoyed at pleasure. Down he sat that day, painfully learned to read Welsh, and returned to borrow the book. It had been lost, nor could he find another copy but one that was in English. Down he sat once more, learned English, and at length, and with entire delight, read *Robinson*. It is like the story of a love-chase. If he had heard a letter from *Clarissa*, would he have been fired with the same chivalrous ardour? I wonder. Yet *Clarissa* has every quality that can be shown in prose, one alone excepted—pictorial or picture-making romance. While *Robinson* depends, for the most part and with the overwhelming majority of its readers, on the charm of circumstance.

In the highest achievements of the art of words, the dramatic and the pictorial, the moral and romantic interest, rise and fall together by a common and organic law. Situation is animated with passion, passion clothed upon with situation. Neither exists for itself, but each inheres indissolubly with the other. This is high art; and not only the highest art possible in words, but the highest art of all, since it combines the greatest mass and diversity of the elements of truth and pleasure. Such are epics, and the few prose tales that have the epic weight. But as from a school of works, aping the creative, incident and romance are ruthlessly discarded, so may character and drama be omitted or subordinated to romance. There is one book, for example, more generally loved than Shakespeare, that captivates in childhood, and still delights in age—I mean the *Arabian Nights*—where you shall look in vain for moral or for intellectual interest. No human face or voice greets us among that wooden

crowd of kings and genies, sorcerers and beggar-
men. Adventure, on the most naked terms,
furnishes forth the entertainment and is found
enough. Dumas approaches perhaps nearest of
any modern to these Arabian authors in the
purely material charm of some of his romances.
The early part of *Monte Cristo*, down to the
finding of the treasure, is a piece of perfect story-
telling; the man never breathed who shared these
moving incidents without a tremor; and yet Faria
is a thing of packthread and Dantès little more
than a name. The sequel is one long-drawn error,
gloomy, bloody, unnatural and dull; but as for
these early chapters, I do not believe there is
another volume extant where you can breathe the
same unmingled atmosphere of romance. It is
very thin and light, to be sure, as on a high
mountain; but it is brisk and clear and sunny in
proportion. I saw the other day, with envy, an
old and a very clever lady setting forth on a
second or third voyage into *Monte Cristo*. Here
are stories which powerfully affect the reader,
which can be reperused at any age, and where
the characters are no more than puppets. The
bony fist of the showman visibly propels them;
their springs are an open secret; their faces are
of wood, their bellies filled with bran; and yet
we thrillingly partake of their adventures. And
the point may be illustrated still further. The last
interview between Lucy and Richard Feveril is
pure drama; more than that, it is the strongest
scene, since Shakespeare, in the English tongue.
Their first meeting by the river, on the other

hand, is pure romance; it has nothing to do with character; it might happen to any other boy or maiden, and be none the less delightful for the change. And yet I think he would be a bold man who should choose between these passages. Thus, in the same book, we may have two scenes, each capital in its order: in the one, human passion, deep calling unto deep, shall utter its genuine voice; in the second, according circumstances, like instruments in tune, shall build up a trivial but desirable incident, such as we love to prefigure for ourselves; and in the end, in spite of the critics, we may hesitate to give the preference to either. The one may ask more genius—I do not say it does; but at least the other dwells as clearly in the memory.

True romantic art, again, makes a romance of all things. It reaches into the highest abstraction of the ideal; it does not refuse the most pedestrian realism. *Robinson Crusoe* is as realistic as it is romantic; both qualities are pushed to an extreme, and neither suffers. Nor does romance depend upon the material importance of the incidents. To deal with strong and deadly elements, banditti, pirates, war and murder, is to conjure with great names, and, in the event of failure, to double the disgrace. The arrival of Haydn and Consuelo at the Canon's villa is a very trifling incident; yet we may read a dozen boisterous stories from beginning to end, and not receive so fresh and stirring an impression of adventure. It was the scene of Crusoe at the wreck, if I remember rightly, that so bewitched my blacksmith. Nor is the fact surprising. Every single article the castaway recovers from the hulk is "a joy for ever" to the man who reads of them. They are the things that should be found, and the bare enumeration stirs the blood. I found a glimmer of the same interest the other day in a new book, *The Sailor's Sweetheart*, by Mr. Clark Russell. The whole business of the brig *Morning Star* is very rightly felt and spiritedly written; but the clothes, the books and the money satisfy the reader's mind like things to eat. We are dealing here with the old cut-and-dry, legitimate interest of treasure trove. But even treasure trove can be made dull. There are few people who have not groaned under the plethora of goods that fell to the lot of the *Swiss Family Robinson*, that dreary family. They found article after article, creature after creature, from milk kine to pieces of ordnance, a whole consignment; but no informing taste had presided over the selection, there was no smack or relish in the invoice; and these riches left the fancy cold. The box of goods in Verne's *Mysterious Island* is another case in point: there was no gusto and no glamour about that; it might have come from a shop. But the two hundred and seventy-eight Australian sovereigns on board the *Morning Star* fell upon me like a surprise that I had expected; whole vistas of secondary stories, beside the one in hand, radiated forth from that discovery, as they radiate from a striking particular in life; and I was made for the moment as happy as a reader has the right to be.

To come at all at the nature of this quality of romance, we must bear in mind the peculiarity of our attitude to any art. No art produces illusion; in the theatre we never forget that we are in the theatre; and while we read a story, we sit wavering between two minds, now merely clapping our hands at the merit of the performance, now condescending to take an active part in fancy with the characters. This last is the triumph of romantic story-telling: when the reader consciously plays at being the hero, the scene is a good scene. Now in character-studies the pleasure that we take is critical; we watch, we approve, we smile at incongruities, we are moved to sudden heats of sympathy with courage, suffering or virtue. But the characters are still themselves, they are not us; the more clearly they are depicted, the more widely do they stand away from us, the more imperiously do they thrust us back into our place as a spectator. I cannot identify myself with Rawdon Crawley or with Eugène de Rastignac, for I have scarce a hope or fear in common with them. It is not character but incident that woos us out of our reserve. Something happens as we desire to have it happen to ourselves; some situation, that we have long dallied with in fancy, is realised in the story with enticing and appropriate details. Then we forget the characters; then we push the hero aside; then we plunge into the tale in our own person and bathe in fresh experience; and then, and then only, do we say we have been reading a romance. It is not only pleasurable things that

we imagine in our day-dreams; there are lights
in which we are willing to contemplate even the
idea of our own death; ways in which it seems
as if it would amuse us to be cheated, wounded
or calumniated. It is thus possible to construct
a story, even of tragic import, in which every
incident, detail and trick of circumstance shall
be welcome to the reader's thoughts. Fiction is to
the grown man what play is to the child; it is
there that he changes the atmosphere and tenor
of his life; and when the game so chimes with his
fancy that he can join in it with all his heart,
when it pleases him with every turn, when he
loves to recall it and dwells upon its recollection
with entire delight, fiction is called romance.

Walter Scott is out and away the king of the
romantics. *The Lady of the Lake* has no indisputable claim to be a poem beyond the inherent
fitness and desirability of the tale. It is just such
a story as a man would make up for himself,
walking, in the best health and temper, through
just such scenes as it is laid in. Hence it is that a
charm dwells undefinable among these slovenly
verses, as the unseen cuckoo fills the mountains
with his note; hence, even after we have flung
the book aside, the scenery and adventures remain present to the mind, a new and green possession, not unworthy of that beautiful name,
The Lady of the Lake, or that direct, romantic
opening—one of the most spirited and poetical in
literature—"The stag at eve had drunk his fill."
The same strength and the same weaknesses
adorn and disfigure the novels. In that ill-written,

ragged book, *The Pirate*, the figure of Cleveland
—cast up by the sea on the resounding foreland
of Dunrossness—moving, with the blood on his
hands and the Spanish words on his tongue,
among the simple islanders—singing a serenade
under the window of his Shetland mistress—is
conceived in the very highest manner of romantic
invention. The words of his song, "Through
groves of palm," sung in such a scene and by such
a lover, clench, as in a nutshell, the emphatic
contrast upon which the tale is built. In *Guy
Mannering*, again, every incident is delightful to
the imagination; and the scene when Harry
Bertram lands at Ellangowan is a model instance
of romantic method.

"'I remember the tune well,' he says 'though
I cannot guess what should at present so strongly
recall it to my memory.' He took his flageolet
from his pocket and played a simple melody.
Apparently the tune awoke the corresponding
associations of a damsel. . . . She immediately
took up the song—

"'Are these the links of Forth, she said;
　　Or are they the crooks of Dee,
　Or the bonny woods of Warroch Head
　　That I so fain would see?'

"'By heaven!' said Bertram, 'it is the very
ballad.'"

On this quotation two remarks fall to be made.
First, as an instance of modern feeling for romance, this famous touch of the flageolet and the
old song is selected by Miss Braddon for omis-

sion. Miss Braddon's idea of a story, like Mrs. Todger's idea of a wooden leg, were something strange to have expounded. As a matter of personal experience, Meg's appearance to old Mr. Bertram on the road, the ruins of Derncleugh, the scene of the flageolet, and the Dominie's recognition of Harry, are the four strong notes that continue to ring in the mind after the book is laid aside. The second point is still more curious. The reader will observe a mark of excision in the passage as quoted by me. Well, here is how it runs in the original: "a damsel, who, close behind a fine spring about half-way down the descent, and which had once supplied the castle with water, was engaged in bleaching linen." A man who gave in such copy would be discharged from the staff of a daily paper. Scott has forgotten to prepare the reader for the presence of the "damsel"; he has forgotten to mention the spring and its relation to the ruin; and now, face to face with his omission, instead of trying back and starting fair, crams all this matter, tail foremost, into a single shambling sentence. It is not merely bad English, or bad style; it is abominably bad narrative besides.

Certainly the contrast is remarkable; and it is one that throws a strong light upon the subject of this paper. For here we have a man of the finest creative instinct touching with perfect certainty and charm the romantic junctures of his story; and we find him utterly careless, almost, it would seem, incapable, in the technical matter of style, and not only frequently weak, but frequently wrong in points of drama. In character parts, indeed, and particularly in the Scotch, he was delicate, strong and truthful; but the trite, obliterated features of too many of his heroes have already wearied two generations of readers. At times his characters will speak with something far beyond propriety with a true heroic note; but on the next page they will be wading wearily forward with an ungrammatical and undramatic rigmarole of words. The man who could conceive and write the character of Elspeth of the Craigburnfoot, as Scott has conceived and written it, had not only splendid romantic, but splendid tragic gifts. How comes it, then, that he could so often fob us off with languid, inarticulate twaddle?

It seems to me that the explanation is to be found in the very quality of his surprising merits. As his books are play to the reader, so were they play to him. He conjured up the romantic with delight, but he had hardly patience to describe it. He was a great daydreamer, a seer of fit and beautiful and humorous visions, but hardly a great artist; hardly, in the manful sense, an artist at all. He pleased himself, and so he pleases us. Of the pleasures of his art he tasted fully; but of its toils and vigils and distresses never man knew less. A great romantic—an idle child.

A NOTE ON REALISM

STYLE is the invariable mark of any master; and for the student who does not aspire so high as to be numbered with the giants, it is still the one quality in which he may improve himself at will. Passion, wisdom, creative force, the power of mystery or colour, are allotted in the hour of birth, and can be neither learned nor simulated. But the just and dexterous use of what qualities we have, the proportion of one part to another and to the whole, the elision of the useless, the accentuation of the important, and the preservation of a uniform character from end to end— these, which taken together constitute technical perfection, are to some degree within the reach of industry and intellectual courage. What to put in and what to leave out; whether some particular fact be organically necessary or purely ornamental; whether, if it be purely ornamental, it may not weaken or obscure the general design; and finally, whether, if we decide to use it, we should do so grossly and notably or in some conventional disguise: are questions of plastic style continually re-arising. And the sphinx that patrols the highways of executive art has no more unanswerable riddle to propound.

In literature (from which I must draw my instances) the great change of the past century has been effected by the admission of detail. It was inaugurated by the romantic Scott; and at length, by the semi-romantic Balzac and his more or less wholly unromantic followers, bound like a duty on the novelist. For some time it signified and expressed a more ample contemplation of the conditions of man's life; but it has recently (at least in France) fallen into a merely technical and decorative stage, which it is, perhaps, still too harsh to call survival. With a movement of alarm, the wiser or more timid begin to fall a little back from these extremities; they begin to aspire after a more naked, narrative articulation; after the succinct, the dignified, and the poetic; and as a means to this, after a general lightening of this baggage of detail. After Scott we beheld the starveling story—once, in the hands of Voltaire, as abstract as a parable—begin to be pampered upon facts. The introduction of these details developed a particular ability of hand; and that ability, childishly indulged, has led to the works that now amaze us on a railway journey. A man of the unquestionable force of M. Zola spends himself on technical successes. To afford a popular flavour and attract the mob, he adds a steady current of what I may be allowed to call the rancid. That is exciting to the moralist; but what more particularly interests the artist is this tendency of the extreme of detail, when followed as a principle, to degenerate into mere *feux-de-joie* of literary tricking. The other day even M. Daudet was to be heard babbling of audible colours and visible sounds.

This odd suicide of one branch of the realists

may serve to remind us of the fact which under-
lies a very dusty conflict of the critics. All repre-
sentative art, which can be said to live, is both
realistic and ideal; and the realism about which
we quarrel is a matter purely of externals. It is
no especial cultus of nature and veracity, but a
mere whim of veering fashion, that has made us
turn our back upon the larger, more various,
and more romantic art of yore. A photographic
exactitude in dialogue is now the exclusive
fashion; but even in the ablest hands it tells us
no more—I think it even tells us less—than
Molière, wielding his artificial medium, has told
us and to all time of Alceste or Orgon, Dorine
or Chrysale. The historical novel is forgotten.
Yet truth to the conditions of man's nature and
the conditions of man's life, the truth of literary
art, is free of the ages. It may be told us in a
carpet comedy, in a novel of adventure, or a
fairy tale. The scene may be pitched in London,
on the sea-coast of Bohemia, or away on the
mountains of Beulah. And by an odd and luminous accident, if there is any page of literature
calculated to awake the envy of M. Zola, it must
be that *Troilus and Cressida* which Shakespeare,
in a spasm of unmanly anger with the world,
grafted on the heroic story of the siege of Troy.

This question of realism, let it be then clearly
understood, regards not in the least degree the
fundamental truth, but only the technical
method, of a work of art. Be as ideal or as
abstract as you please, you will be none the less
veracious; but if you be weak, you run the risk

of being tedious and inexpressive; and if you be very strong and honest, you may chance upon a masterpiece.

A work of art is first cloudily conceived in the mind; during the period of gestation it stands more clearly forward from these swaddling mists, puts on expressive lineaments, and becomes at length that most faultless, but also, alas! that incommunicable product of the human mind, a perfected design. On the approach to execution all is changed. The artist must now step down, don his working clothes, and become the artisan. He now resolutely commits his airy conception, his delicate Ariel, to the touch of matter; he must decide, almost in a breath, the scale, the style, the spirit, and the particularity of execution of his whole design.

The engendering idea of some works is stylistic; a technical preoccupation stands them instead of some robuster principle of life. And with these the execution is but play; for the stylistic problem is resolved beforehand, and all large originality of treatment wilfully foregone. Such are the verses, intricately designed, which we have learnt to admire, with a certain smiling admiration, at the hands of Mr. Lang and Mr. Dobson; such, too, are those canvases where dexterity or even breadth of plastic style takes the place of pictorial nobility of design. So, it may be remarked, it was easier to begin to write *Esmond* than *Vanity Fair*, since, in the first, the style was dictated by the nature of the plan; and Thackeray, a man probably of some indolence of mind, enjoyed and got good profit of this economy of effort. But the case is exceptional. Usually in all works of art that have been conceived from within outwards, and generously nourished from the author's mind, the moment in which he begins to execute is one of extreme perplexity and strain. Artists of indifferent energy and an imperfect devotion to their own ideal make this ungrateful effort once for all; and, having formed a style, adhere to it through life. But those of a higher order cannot rest content with a process which, as they continue to employ it, must infallibly degenerate toward the academic and the cut-and-dried. Every fresh work in which they embark is the signal for a fresh engagement of the whole forces of their mind; and the changing views which accompany the growth of their experience are marked by still more sweeping alterations in the manner of their art. So that criticism loves to dwell upon and distinguish the varying periods of a Raphael, a Shakespeare, or a Beethoven.

It is, then, first of all, at this initial and decisive moment when execution is begun, and thenceforth only in a less degree, that the ideal and the real do indeed, like good and evil angels, contend for the direction of the work. Marble, paint, and language, the pen, the needle, and the brush, all have their grossnesses, their ineffable impotences, their hours, if I may so express myself, of insubordination. It is the work and it is a great part of the delight of any artist to contend with these unruly tools, and now

by brute energy, now by witty expedient, to drive
and coax them to effect his will. Given these
means, so laughably inadequate, and given the
interest, the intensity, and the multiplicity of the
actual sensation whose effect he is to render with
their aid, the artist has one main and necessary
resource which he must, in every case and upon
any theory, employ. He must, that is, suppress
much and omit more. He must omit what is
tedious or irrelevant, and suppress what is tedious
and necessary. But such facts as, in regard to the
main design, subserve a variety of purposes, he
will perforce and eagerly retain. And it is the
mark of the very highest order of creative art to
be woven exclusively of such. There, any fact that
is registered is contrived a double or a treble debt
to pay, and is at once an ornament in its place
and a pillar in the main design. Nothing would
find room in such a picture that did not serve,
at once, to complete the composition, to accentuate the scheme of colour, to distinguish the
planes of distance, and to strike the note of the
selected sentiment; nothing would be allowed in
such a story that did not, at the same time,
expedite the progress of the fable, build up the
characters, and strike home the moral or the
philosophical design. But this is unattainable. As
a rule, so far from building the fabric of our
works exclusively with these, we are thrown into
a rapture if we think we can muster a dozen or
a score of them, to be the plums of our confec-
tion. And hence, in order that the canvas may be
filled or the story proceed from point to point,

267

other details must be admitted. They must be admitted, alas! upon a doubtful title; many without marriage robes. Thus any work of art, as it proceeds toward completion, too often—I had almost written always—loses in force and poignancy of main design. Our little air is swamped and dwarfed among hardly relevant orchestration; our little passionate story drowns in a deep sea of descriptive eloquence or slipshod talk.

But again, we are rather more tempted to admit those particulars which we know we can describe; and hence those most of all which, having been described very often, have grown to be conventionally treated in the practice of our art. These we choose, as the mason chooses the acanthus to adorn his capital, because they come naturally to the accustomed hand. The old stock incidents and accessories, tricks of workmanship and schemes of composition (all being admirably good, or they would long have been forgotten) haunt and tempt our fancy, offer us ready-made but not perfectly appropriate solutions for any problem that arises, and wean us from the study of nature and the uncompromising practice of art. To struggle, to face nature, to find fresh solutions, and give expression to facts which have not yet been adequately or not yet elegantly expressed, is to run a little upon the danger of extreme self-love. Difficulty sets a high price upon achievement; and the artist may easily fall into the error of the French naturalists, and consider any fact as welcome to admission if it be the ground of brilliant handiwork; or, again, into the error of the modern landscape-painter, who is apt to think that difficulty overcome and science well displayed can take the place of what is, after all, the one excuse and breath of art—charm. A little further, and he will regard charm in the light of an unworthy sacrifice to prettiness, and the omission of a tedious passage as an infidelity to art.

We have now the matter of this difference before us. The idealist, his eye singly fixed upon the greater outlines, loves rather to fill up the interval with detail of the conventional order, briefly touched, soberly suppressed in tone, courting neglect. But the realist, with a fine intemperance, will not suffer the presence of anything so dead as a conversation; he shall have all fiery, all hot-pressed from nature, all charactered and notable, seizing the eye. The style that befits either of these extremes, once chosen, brings with it its necessary disabilities and dangers. The immediate danger of the realist is to sacrifice the beauty and significance of the whole to local dexterity, or, in the insane pursuit of completion, to immolate his readers under facts; but he comes in the last resort, and as his energy declines, to discard all design, abjure all choice, and, with scientific thoroughness, steadily to communicate matter which is not worth learning. The danger of the idealist is, of course, to become merely null and lose all grip of fact, particularity, or passion.

We talk of bad and good. Everything, indeed, is good which is conceived with honesty and executed with communicative ardour. But though on neither side is dogmatism fitting, and though in every case the artist must decide for himself, and decide afresh and yet afresh for each succeeding work and new creation; yet one thing may be generally said, that we of the last quarter of the nineteenth century, breathing as we do the intellectual atmosphere of our age, are more apt to err upon the side of realism than to sin in quest of the ideal. Upon that theory it may be well to watch and correct our own decisions, always holding back the hand from the least appearance of irrelevant dexterity, and resolutely fixed to begin no work that is not philosophical, passionate, dignified, happily mirthful, or, at the last and least, romantic in design.

MEMOIRS OF AN ISLET

THOSE who try to be artists use, time after time, the matter of their recollections, setting and resetting little coloured memories of men and scenes, rigging up (it may be) some especial friend in the attire of a buccaneer, and decreeing armies to manœuvre, or murder to be done, on the playground of their youth. But the memories are a fairy gift which cannot be worn out in using. After a dozen services in various tales, the little sunbright pictures of the past still shine in the mind's eye with not a lineament defaced, not a tint impaired. *Glück und Unglück wird Gesang*, if Goethe pleases; yet only by endless avatars, the original re-embodying after each. So that a writer, in time, begins to wonder at the perdurable life of these impressions; beings, perhaps, to fancy that he wrongs them when he weaves them in with fiction; and looking back on them with evergrowing kindness, puts them at last, substantive jewels, in a setting of their own.

One or two of these pleasant spectres I think I have laid. I used one but the other day: a little eyot of dense, freshwater sand, where I once waded deep in butterburrs, delighting to hear the song of the river on both sides, and to tell myself that I was indeed and at last upon an island. Two of my puppets lay there a summer's day, hearkening to the shearers at work in riverside

271

fields and to the drums of the gray old garrison upon the neighbouring hill. And this was, I think, done rightly: the place was rightly peopled —and now belongs not to me but to my puppets —for a time at least. In time, perhaps, the puppets will grow faint; the original memory swim up instant as ever; and I shall once more lie in bed, and see the little sandy isle in Allan Water as it is in nature, and the child (that once was me) wading there in butterburrs; and wonder at the instancy and virgin freshness of that memory; and be pricked again, in season and out of season, by the desire to weave it into art.

There is another isle in my collection, the memory of which besieges me. I put a whole family there, in one of my tales; and later on, threw upon its shores, and condemned to several days of rain and shellfish on its tumbled boulders, the hero of another. The ink is not yet faded; the sound of the sentences is still in my mind's ear; and I am under a spell to write of that island again.

I

The little isle of Earraid lies close in to the southwest corner of the Ross of Mull: the sound of Iona on one side, across which you may see the isle and church of Columba; the open sea to the other, where you shall be able to mark, on a clear, surfy day, the breakers running white on many sunken rocks. I first saw it, or first remembered seeing it, framed in the round bull's-eye of a cabin port, the sea lying smooth along its shores like the waters of a lake, the colourless, clear light of the early morning making plain its heathery and rocky hummocks. There stood upon it, in these days, a single rude house of uncemented stones, approached by a pier of wreckwood. It must have been very early, for it was then summer, and in summer, in that latitude, day scarcely withdraws; but even at that hour the house was making a sweet smoke of peats which came to me over the bay, and the bare-legged daughters of the cotter were wading by the pier. The same day we visited the shores of the isle in the ship's boats; rowed deep into Fiddler's Hole, sounding as we went; and having taken stock of all possible accommodation, pitched on the northern inlet as the scene of operations. For it was no accident that had brought the lighthouse steamer to anchor in the Bay of Earraid. Fifteen miles away to seaward, a certain black rock stood environed by the Atlantic rollers, the outpost of the Torran reefs. Here was a tower to be built, and a star lighted, for the conduct of seamen. But as the rock was small, and hard of access, and far from land, the work would be one of years; and my father was now looking for a shore station, where the stones might be quarried and dressed, the men live, and the tender, with some degree of safety, lie at anchor.

I saw Earraid next from the stern thwart of an Iona lugger, Sam Bough and I sitting there cheek by jowl, with our feet upon our baggage, in a beautiful, clear, northern summer eve. And behold! there was now a pier of stone, there were rows of sheds, railways, travelling-cranes, a street of cottages, an iron house for the resident engineer, wooden bothies for the men, a stage where the courses of the tower were put together experimentally, and behind the settlement a great gash in the hillside where granite was quarried. In the bay, the steamer lay at her moorings. All day long there hung about the place the music of chinking tools; and even in the dead of night, the watchman carried his lantern to and fro in the dark settlement, and could light the pipe of any midnight muser. It was, above all, strange to see Earraid on the Sunday, when the sound of the tools ceased and there fell a crystal quiet. All about the green compound men would be saun-tering in their Sunday's best, walking with those lax joints of the reposing toiler, thoughtfully smoking, talking small, as if in honour of the stillness, or hearkening to the wailing of the gulls. And it was strange to see our Sabbath services, held, as they were, in one of the bothies, with Mr. Brebner reading at a table, and the con-gregation perched about in the double tier of sleeping bunks; and to hear the singing of the psalms, "the chapters," the inevitable Spurgeon's sermon, and the old, eloquent lighthouse prayer.

In fine weather, when by the spy-glass on the hill the sea was observed to run low upon the reef, there would be a sound of preparation in the very early morning; and before the sun had risen from behind Ben More, the tender would steam out of the bay. Over fifteen sea-miles of the great blue Atlantic rollers she ploughed her way, trailing at her tail a brace of wallowing stone-lighters. The open ocean widened upon either board, and the hills of the mainland began to go down on the horizon, before she came to her unhomely destination, and lay-to at last where the rock clapped its black head above the swell, with the tall iron barrack on its spider legs, and the truncated tower, and the cranes waving their arms, and the smoke of the engine-fire rising in the mid-sea. An ugly reef is this of the Dhu Heartach; no pleasant assemblage of shelves, and pools, and creeks, about which a child might play for a whole summer without weariness, like the Bell Rock or the Skerryvore, but one oval nodule of black-trap, sparsely bedab-bled with an inconspicuous fucus, and alive in every crevice with a dingy insect between a slater and a bug. No other life was there but that of sea-birds, and of the sea itself, that here ran like a mill race, and growled about the outer reef for ever, and ever and again, in the calmest weather, roared and spouted on the rock itself. Times were different upon Dhu-Heartach when it blew, and the night fell dark, and the neighbour lights of Skerryvore and Rhu-val were quenched in fog, and the men sat prisoned high up in their iron drum, that, then resounded with the lashing of the sprays. Fear sat with them in their sea-beleaguered dwelling; and the colour changed in anxious faces when some greater billow struck the barrack, and its pillars quivered and sprang under the blow. It was then that the foreman builder, Mr. Goodwillie, whom I see before me still in his rock-habit of undecipherable rags, would get his fiddle down and strike up human minstrelsy amid the music of the storm. But it was in sunshine only that I saw Dhu-Heartach; and it was in sunshine, or the yet lovelier summer afterglow, that the steamer would return to Earraid, ploughing an enchanted sea; the obedient lighters, relieved of their deck cargo, riding in her wake more quietly; and the steersman upon each, as she rose on the long swell, standing tall and dark against the shining west.

II

But it was in Earraid itself that I delighted chiefly. The lighthouse settlement scarce encroached beyond its fences; over the top of the first brae the ground was all virgin, the world all shut out, the face of things unchanged by any of man's doings. Here was no living presence, save for the limpets on the rocks, for some old, gray, rain-beaten ram that I might rouse out of a ferry den betwixt two boulders, or for the haunting and the piping of the gulls. It was older than man; it was found so by incoming Celts, and seafaring Norsemen, and Columba's priests. The earthy savour of the bog-plants, the rude disorder of the boulders, the inimitable seaside brightness of the air, the brine and the iodine, the lap of the billows among the weedy reefs, the sudden springing up of a great run of dashing surf along the seafront of the isle, all that I saw and felt my predecessors must have seen and felt with scarce a difference. I steeped myself in open air and in past ages.

"Delightful would it be to me to be in *Uchd
 Ailiun*
  On the pinnacle of a rock,
That I might often see
  The face of the ocean;
That I might hear the song of the wonderful
  birds,
  Source of happiness;
That I might hear the thunder of the crowding
  waves
  Upon the rocks:
At times at work without compulsion—
  This would be delightful;
At times plucking dulse from the rocks
  At times at fishing."

So, about the next island of Iona, sang Columba himself twelve hundred years before. And so might I have sung of Earraid.

And all the while I was aware that this life of sea-bathing and sun-burning was for me but a holiday. In that year cannon were roaring for days together on French battlefields; and I would sit in my isle (I call it mine, after the use of lovers) and think upon the war, and the loudness of these far-away battles, and the pain of the men's wounds, and the weariness of their marching. And I would think too of that other war which is as old as mankind, and is indeed the life of man: the unsparing war, the grinding slavery of competition; the toil of seventy years, dear-bought bread, precarious honour, the perils and pitfalls, and the poor rewards. It was a long look forward; the future summoned me as with trumpet calls, it warned me back as with a voice of weeping and beseeching; and I thrilled and trembled on the brink of life, like a childish bather on the beach.

There was another young man on Earraid in these days, and we were much together, bathing, clambering on the boulders, trying to sail a boat and spinning round instead in the oily whirlpools of the roost. But the most part of the time we spoke of the great uncharted desert of our futures; wondering together what should there befall us; hearing with surprise the sound of our own voices in the empty vestibule of youth. As far, and as hard, as it seemed then to look forward to the grave, so far it seems now to look backward upon these emotions; so hard to recall justly that loath submission, as of the sacrificial bull, with which we stooped our necks under the yoke of destiny. I met my old companion but the other day; I cannot tell of course what he was thinking; but, upon my part, I was wondering to see us both so much at home, and so composed and sedentary in the world; and how much we had gained, and how much we had lost, to attain to that composure; and which had been upon the whole our best estate: when we sat there prating sensibly like men of some experience, or when we shared our timorous and hopeful counsels in a western islet.

FATHER DAMIEN

An Open Letter to the Reverend Dr. Hyde of Honolulu

Sydney,
February 25, 1890.

Sir,—It may probably occur to you that we have
met, and visited, and conversed; on my side, with
interest. You may remember that you have done
me several courtesies, for which I was prepared
to be grateful. But there are duties which come
before gratitude, and offences which justly divide
friends, far more acquaintances. Your letter to
the Reverend H. B. Gage is a document which,
in my sight, if you had filled me with bread
when I was starving, if you had sat up to nurse
my father when he lay a-dying, would yet absolve
me from the bonds of gratitude. You know
enough, doubtless, of the process of canonisation
to be aware that, a hundred years after the death
of Damien, there will appear a man charged
with the painful office of the *devil's advocate*.
After that noble brother of mine, and of all
frail clay, shall have lain a century at rest, one
shall accuse, one defend him. The circumstance
is unusual that the devil's advocate should be a
volunteer, should be a member of a sect immediately rival, and should make haste to take upon
himself his ugly office ere the bones are cold;

unusual, and of a taste which I shall leave my
readers free to qualify; unusual, and to me in-
spiring. If I have at all learned the trade of using
words to convey truth and to arouse emotion,
you have at last furnished me with a subject. For
it is in the interest of all mankind, and the cause
of public decency in every quarter of the world,
not only that Damien should be righted, but that
you and your letter should be displayed at length,
in their true colours, to the public eye.

To do this properly, I must begin by quoting
you at large: I shall then proceed to criticise
your utterance from several points of view, divine
and human, in the course of which I shall attempt to draw again, and with more specification,
the character of the dead saint whom it has
pleased you to vilify: so much being done, I shall
say farewell to you for ever.

HONOLULU,
August 2, 1889.

REV. H. B. GAGE.

DEAR BROTHER,—In answer to your inquiries
about Father Damien, I can only reply that we
who knew the man are surprised at the extravagant newspaper laudations, as if he was a most
saintly philanthropist. The simple truth is, he
was a coarse, dirty man, headstrong and bigoted.
He was not sent to Molokai, but went there without orders; did not stay at the leper settlement
(before he became one himself), but circulated
freely over the whole island (less than half the
island is devoted to the lepers), and he came

often to Honolulu. He had no hand in the reforms and improvements inaugurated, which
were the work of our Board of Health, as occasion required and means were provided. He was
not a pure man in his relations with women,
and the leprosy of which he died should be
attributed to his vices and carelessness. Others
have done much for the lepers, our own ministers, the government physicians, and so forth,
but never with the Catholic idea of meriting
eternal life.—Yours, etc.,

C. M. HYDE[1]

To deal fitly with a letter so extraordinary, I
must draw at the outset on my private knowledge of the signatory and his sect. It may offend
others; scarcely you, who have been so busy to
collect, so bold to publish, gossip on your rivals.
And this is perhaps the moment when I may
best explain to you the character of what you are
to read: I conceive you as a man quite beyond
and below the reticences of civility: with what
measure you mete, with that shall it be measured
you again; with you, at last, I rejoice to feel the
button off the foil and to plunge home. And if
in aught that I shall say I should offend others,
your colleagues, whom I respect and remember
with affection, I can but offer them my regret; I
am not free, I am inspired by the consideration
of interests far more large; and such pain as
can be inflicted by anything from me must be
indeed trifling when compared with the pain

[1] From the Sydney *Presbyterian*, October 26, 1889.

with which they read your letter. It is not the hangman, but the criminal, that brings dishonour on the house.

You belong, sir, to a sect—I believe my sect, and that in which my ancestors laboured—which has enjoyed, and partly failed to utilise, an exceptional advantage in the islands of Hawaii. The first missionaries came; they found the land already self-purged of its old and bloody faith; they were embraced, almost on their arrival, with enthusiasm; what troubles they supported came far more from whites than from Hawaiians; and to these last they stood (in a rough figure) in the shoes of God. This is not the place to enter into the degree or causes of their failure, such as it is. One element alone is pertinent, and must here be plainly dealt with. In the course of their evangelical calling, they—or too many of them—grew rich. It may be news to you that the houses of missionaries are a cause of mocking on the streets of Honolulu. It will at least be news to you, that when I returned your civil visit, the driver of my cab commented on the size, the taste, and the comfort of your home. It would have been news certainly to myself, had any one told me that afternoon that I should live to drag such matter into print. But you see, sir, how you degrade better men to your own level; and it is needful that those who are to judge betwixt you and me, betwixt Damien and the devil's advocate, should understand your letter to have been penned in a house which could raise, and that very justly, the envy and the comments of the passers-by. I think (to employ a phrase of yours which I admire) it "should be attributed" to you that you have never visited the scene of Damien's life and death. If you had, and had recalled it, and looked about your pleasant rooms, even your pen perhaps would have been stayed.

Your sect (and remember, as far as any sect avows me, it is mine) has not done ill in a worldly sense in the Hawaiian Kingdom. When calamity befell their innocent parishioners, when leprosy descended and took root in the Eight Islands, a *quid pro quo* was to be looked for. To that prosperous mission, and to you, as one of its adornments, God had sent at last an opportunity. I know I am touching here upon a nerve acutely sensitive. I know that others of your colleagues look back on the inertia of your Church, and the intrusive and decisive heroism of Damien, with something almost to be called remorse. I am sure it is so with yourself; I am persuaded your letter was inspired by a certain envy, not essentially ignoble, and the one human trait to be espied in that performance. You were thinking of the lost chance, the past day; of that which should have been conceived and was not; of the service due and not rendered. *Time was*, said the voice in your ear, in your pleasant room, as you sat raging and writing; and if the words written were base beyond parallel, the rage, I am happy to repeat—it is the only compliment I shall pay you—the rage was almost virtuous. But, sir, when we have failed, and another has succeeded; when we have stood by, and another has

284

stepped in; when we sit and grow bulky in our charming mansions, and a plain, uncouth peasant steps into the battle, under the eyes of God, and succours the afflicted, and consoles the dying, and is himself afflicted in his turn, and dies upon the field of honour—the battle cannot be retrieved as your unhappy irritation has suggested. It is a lost battle, and lost for ever. One thing remained to you in your defeat—some rags of common honour; and these you have made haste to cast away.

Common honour; not the honour of having done anything right, but the honour of not having done aught conspicuously foul; the honour of the inert: that was what remained to you. We are not all expected to be Damiens; a man may conceive his duty more narrowly, he may love his comforts better; and none will cast a stone at him for that. But will a gentleman of your reverend profession allow me an example from the fields of gallantry? When two gentlemen compete for the favour of a lady, and the one succeeds and the other is rejected, and (as will sometimes happen) matter damaging to the successful rival's credit reaches the ear of the defeated, it is held by plain men of no pretensions that his mouth is, in the circumstance, almost necessarily closed. Your Church and Damien's were in Hawaii upon a rivalry to do well: to help, to edify, to set divine examples. You having (in one huge instance) failed, and Damien succeeded, I marvel it should not have occurred to you that you were doomed to silence; that when you had been outstripped in that high rivalry,

and sat inglorious in the midst of your wellbeing,
in your pleasant room—and Damien, crowned
with glories and horrors, toiled and rotted in that
pigsty of his under the cliffs of Kalawao—you,
the elect who would not, were the last man on
earth to collect and propagate gossip on the
volunteer who would and did.

I think I see you—for I try to see you in the
flesh as I write these sentences—I think I see
you leap at the word pigsty, a hyperbolical expression at the best. "He had no hand in the
reforms," he was "a coarse, dirty man"; these
were your own words; and you may think it
possible that I am come to support you with fresh
evidence. In a sense, it is even so. Damien has
been too much depicted with a conventional halo
and conventional features; so drawn by men who
perhaps had not the eye to remark or the pen
to express the individual; or who perhaps were
only blinded and silenced by generous admiration, such as I partly envy for myself—such as
you, if your soul were enlightened, would envy
on your bended knees. It is the least defect of
such a method of portraiture that it makes the
path easy for the devil's advocate, and leaves
for the misuse of the slanderer a considerable
field of truth. For the truth that is suppressed by
friends is the readiest weapon of the enemy. The
world, in your despite, may perhaps owe you
something, if your letter be the means of sub-
stituting once for all a credible likeness for a wax
abstraction. For, if that world at all remember
you, on the day when Damien of Molokai shall

be named Saint, it will be in virtue of one work: your letter to the Reverend H. B. Gage.

You may ask on what authority I speak. It was my inclement destiny to become acquainted, not with Damien, but with Dr. Hyde. When I visited the lazaretto, Damien was already in his resting grave. But such information as I have, I gathered on the spot in conversation with those who knew him well and long: some indeed who revered his memory; but others who had sparred and wrangled with him, who beheld him with no halo, who perhaps regarded him with small respect, and through whose unprepared and scarcely partial communications the plain, human features of the man shone on me convincingly. These gave me what knowledge I possess; and I learnt it in that scene where it could be most completely and sensitively understood—Kalawao, which you have never visited, about which you have never so much as endeavoured to inform yourself; for, brief as your letter is, you have found the means to stumble into that confession. "*Less than one-half* of the island," you say, "is devoted to the lepers." Molokai—"*Molokai ahina*," the "grey," lofty, and most desolate island—along all its northern side plunges a front of precipice into a sea of unusual profundity. This range of cliff is, from east to west, the true end and frontier of the island. Only in one spot there projects into the ocean a certain triangular and rugged down, grassy, stony, windy, and rising in the midst into a hill with a dead crater: the whole bearing to the cliff that overhangs it some-

what the same relation as a bracket to a wall.
With this hint you will now be able to pick out
the leper station on a map; you will be able to
judge how much of Molokai is thus cut off between the surf and precipice, whether less than
a half, or less than a quarter, or a fifth, or a
tenth—or, say, a twentieth; and the next time
you burst into print you will be in a position to
share with us the issue of your calculations.

I imagine you to be one of those persons who
talk with cheerfulness of that place which oxen
and wainropes could not drag you to behold.
You, who do not even know its situation on the
map, probably denounce sensational descriptions,
stretching your limbs the while in your pleasant
parlour on Beretania Street. When I was pulled
ashore there one early morning, there sat with
me in the boat two sisters, bidding farewell (in
humble imitation of Damien) to the lights and
joys of human life. One of these wept silently; I
could not withhold myself from joining her. Had
you been there, it is my belief that nature would
have triumphed even in you; and as the boat
drew but a little nearer, and you beheld the stairs
crowded with abominable deformations of our
common manhood, and saw yourself landing in
the midst of such a population as only now and
then surrounds us in the horror of a nightmare—
what a haggard eye you would have rolled over
your reluctant shoulder towards the house on
Beretania Street. Had you gone on; had you
found every fourth face a blot upon the landscape; had you visited the hospital and seen the

butt-ends of human beings lying there almost unrecognisable, but still breathing, still thinking, still remembering: you would have understood that life in the lazaretto is an ordeal from which the nerves of a man's spirit shrink, even as his eye quails under the brightness of the sun; you would have felt it was (even to-day) a pitiful place to visit and a hell to dwell in. It is not the fear of possible infection. That seems a little thing when compared with the pain, the pity, and the disgust of the visitor's surroundings, and the atmosphere of affliction, disease, and physical disgrace in which he breathes. I do not think I am a man more than usually timid; but I never recall the days and nights I spent upon that island promontory (eight days and seven nights), without heartfelt thankfulness that I am somewhere else. I find in my diary that I speak of my stay as a "grinding experience": I have once jotted in the margin, "*Harrowing* is the word"; and when the *Mokolii* bore me at last towards the outer world, I kept repeating to myself, with a new conception of their pregnancy, those simple words of the song—

'Tis the most distressful country that ever yet was seen.

And observe: that which I saw and suffered from was a settlement purged, bettered, beautified; the new village built, the hospital and the Bishop-Home excellently arranged; the sisters, the doctor, and the missionaries, all indefatigable in their noble tasks. It was a different place when Damien came there and made his great renunciation, and slept that first night under a tree amidst his rotting brethren: alone with pestilence; and looking forward (with what courage, with what pitiful sinkings of dread, God only knows) to a lifetime of dressing sores and stumps.

You will say, perhaps, I am too sensitive, that sights as painful abound in cancer hospitals and are confronted daily by doctors and nurses. I have long learned to admire and envy the doctors and the nurses. But there is no cancer hospital so large and populous as Kalawao and Kalaupapa; and in such a matter every fresh case, like every inch of length in the pipe of an organ, deepens the note of the impression; for what daunts the onlooker is that monstrous sum of human suffering by which he stands surrounded. Lastly, no doctor or nurse is called upon to enter once for all the doors of that gehenna; they do not say farewell, they need not abandon hope, on its sad threshold; they but go for a time to their high calling, and can look forward as they go to relief, to recreation, and to rest. But Damien shut-to with his own hand the doors of his own sepulchre.

I shall now extract three passages from my diary at Kalawao.

A. "Damien is dead and already somewhat ungratefully remembered in the field of his labours and sufferings. 'He was a good man, but very officious,' says one. Another tells me he had fallen (as other priests so easily do) into something of the ways and habits of thought of a

Kanaka; but he had the wit to recognise the fact, and the good sense to laugh at [over] it. A plain man it seems he was; I cannot find he was a popular."

B. "After Ragsdale's death" [Ragsdale was a famous Luna, or overseer, of the unruly settlement] "there followed a brief term of office by Father Damien which served only to publish the weakness of that noble man. He was rough in his ways, and he had no control. Authority was relaxed; Damien's life was threatened, and he was soon eager to resign."

C. "Of Damien I begin to have an idea. He seems to have been a man of the present class, certainly of the peasant type: shrewd, ignorant and bigoted, yet with an open mind, and capable of receiving and digesting a reproof if it were bluntly administered; superbly generous in the least thing as well as in the greatest, and as ready to give his last shirt (although not without human grumbling) as he had been to sacrifice his life; essentially indiscreet and officious, which made him a troublesome colleague; domineering in all his ways, which made him incurably unpopular with the Kanakas, but yet destitute of real authority, so that his boys laughed at him and he must carry out his wishes by the means of bribes. He learned to have a mania for doctoring; and set up the Kanakas against the remedies of his regular rivals: perhaps (if anything matter at all in the treatment of such a disease) the worst thing that he did, and certainly the easiest. The best and worst of the man appear very plainly in his dealings with Mr. Chapman's money; he had originally laid it out [intended to lay it out] entirely for the benefit of Catholics, and even so not wisely; but after a long, plain talk, he admitted his error fully and revised the list. The sad state of the boys' home is in part the result of his lack of control; in part, of his own slovenly ways and false ideas of hygiene. Brother officials used to call it 'Damien's Chinatown.' 'Well,' they would say, 'your Chinatown keeps growing.' And he would laugh with perfect good-nature, and adhere to his errors with perfect obstinacy. So much I have gathered of truth about this plain, noble human brother and father of ours; his imperfections are the traits of his face, by which we know him for our fellow; his martyrdom and his example nothing can lessen or annul; and only a person here on the spot can properly appreciate their greatness."

I have set down these private passages, as you perceive, without correction; thanks to you, the public has them in their bluntness. They are almost a list of the man's faults, for it is rather these that I was seeking: with his virtues, with the heroic profile of his life, I and the world were already sufficiently acquainted. I was besides a little suspicious of Catholic testimony; in no ill sense, but merely because Damien's admirers and disciples were the least likely to be critical. I know you will be more suspicious still; and the facts set down above were one and all collected from the lips of Protestants who had opposed the father in his life. Yet I am strangely deceived, or they build up the image of a man, with all his weaknesses, essentially heroic, and alive with rugged honesty, generosity, and mirth.

Take it for what it is, rough private jottings of the worst sides of Damien's character, collected from the lips of those who had laboured with and (in your own phrase) "knew the man";—though I question whether Damien would have said that he knew you. Take it, and observe with wonder how well you were served by your gossips, how ill by your intelligence and sympathy; in how many points of fact we are at one, and how widely our appreciations vary. There is something wrong here; either with you or me. It is possible, for instance, that you, who seem to have so many ears in Kalawao, had heard of the affair of Mr. Chapman's money, and were singly struck by Damien's intended wrong-doing. I was struck with that also, and set it fairly down; but I was struck much more by the fact that he had the honesty of mind to be convinced. I may here tell you that it was a long business; that one of his colleagues sat with him late into the night, multiplying arguments and accusations; that the father listened as usual with "perfect good-nature and perfect obstinacy"; but at the last, when he was persuaded—"Yes," said he, "I am very much obliged to you; you have done me a service; it would have been a theft." There are many (not Catholics merely) who require their heroes and saints to be infallible; to these the story will be painful; not to the true lovers, patrons, and servants of mankind.

And I take it, this is a type of our division; that you are one of those who have an eye for faults and failures; that you take a pleasure to find and publish them; and that, having found them, you make haste to forget the overvailing virtues and the real success which had alone introduced them to your knowledge. It is a dangerous frame of mind. That you may understand how dangerous, and into what a situation it has already brought you, we will (if you please) go hand-in-hand through the different phrases of your letter, and candidly examine each from the point of view of its truth, its appositeness, and its charity.

Damien was *coarse.*

It is very possible. You make us sorry for the lepers, who had only a coarse old peasant for their friend and father. But you, who were so refined, why were you not there, to cheer them with the lights of culture? Or may I remind you that we have some reason to doubt if John the Baptist were genteel; and in the case of Peter, on whose career you doubtless dwell approvingly in the pulpit, no doubt at all he was a "coarse, headstrong" fisherman! Yet even in our Protestant Bibles Peter is called Saint.

Damien was *dirty.*

He was. Think of the poor lepers annoyed with this dirty comrade! But the clean Dr. Hyde was at his food in a fine house.

Damien was *headstrong*.

I believe you are right again; and I thank God for his strong head and heart.

Damien was *bigoted*.

I am not fond of bigots myself, because they are not fond of me. But what is meant by bigotry, that we should regard it as a blemish in a priest? Damien believed his own religion with the simplicity of a peasant or a child; as I would I could suppose that you do. For this, I wonder at him some way off; and had that been his only character, should have avoided him in life. But the point of interest in Damien, which has caused him to be so much talked about and made him at last the subject of your pen and mine, was that, in him, his bigotry, his intense and narrow faith, wrought potently for good, and strengthened him to be one of the world's heroes and exemplars.

Damien *was not sent to Molokai, but went there without orders*.

Is this a misreading? or do you really mean the words for blame? I have heard Christ, in the pulpits of our Church, held up for imitation on the ground that His sacrifice was voluntary. Does Dr. Hyde think otherwise?

Damien *did not stay at the settlement, etc*.

It is true he was allowed many indulgences. Am I to understand that you blame the father for profiting by these, or the officers for granting them? In either case, it is a mighty Spartan standard to issue from the house on Beretania Street; and I am convinced you will find yourself with few supporters.

Damien *had no hand in the reforms, etc.*

I think even you will admit that I have already been frank in my description of the man I am defending; but before I take you up upon this head, I will be franker still, and tell you that perhaps nowhere in the world can a man taste a more pleasurable sense of contrast than when he passes from Damien's "Chinatown" at Kala-wao to the beautiful Bishop-Home at Kalaupapa. At this point, in my desire to make all fair for you, I will break my rule and adduce Catholic testimony. Here is a passage from my diary about my visit to the Chinatown, from which you will see how it is (even now) regarded by its own officials: "We went round all the dormitories, refectories, etc.—dark and dingy enough, with a superficial cleanliness, which he [Mr. Dutton, the lay-brother] did not seek to defend. 'It is almost decent,' said he; 'the sisters will make that all right when we get them here.'" And yet I gathered it was already better since Damien was dead, and far better than when he was there alone and had his own (not always excellent) way. I have now come far enough to meet you on a common ground of fact; and I tell you that, to a mind not prejudiced by jealousy, all the reforms of the lazaretto, and even those which he most

296

vigorously opposed, are properly the work of Damien. They are the evidence of his success; they are what his heroism provoked from the reluctant and the careless. Many were before him in the field, Mr. Meyer, for instance, of whose faithful work we hear too little: there have been many since; and some had more worldly wisdom, though none had more devotion, than our saint. Before his day, even you will confess, they had effected little. It was his part, by one striking act of martyrdom, to direct all men's eyes on that distressful country. At a blow, and with the price of his life, he made the place illustrious and public. And that, if you will consider largely, was the one reform needful; pregnant of all that should succeed. It brought money; it brought (best individual addition of them all) the sisters; it brought supervision, for public opinion and public interest landed with the man at Kalawao. If ever any man brought reforms, and died to bring them, it was he. There is not a clean cup or towel in the Bishop-Home, but dirty Damien washed it.

Damien *was not a pure man in his relations with women, etc.*

How do you know that? Is this the nature of the conversation in that house on Beretania Street which the cabman envied, driving past?— racy details of the misconduct of the poor peasant priest, toiling under the cliffs of Molokai?

Many have visited the station before me; they seem not to have heard the rumour. When I was there I heard many shocking tales, for my informants were men speaking with the plainness of the laity; and I heard plenty of complaints of Damien. Why was this never mentioned? and how came it to you in the retirement of your clerical parlour?

But I must not even seem to deceive you. This scandal, when I read it in your letter, was not new to me. I had heard it once before; and I must tell you how. There came to Samoa a man from Honolulu; he, in a public-house on the beach, volunteered the statement that Damien had "contracted the disease from having connection with the female lepers"; and I find a joy in telling you how the report was welcomed in a public-house. A man sprang to his feet; I am not at liberty to give his name, but from what I heard I doubt if you would care to have him to dinner in Beretania Street. "You miserable little ——" (here is a word I dare not print, it would so shock your ears). "You miserable little ——," he cried, "if the story were a thousand times true, can't you see you are a million times a lower —— for daring to repeat it?" I wish it could be told of you that when the report reached you in your house, perhaps after family worship, you had found in your soul enough holy anger to receive it with the same expressions; ay, even with that one which I dare not print; it would not need to have been blotted away, like Uncle Toby's oath, by the tears of the recording angel; it would have been counted to you for your brightest righteousness. But you have deliberately

298

chosen the part of the man from Honolulu, and
you have played it with improvements of your
own. The man from Honolulu—miserable, leer-
ing creature—communicated the tale to a rude
knot of beach-combing drinkers in a public-
house, where (I will so far agree with your temperance opinions) man is not always at his
noblest; and the man from Honolulu had himself been drinking—drinking, we may charitably
fancy, to excess. It was to your "Dear Brother,
the Reverend H. B. Gage," that you chose to
communicate the sickening story; and the blue
ribbon which adorns your portly bosom forbids
me to allow you the extenuating plea that you
were drunk when it was done. Your "dear
brother"—a brother indeed—made haste to deliver up your letter (as a means of grace, perhaps)
to the religious papers; where, after many
months, I found and read and wondered at it;
and whence I have now reproduced it for the
wonder of others. And you and your dear brother
have, by this cycle of operations, built up a contrast very edifying to examine in detail. The man
whom you would not care to have to dinner, on
the one side; on the other, the Reverend Dr.
Hyde and the Reverend H. B. Gage: the Apia
bar-room, the Honolulu manse.

But I fear you scarce appreciate how you appear to your fellow-men; and to bring it home
to you, I will suppose your story to be true. I
will suppose—and God forgive me for supposing
it—that Damien faltered and stumbled in his
narrow path of duty; I will suppose that, in the

horror of his isolation, perhaps in the fever of incipient disease, he, who was doing so much more than he had sworn, failed in the letter of his priestly oath—he, who was so much a better man than either you or me, who did what we have never dreamed of daring—he too tasted of our common frailty. "O, Iago, the pity of it!" The least tender should be moved to tears; the most incredulous to prayer. And all that you could do was to pen your letter to the Reverend H. B. Gage!

Is it growing at all clear to you what a picture you have drawn of your own heart? I will try yet once again to make it clearer. You had a father: suppose this tale were about him, and some informant brought it to you, proof in hand: I am not making too high an estimate of your emotional nature when I suppose you would regret the circumstance? that you would feel the tale of frailty the more keenly since it shamed the author of your days? and that the last thing you would do would be to publish it in the religious press? Well, the man who tried to do what Damien did, is my father, and the father of the man in the Apia bar, and the father of all who love goodness; and he was your father too, if God had given you grace to see it.